Pastoral Care in the Protestant Tradition

Pastoral Care in the Protestant Tradition

Essays in Honor of Scott M. Manetsch

EDITED BY
JEFFREY A. FISHER
MARTIN I. KLAUBER

Foreword by John D. Woodbridge
Afterword by Douglas A. Sweeney

◆PICKWICK *Publications* • Eugene, Oregon

PASTORAL CARE IN THE PROTESTANT TRADITION
Essays in Honor of Scott M. Manetsch

Copyright © 2026 Wipf and Stock Publishers. All rights reserved. Except for brief quotations in critical publications or reviews, no part of this book may be reproduced in any manner without prior written permission from the publisher. Write: Permissions, Wipf and Stock Publishers, 199 W. 8th Ave., Suite 3, Eugene, OR 97401.

Pickwick Publications
An Imprint of Wipf and Stock Publishers
199 W. 8th Ave., Suite 3
Eugene, OR 97401

www.wipfandstock.com

PAPERBACK ISBN: 979-8-3852-3361-8
HARDCOVER ISBN: 979-8-3852-3362-5
EBOOK ISBN: 979-8-3852-3363-2

Cataloguing-in-Publication data:

Names: Fisher, Jeffrey A. [editor]. | Klauber, Martin I. [editor].

Title: Pastoral care in the Protestant tradition : essays in Honor of Scott M. Manetsch / edited by Jeffrey A. Fisher and Martin I. Klauber.

Description: Eugene, OR: Pickwick Publications, 2026 | Includes bibliographical references.

Identifiers: ISBN 979-8-3852-3361-8 (paperback) | ISBN 979-8-3852-3362-5 (hardcover) | ISBN 979-8-3852-3363-2 (ebook)

Subjects: LCSH: Pastoral theology. | Pastoral theology—Reformed Church. | Pastoral theology—History. | Pastoral care—History. | Bible—Hermeneutics.

Classification: BV4010 F574 2026 (paperback) | BV4010 (ebook)

01/15/26

Scripture quotations in the introduction are taken from the King James Version.
Scripture quotations in chapter 1 are the author's translation of Martin Luther's translation of the Bible, as reproduced in *D. Martin Luthers Werke, Kritische Gesamtausgabe: Deutsche Bibel*, 12 vols. (Weimar: Hermann Böhlaus Nachfolger, 1906–61).
Scripture quotations in chapters 3 and 7 are taken from The Holy Bible, New International Version®, NIV®. Copyright © 1973, 1978, 1984, 2011 by Biblica, Inc. Used with permission of Zondervan. All rights reserved worldwide. www.zondervan.com.
Scripture quotations in chapter 6 are taken from Matthew Henry's *Exposition of All the Books of the Old and New Testament*, 6 vols., 3rd ed. (London: for J. Clark et al., 1725).
Scripture quotations in chapter 9 are the author's translation of the Vulgate.
Unless otherwise noted, Scripture quotations in chapter 10 are either the author's own translation or the author's translation of the cited writers' respective translations.

> The pastor ought to have two voices:
> one, for gathering the sheep; and another,
> for warding off and driving away wolves and thieves.
>
> JOHN CALVIN, COMMENTARY ON TITUS 1:9

Contents

Contributors | ix

Foreword | xi
    John D. Woodbridge

Abbreviations | xvii

PART 1. PASTORAL CARE IN THE REFORMATION ERA

1. By the Word Alone: Martin Luther's Pastoral Care in His Sermons on the Temptation of Jesus | 3
    Todd R. Hains

2. Pastoral Care in the Swiss Reformation | 26
    Amy Nelson Burnett

3. Pastoral Care in the French Reformation | 40
    Martin I. Klauber

4. "Committed by Us to Their Spiritual Charge": The Pastoral Theology of the Tudor Royal Ecclesiastical Injunctions | 52
    Andre A. Gazal

5. Bénédict Pictet (1655–1724): A Case Study in Pastoral Care | 82
    Jonathon Beeke

PART 2. PASTORAL CARE IN REFORMATION READINGS OF SCRIPTURE

6   Religion, Revelation, and the People of God in Matthew Henry's Commentary on the Psalms | 105
    RICHARD A. MULLER

7   Pastoral Care in Reformed Interpretations of Isaiah: Comforting God's People in the Reformation from Isaiah 40–66 | 131
    JEFFREY A. FISHER

8   Prophets, Preachers, and Potentates: Nikolaus Selnecker and the Late Lutheran Reformation | 150
    J. JEFFERY TYLER

9   Pastoral Insights from Reformation Readings on Romans: Reigning Sin, Concupiscence, and the Mortal/Venial Distinction | 167
    JEB RALSTON

10 "Do Not Many of You Become Teachers": Interpreting James's Directive About Teaching (3:1) in the Reformation | 193
    KIRK SUMMERS

Afterword | 215
    DOUGLAS A. SWEENEY

Contributors

JOHN D. WOODBRIDGE, research professor of church history and the history of Christian thought at Trinity Evangelical Divinity School

TODD R. HAINS, executive editor of Bibles at Baker Publishing Group

AMY NELSON BURNETT, Paula and D. B. Varner University Emerita Professor of History at the University of Nebraska–Lincoln

MARTIN I. KLAUBER, affiliate professor of church history at Trinity Evangelical Divinity School; scholar in residence at Puritan Reformed Theological Seminary

ANDRE A. GAZAL, vice president of academic affairs and professor of church history and theology at Montana Bible College

JONATHON BEEKE, academic dean and associate professor of historical theology at Puritan Reformed Theological Seminary

RICHARD A. MULLER, senior fellow at the Junius Institute for Digital Reformation Research; scholar in residence at Puritan Reformed Theological Seminary

JEFFREY A. FISHER, professor of theology at The Foundry

J. JEFFERY TYLER, professor of religion at Hope College

JEB RALSTON, PhD candidate in historical theology at Trinity Evangelical Divinity School and the University of Geneva

KIRK SUMMERS, professor of classics at the University of Alabama

DOUGLAS A. SWEENEY, dean and professor of divinity at Beeson Divinity School

Foreword

JOHN D. WOODBRIDGE

"For what shall it profit a man, if he shall gain the whole world, and lose his own soul? Or what shall a man give in exchange for his soul?" (Mark 8:36–37). These questions asked by Jesus Christ contain critically important counsel. Christ made the care of souls a premium concern for everyone, whether man or woman, boy or girl. By comparison, all substitute earthly "gains," such as the acquisition of fame or wealth, pale into insignificance. They are mere baubles and trinkets. They are fleeting. They can also be dangerous if they divert us from weighing our own soul's eternal state. Soul care should be a top priority for us as we soldier on through this life.

How do we "gain our own souls"? Answering this query has been a major quest in the Christian West and East for more than two millennia. From the patristic era to the time of the sixteenth-century Protestant Reformation, various theologians, priests, popes, and patriarchs proffered their own answers to this important question. In both the Western and Eastern churches, Pope Gregory the Great's *Pastoral Rule*—which offered consolation and spiritual medicine—stood out as an especially esteemed pastoral reflection on this topic.

Upon reading a copy of this book in AD 590, Licinianus, the bishop of Cartagena, wrote to Gregory the Great, "Who would not read with consolation a book which, if meditated on perseveringly, is a medicine for the soul, and which, by inspiring contempt for the decrepit, fluctuating, and ever changing things of this world, opens the eyes of the mind to the stability of the life eternal!"[1]

Many Protestant pastor-theologians of the sixteenth century likewise put the soul's welfare at the heart of their ministries. They sought to teach and preach what their parishioners needed to know and believe about the gospel to possess a right standing before God. They, too, understood our primordial responsibility to prepare for death and for eternity. John Calvin appreciated Gregory the Great's counsel regarding pastoral care. He cited most frequently the writings of St. Augustine and Gregory from among the patristic theologians, and he even considered Gregory the last good pope.[2] Gregory had written that "the government [or care] of souls is the art of arts."[3]

Professor Scott Manetsch's *Calvin's Company of Pastors: Pastoral Care and the Emerging Reformed Church, 1536–1609*, is a magisterial study of pastoral care during the Protestant Reformation.[4] It is beautifully written. It is thoroughly researched in primary sources. It reveals a mastery of the secondary literature. And it highlights Calvin's own conviction that to be a pastor is to fulfill an apostolic calling.

Professor Manetsch describes the aim of his book as follows: "The central purpose of this book is to examine the pastoral theology and practical ministry activities of this cadre of men who served as pastors in Geneva's churches during nearly three-quarters of a century from 1536 to 1609."[5] He observes, "Not surprisingly, Calvin and his colleagues believed that the vocation of the Christian minister was of critical importance for the spiritual well-being of God's people on earth. For Calvin, the office of the minister of the word was the 'chief sinew by which believers are held together in one body.'" Indeed, "neither the light and heat of the sun, nor food and drink, are as necessary to nourish and sustain the present life as the apostolic office and pastoral office is necessary to preserve the church on earth."[6]

The present volume in hand brings together essays that nicely complement Professor Manetsch's field of research and findings. They provide

1. Davis, introduction to *St. Gregory the Great*, 3.
2. See Little, "Appreciation of Gregory," 155; Calvin, *Institutes* IV.18.47 (*CO* 1:1022).
3. Gregory, *Pastoral Care*, 21.
4. See Manetsch, *Calvin's Company of Pastors*.
5. Manetsch, *Calvin's Company of Pastors*, 2.
6. Manetsch, *Calvin's Company of Pastors*, 71.

additional insights into the way Protestant reformers of the sixteenth century thought about pastoral theology and practiced pastoral care.

To parachute back into the Protestant Reformation may offer several surprises upon our safe landing. The Constantinian sixteenth-century world we enter, in which church and state were closely linked together, could strike a modern visitor as quite strange. What was living and dying like in sixteenth-century Geneva? Professor Manetsch vividly paints a picture of the harsh realities besetting the Genevan citizenry: "To live in sixteenth-century Geneva was to live in a precarious existence. The world of Calvin, Beza, and Goulart was a world of wars and rumblings of war; it was a world populated by witches and demoniacs; a world where people were afflicted by disease, famine, and sudden disaster."[7] In this world the inevitability and reality of death were not covered up, nor were they downplayed by using verbal euphemisms for death. The care of parishioners' souls in such an unsettled and precarious environment could be a daunting challenge for pastors.

Some swaths of the Protestant Reformation might look familiar to us. But other territories, such as the reformers' thinking about pastoral care and pastoral theology, may seem like foreign regions to explore. We need expert pathfinders to guide us into these territories. In his study *Calvin's Company of Pastors*, Professor Manetsch, as a seasoned pathfinder, provides us with a veritable storehouse of rich insights. The essayists in this volume are also expert pathfinders. They know well the topography of their respective fields of historical competency, and so they afford additional exceptional insights into the pastoral theology and pastoral practice of the Protestant reformers of the sixteenth century.

The subject matters broached in this volume fall under two rubrics: The first, "Pastoral Care in the Reformation Era," includes regional studies highlighting what leading Protestant reformers of various theological confessions taught and practiced with respect to pastoral care. The second rubric, "Pastoral Care in Reformation Readings of Scripture," includes case studies of individual pastors who faithfully sought to pursue scriptural teaching in their theology and ministries. For example, Reformation pastors disputed Roman Catholic doctrinal distinctives regarding venial and mortal sins (see chapter 9).

The Protestant reformers did not always treat the issues of pastoral practice and pastoral theology in exactly the same manner. Sometimes

---

7. Manetsch, *Calvin's Company of Pastors*, 289.

their debates were bitter and caused breaches in fellowship. Nonetheless, the essays in this volume do make it clear that the Protestant reformers were unified in advocating the important Protestant solas, such as *sola scriptura* and *sola fide*. They rejected the pope's claim to be the *infallible* teacher of the church. They said that the popes and councils had erred, whereas Scripture had not. They denied the premise that they, as pastors, enjoyed a higher spiritual rank than members of the laity. They sharply criticized the Roman Catholic eucharistic teachings regarding the Mass. They disputed the biblical and historical warrant for the Roman Catholic doctrine of transubstantiation.

Whereas Roman Catholic priests often assumed they were providing pastoral care through the administration of the sacraments of their church, the reformers, though not at all dismissive of the benefits of the Christian ordinances, believed they were providing essential pastoral care through the faithful preaching of Holy Scripture, God's written word. For example, in exegeting the book of Isaiah, several reformers emphasized passages assuring the faithful of the Lord's comfort, protection, peace, and providential care (see chapter 7).

Even if a pastor were a gifted theologian and biblical scholar, he might still confront trying circumstances that tested his faith to its very core: The tragic death of a parishioner's child or spouse. A boating accident on the Seine River that took the lives of over fifty Huguenot parishioners on a Sunday morning (see chapter 3).

The pastor's care of his parishioners' souls and physical needs could be joyful and satisfying. But the responsibility could also be overwhelming, dispiriting, and exhausting. It could lay bare the pastor's own weaknesses and need for enduements of divine wisdom and spiritual power. It could lead him to seek the fellowship and encouragement of his pastoral colleagues. It could prompt him to confess his own sins and be more attentive to his own soul's spiritual well-being. It could induce him to pray more fervently the Lord's Prayer.

John Calvin and the company of pastors in Geneva realized it was critically important to approve only those candidates for the ministry who gave convincing evidence that they were called of God to the apostolic position (see chapter 10). These pastors needed to be evangelically orthodox and trustworthy. They needed to flee sin. They needed to stay the course despite the hardships of ministry. They should not run away or flee their posts, even if their community were stricken by the plague or besieged by foreign enemies. They should be generous and walk humbly before the parishioners under their care. The apostolic ministry of being a pastor was not for the faint of heart, nor was it for candidates vacillating in their evangelical convictions.

"For what shall it profit a man, if he shall gain the whole world, and lose his own soul? Or what shall a man give in his exchange for his soul?" Jesus Christ made the care of souls a primary concern for his disciples. Protestant Reformation pastors of the sixteenth century realized that in their apostolic office, they needed to provide soul care for their parishioners and for themselves. Professor Manetsch's magisterial book and the present volume give us welcome and insightful apertures into their dedicated efforts to do so in Christ's name.

BIBLIOGRAPHY

Calvin, John. *Institutes of the Christian Religion*. In CO 1.
Davis, Henry. Introduction to *St. Gregory the Great: Pastoral Care*, translated by Henry Davis, 3–15. Vol. 11 of *Ancient Christian Writers: The Works of the Fathers in Translation*. Westminster, MD: Newman, 1950.
Gregory the Great. *St. Gregory the Great: Pastoral Care*. Translated by Henry Davis. Vol. 11 of *Ancient Christian Writers: The Works of the Fathers in Translation*. Westminster, MD: Newman, 1950.
Little, Lester K. "Calvin's Appreciation of Gregory the Great." *Harvard Theological Review* 56 (Apr. 1963) 145–57.
Manetsch, Scott M. *Calvin's Company of Pastors: Pastoral Care and the Emerging Reformed Church, 1536–1609*. Oxford Studies in Historical Theology. Oxford: Oxford University Press, 2013.

Abbreviations

BoC 1959 Tappert, Theodore G., ed. and trans. *The Book of Concord: The Confessions of the Evangelical Lutheran Church.* Philadelphia: Fortress, 1959.

BSELK Müller, J. T., ed. *Die Symbolischen Bücher Der Evangelisch-Lutherischen Kirche.* München: Bayerische Staatsbibliothek, 1882.

CB Aubert, Hippolyte, et al., eds. *Correspondance de Théodore de Bèze.* 43 vols. Geneva: Droz, 1960–2017.

CHC Ursinus, Zacharias. *Corpus doctrinae Orthodoxae Sive Catecheticarum Explicationum D. Zachariae Ursini Opus absolutum.* Edited by David Pareus. Heidelberg: Jonas Rhodius, 1612.

CO Calvin, John. *Ioannis Calvini Opera Quae Supersunt Omnia.* Edited by Guilielmus Baum, Eduardus Cunitz, Eduardus Reuss. 59 vols. Brunswick and Berlin: C. A. Schwetschke and Sons, 1863–1900.

CR *Corpus Reformatorum.* Edited by Carl Gottlieb Bretschneider, Heinrich Ernst Bindseil. Halle: C. A. Schwetschke and Sons, 1834–1900.

CSEL *Corpus Scriptorum Ecclesiasticorum Latinorum.* 85 vols. Vienna, 1866–.

CTS Calvin, John. *Commentary on the Book of Isaiah.* Translated and edited by John Pringle. Calvin Translation Society vols. 13–16. Edinburgh: Calvin Translation Society, 1850–53.

ECM	Aland, Barbara, et al., eds. *Novum Testamentum Graecum: Editio Critica Maior*. Vol. 4, *Catholic Letters*. Part 1, *James*; Part 2, *Supplementary Material*. Stuttgart: Editorial Verbo Divino, 1997–98. Indispensable for understanding how to use the *ECM* is Peter Head's article "Editio Critica Maior: An Introduction and Assessment," *Tyndale Bulletin* 61 (2010) 131–52.
HZW	Zwingli, Ulrich. *Huldrych Zwingli: Writings*. Translated by E. J. Furcha and H. Wayne Pipkin. 2 vols. Allison Park, PA: Pickwick, 1984.
LW	Luther, Martin. *Luther's Works* [American Edition]. Edited by Jaroslav Pelikan et al. St. Louis: Concordia, 1955–86 [vols. 1–30]; Philadelphia: Fortress, 1957–86 [vols. 31–56]; St. Louis: Concordia, 2009– [vols. 56–].
MBDS	Bucer, Martin. *Deutsche Schriften. Opera omnia*. Series 1. Edited by Robert Stupperich et al. 19 vols. Gütersloh: Gütersloher Verlagshaus G. Mohn, 1960–2016.
PL	Migne, J.-P., ed. *Patrologiae cursus completus. Series Latina*. 221 vols. Paris and Turnhout, 1857–79.
PRRD	Muller, Richard A. *Post-Reformation Reformed Dogmatics: The Rise and Development of Reformed Orthodoxy, ca. 1520 to ca. 1725*. 4 vols. 2nd ed. Grand Rapids: Baker Academic, 2003.
TAL	Luther, Martin. *The Annotated Luther*. 6 vols. Edited by Hans J. Hillerbrand, Kirsi I. Stjerna, and Timothy J. Wengert. Minneapolis: Fortress, 2015–17.
WA	Luther, Martin. *D. Martin Luthers Werke, Kritische Gesamtausgabe: [Schriften]*. Weimar: Hermann Böhlaus Nachfolger, 1883–2009.
WATR	Luther, Martin. *D. Martin Luthers Werke, Kritische Gesamtausgabe: Tischreden*. 6 vols. Weimar: Hermann Böhlaus Nachfolger, 1912–21.
Z	Zwingli, Ulrich. *Huldreich Zwinglis sämtliche Werke*. Edited by Emil Egli et al. 21 vols. Corpus Reformatorum 88–108. Leipzig/Zurich: Heinsius/TVZ, 1905–2013.

PART 1

Pastoral Care in the Reformation Era

1

By the Word Alone

Martin Luther's Pastoral Care in His Sermons on the Temptation of Jesus

TODD R. HAINS

> My zeal has brought me to death's door,
>
> for my adversaries forget your word.
>
> Your word has been tried so purely,
>
> and your servant loves it.
>
> PSALM 119:139–40[1]

A PASTORAL CRISIS SPARKED the Reformation.

The church's faithful were uncertain. They were uncertain what pleased God. Were the ordinary lives of ordinary men and women pleasing to God? Or did he require something more—more works, more self-denial, something more like monastic vows and monastic lives? They were uncertain whether and how God forgives sins. Was the ordinary absolution spoken by ordinary men and women enough for God to forgive

---

1. All Scripture quotations are my translation of Luther's translation of the Bible. I have leaned on Myles Coverdale's rendering of the Psalms, since he himself leaned on Luther's 1524 Psalter. See, for example, Clapton, *Our Prayer Book Psalter*, x.

sins? Or did he require something more—pilgrimages and payments, something more like Rome's indulgences?[2] They were also uncertain what founded the church on earth. Was the ordinary word of God, heard by ordinary men and women, enough for God to establish his church? Or did he require something more—a representative on earth, something more like the Roman papacy?

Martin Luther cut this crisis down to size with one question: Where is this written? He didn't come up with that question on his own; he borrowed it from his dear Lord. Jesus Christ responded to the three trials of Satan with the unadorned phrase "It is written" (Matt 4:4, 7, 10; Luke 4:4, 8, 12). The words of God that Jesus quoted against Satan revealed what was really at stake. Was the word enough?

Jesus's trials in the wilderness, Luther preached, hold in them every trial and affliction faced by every believer. And every believer can and must find the antidote to these trials and afflictions in Jesus's own trials. Unfortunately, that antidote had been hidden, typical of the medieval pastoral crisis, under the muck of human teaching. Matthew 4:1–11, the Gospel reading for Invocavit Sunday—that is, the First Sunday in Lent—had come to be taught as a justification for forty days of Lenten fasting.[3] Luther saw the medieval church's mandate for fasting as neither meritorious nor helpful. Worse yet, it distracted from the gift and example of our Lord Jesus Christ for our life, forgiveness, and salvation. "I refuse to institute fasting," Luther said. "Instead, I will preach the gospel."[4]

---

2. The logic of indulgences was highly nuanced. Our sins result in eternal and temporal punishment. The absolution deletes any and all eternal punishment, but to remove temporal punishment was another matter. That's where indulgences stepped in. This sort of scholastic parsing obfuscated the clear, scriptural proclamation of the forgiveness of sins. And that was Luther's concern: the plain and simple forgiveness of sins according to the word of God. For more on indulgences, see Tentler, *Sin and Confession*.

3. The First Sunday in Lent takes its nickname Invocabit, or the softened form Invocavit, from the first word of its introit: "Invocabit me et exaudiam eum"; "He shall call upon me, and I will hear him" (Ps 91:15). The Collect of the Day unapologetically pushed the works-focused understanding of the readings of the First Sunday in Lent. Here's the address and doctrine: "O God, you purify your Christian Church through the annual observance of the forty-day fast." Legg, ed., *The Sarum Missal*, 56; *Ewangeli und Epistel*, XXXIr.

4. *WA* 46:203.19–20. In his teaching on fasting, Luther is counteracting medieval abuses: those that offered works as meritorious but also harmed the physical health and well-being of pregnant mothers, of children, of the elderly, weak, and infirm. Luther teaches that Scripture commands but does not praise fasting. Fasting is worth nothing to God; it merely helps us to train our flesh, lest our passions master us. And God often sends forced fasting because of poverty or lack. This, for Luther, is the highest form of fasting. He leaves the demands and regulations of fasting with rulers of the

Luther labored to lay bare the true teaching and example of Matt 4. Throughout his life, he preached eighteen times on the First Sunday in Lent. Fourteen times he took as his text the Gospel reading of Matt 4:1–11 (1521–38).[5] (One of these sermons was preached on the following Saturday, 1534; another sermon's transcripts were lost, 1527.[6]) Only four times did he preach another text on this Sunday: once, in 1521, he preached Gen 31, once, in 1539, he preached the Epistle text of 2 Cor 6:1–10; once, in 1540, he preached on Ps 72; and the famous Invocavit Sermons of 1522 did not strictly take a text.[7]

In these labors we can see in miniature Luther's pastoral program for the Reformation: let the pure word shine forth to do the work it alone can do. In Luther's preaching, each trial of Jesus reveals a challenge to the word: first, the insufficiency of the word; second, the word against the word; third, worship without the word.[8]

---

land and fathers of the house. See, for example, *WA* 20:271.12–27; *LW* 57:254–56; *WA* 46:201.25–33, 202.1–26, 203.1–24; *LW* 76:365–66; "The Use and Confession of Christian Freedom" (February 14, 1524), *LW* 56:23–26.

5. Sermon on Invocavit Sunday, February 7, 1521, *WA* 9:588–93; Sermon on Invocavit Sunday, February 23, 1523, *WA* 11:21–27; Sermon on Invocavit Sunday, February 14, 1524, *WA* 15:450–53; Sermon on Invocavit Sunday, March 5, 1525, *WA* 17.1:63–67; Sermon on Invocavit Sunday (Morning), February 18, 1526, *WA* 20:269–75; Sermon on Invocavit Sunday (Afternoon), February 18, 1526, *WA* 20:275–80; Sermon on Invocavit Sunday, March 1, 1528, *WA* 27:61–64; Sermon on Invocavit Sunday, February 14, 1529, *WA* 29:52–62; Sermon on Invocavit Sunday, February 18, 1532, *WA* 36:118–22; Sermon on Invocavit Sunday (At Home), February 22, 1534, *WA* 37:304–7; Sermon on the Saturday after Invocavit Sunday (At the Castle Church), February 28, 1534, *WA* 37:308–12; Sermon on Invocavit Sunday, February 18, 1537, *LW* 57:253–76; *WA* 45:25–47; Sermon on Invocavit Sunday, March 10, 1538, *WA* 46:201–7.

Three postils cover this text, as well as four table talk and annotations on Matthew. The Gospel for the First Sunday in Lent, *Church Postil* (1525, 1540), *LW* 76:365–74 (*WA* 17.2:186–97); The Gospel for the First Sunday in Lent, *House Postil* (1544), *WA* 52:171–77 (revised from Invocavit Sunday 1534); as well as The Gospel for the First Sunday in Lent, Roth's *Winter Postil* (1528), *WA* 21:96–104 (revised from Invocavit Sunday 1523). Luther did not approve of Roth's postils. *WATR* 1:205–6, no. 471; *WATR* 1:350–51, no. 724; *WATR* 1:355, no. 739; *WATR* 2:136, no. 1569. Annotations on Some Chapters of St. Matthew (1538), *LW* 67:25–27 (*WA* 38:453–56).

6. These transcriptions may have been lost in Denmark, *WA* 23:665, 668–69.

7. Sermon on Invocavit Sunday, February 17, 1521, *WA* 9:509; Sermon on Invocavit Sunday (Afternoon), February 23, 1539, *WA* 47:666–71; Fourth Sermon on Psalm 72, on Invocavit Sunday, February 15, 1540, *WA* 49:30–35; The Invocavit Sermons (1522), *TAL* 4:14–45 (*WA* 10.3:1–64; see also *LW* 51:70–100).

8. In the 1530s, Luther maps the three temptations to three ages of the church: persecution under the black devil, heresy under the white devil, and papacy under the divine devil. He does this most explicitly in his 1537 sermon (*LW* 57:253–76), but he also makes comments at table about it in 1533 (*WATR* 1:205.10–19, 206.1–10, no. 471).

JESUS IN THE WILDERNESS: MATTHEW 4:1–11

A reading from the Gospel according to Matthew:

> Then Jesus was led by the Spirit into the wilderness, so that he would be tempted by the devil. And then he fasted forty days and nights. He hungered.
>
> And the tempter came to him and said, "If you really are the Son of God—then speak, that these stones become bread." And he answered and said, "It stands written: Man does not live by bread alone, but by each and every word that comes from the mouth of God."
>
> Then the devil led him into the holy city and placed him on the parapet of the temple and said to him, "If you really are the Son of God, then cast yourself down, for it stands written, 'He will command his angels concerning you, and they will bear you in their hands, so that your foot does not even touch a stone.'" Then Jesus said to him, "But it also stands written, 'You shall not put God your Lord to the test.'"
>
> Again, the devil led him to a very high mountain and showed him all the kingdoms of the world and their glory. And he said to him, "All this I will give to you, if you fall down and worship me." And Jesus said to him, "Get away from me, Satan, for it stands written, 'You shall worship God your Lord and serve him alone.'"
>
> Then the devil left him, and behold, the angels came to him and served him.

STONES TO BREAD: THE INSUFFICIENCY OF THE WORD

Jesus, the Lord of heaven and earth, hungered.[9] He truly feels the pain and desire of hunger here—how our bodies demand and press us for physical and fleshly needs and comforts. These fleshly needs cause our members, muscles, and bones to ache, focusing our thoughts and attention on our bodies alone. "I am feeble and sore smitten, I roar for the disquietness of my heart" (Ps 38:8). He is true man, born of Mary. "Christ is not made of

---

Philip Melanchthon uses this schema in *Treatise on the Power and Primacy of the Pope* (1537), and Bernard of Clairvaux does something similar (*LW* 57:253–54).

9. *WA* 15:451.1–25; *WA* 36:119.10; *WA* 37:308.3–17; *WA* 37:310.24–25; *WA* 46:203.28–29, 204.1.

wood and stone," Luther says, "like the Sophists who feel nothing at all."[10] He is like you and me in every way but one: he is without sin. And still this trial was no trifle.[11] Yes, he holds the field and defeats Satan, but "not without sweat, struggle, and pain."[12]

Satan fashions Jesus's hunger into a weapon.[13] He thrusts it against the word and office written over Christ. "If you really are the Son of God—then speak, that these stones become bread." With this trial Satan deploys a twofold maneuver. First, he pushes Christ to doubt the goodness of his God. It is as if he says, Feel that hunger, that roaring need? Your God doesn't care for you! If he did, the least he could do is give you food. "I think He has abandoned You."[14] Second, he pushes Christ to abuse his office. It is as if he says, If you are really God's Son, surely you can do the things God does; speak, and let there be food. Don't wait around for roasted fowl to fly into your mouth.[15] You can quench your hunger and desire right now: "Cut a slice of rock and eat!"[16]

It doesn't sound like a big deal, but it is! It is a test of faith, Luther says. This test asserts that we live by the material alone and should not attend to God.[17] Here Satan puffs up the flesh and its wants, so that the flesh overtakes the spirit and sends it packing.[18] Don't think of your soul or God, Satan whispers. Just think of gobbling and guzzling. It doesn't matter how many times I hear it: gold doesn't come from the gospel! What I need first is a good house and money enough; then I'll turn to the gospel.[19]

Jesus swats Satan's two poisonous darts to the ground with but a word: "Man does not live by bread alone but by each and every word that comes from the mouth of God." The God who creates by his word also

---

10. *WA* 15:451.18–19.

11. *WA* 46:204.

12. *WA* 46:204.19–20.

13. *WA* 9:591.1–5; *WA* 20:272.5–9; *WA* 27:61.9–14; *WA* 29:53.6–9, 54.1–4, 53.16, 54.8–11; *WA* 37:305.13–19; *WA* 37:309.35–38, 310.1–4; *WA* 45:29.1–3, 30.1; *WA* 46:204.24–26, 205.6–13; *LW* 76:367.

14. *LW* 76:367.

15. *LW* 76:367.

16. *WA* 37:310.1.

17. *WA* 37:305.7–12; *WA* 52:172.30–33.

18. *WA* 11:26.5–17.

19. *WA* 20:272.11–12.

sustains and preserves by his word. It's true; our bodies require nourishment.[20] And that nourishment comes from the word of God.

The word of God comes to us under the mask of bread and other physical goods.[21] "All creatures are God's masks and disguises."[22] He doesn't need these masks and disguises. God could feed us and preserve us without visible, temporal goods. But in his good pleasure, he teaches us his mercy by so miraculously and mysteriously hiding his word underneath humble creatures of wheat and water and the like.[23] "God commands the opposite, so that I believe him."[24] Against all human reason and argument, we must let God's masks remain according to his command.[25] By God's command flesh and blood are made and sustained out of bread.[26] "If it so pleases him, I will use it!"[27]

Whatever physical thing provides the body its needs and comforts is nothing without God's word. Without God's word bread cannot nourish us, and clothes cannot clothe us.[28] Perhaps you are rich and filled with good things to overflowing, perhaps you have one thousand years of food—it is all for nothing.[29] "Even if a church is full of gold and a city is full of grain, nevertheless, there's no life in them even for a moment."[30] Gold and grain and every treasure will not nourish you, and they certainly will not satisfy you. The word must be added. "Unless the word is present, nothing at all will nourish naturally. This [faith and knowledge] alone makes a Christian."[31] "For not the bread but the word of God nourishes also the body naturally, just as it creates and preserves all things."[32]

---

20. *WA* 9:59.32–34.
21. *WA* 17.1:65.16–19; *WA* 20:272.24, 273.1; *LW* 76:369, 370.
22. *LW* 76:370.
23. *WA* 20:274.1–3.
24. *WA* 27:61.19–20.
25. Luther brings up the counterexample of the Radicals. They despised the physical material that God deigned to use: the water of baptism they called a cow's drink or a dog's bath. See, for example, *WA* 20:276.14–22, 277.1–14; 276.35–37.
26. *WA* 20:273.11–13.
27. *WA* 20:277.1.
28. *WA* 17.1:65.2–3.
29. *WA* 17.1:66.13–14.
30. *WA* 20:272.21–23.
31. *WA* 36:119.19–20.
32. *LW* 76:368.

The word of God alone gives life.[33] God's word must fail before stones become bread.[34]

Satan knows this. He wants to make the word nothing.[35] He wants to put a wedge between us and the word, because he knows that only the word has real life and life everlasting.[36] He knows it is his defeat.

Our Lord overcomes this trial for us, modeling how we are to cling to the word even as our bodies cry out for food and drink and whatever other physical comforts we think we need. "You would love to tear me from the word, but you won't be able to! Before I go without God's word, I will sooner go without bread and die of hunger!"[37] Our Lord Jesus seizes the word and forsakes all else. The word is all that he needs. "God nourishes you without bread through His word."[38] "I have his word and live by it, even if my body dies."[39] Jesus holds the word against Satan's lie that the flesh and its wants can give life.

Luther points his hearers to the example of the people of Israel in the wilderness.[40] Their situation was hopeless. Their only hope was the signs and wonders of the word. The word was with them, and they clung to it. By the word alone they received water from rock and bread from cloud. They even won battles by the word alone, not by the strength of horses and the might of warriors (Pss 33:16–17; 44:6). Out of the waterless waste he gave them water. Out of the pathless desert he made them a path. And out of the wilderness God made them a house.[41] Even so, because the body howls with its desire and need, they doubted whether God could sustain them in the desert.

And we are no different.[42] We are surrounded with the wonder and marvel of creation—a world of the word! But we are tempted to explain these wonders and marvels through cold facts and science alone, as if we are masters over them. In contrast, Luther heightens and magnifies the everyday miracles of our ordinary lives. God's word multiplies the harvest

---

33. *WA* 17.1:64.39, 65.1–2.
34. *WA* 37:305.28–29; *WA* 52:173.35–37.
35. *WA* 37:305.19–21.
36. *LW* 57:258; *WA* 45:29.17–20; *WA* 37:305.34–36.
37. *WA* 37:305.21–23.
38. *LW* 76:368.
39. *WA* 46:205.21–22.
40. *WA* 17.1:65.26–27; *WA* 20:273.31–34, 274.3–9; *WA* 37:309.10–13, 26–29.
41. *LW* 76:369.
42. *WA* 37:309.26–29.

in the field and the flour in the sack and the bread in the cupboard.[43] It is not mere heat that transforms what we eat into muscle, sinew, and bone, into our flesh and blood; it is the word and command of God. And how many and diverse things come from one bit of bread by God's command: not just some dung and water but all our members.[44] He can work even greater miracles than our reason can grasp: he brought water out of rock, he can bring heat out of snow.[45] This is true of all our needs.[46] He gladly hides his provision and sustaining power under the masks of creation—even to the point of hiding a blessing under a curse. And he can just as well sustain us without visible, temporal things, using his unmediated word.[47] "The world is brim full with miracles."[48]

That we not forget that our help is in the name of the Lord alone, Luther encourages his hearers to inscribe Matt 4:4 on every article of clothing and in every nook and cranny of the home: "Man does not live by bread alone, but by each and every word that comes from the mouth of God."[49] Like Christ, we must constantly learn to entrust ourselves to the word and mercy of God. Christ was not abandoned—neither shall we be![50]

Of course, Jesus is also true God of true God. He could have marshaled all his divine might against Satan, squashing him like an ant with rank upon rank of angels. But for our sake he did not take advantage of his divinity, and he stands here like any other man or woman. And in the midst of the pain and pining of the flesh, he lands blow after blow against his ancient foe with nothing but the word alone. "Even if you kill me, I am still God's Son, for I have God's word."[51] With only a word our Lord has overcome the devil, the world, and all that we lack. And by his word so can we. His victory is our victory.

And so, we suffer and wait and fast with Christ.[52] It doesn't look good or sound good or feel good. The word doesn't seem to be enough.

43. *WA* 17.1:65.15–16; *LW* 76:369.
44. *WA* 20:273.3–13.
45. *WA* 20:274.22–25.
46. *LW* 76:369.
47. *WA* 27.61.21–23; *WA* 36:119.30–35.
48. *WA* 20:273.17–18.
49. *WA* 20:272.16–17, 34–35.
50. *WA* 27.61.21–23; *WA* 36:119.30–35.
51. *WA* 46:205.20–21.
52. *WA* 52:174.5–6.

Satan magnifies the hunger and howling of our flesh, driving it against God's promises to us, tempting us to use these promises not for faith and life but for sin.[53] Wrap your sin in the cloak of God's word, he says, and satisfy the needs of your belly and loins, your heart and flesh. The word isn't enough—it won't do it, so take action and live! This temptation hurts. It hurts to fast, but our God has led us, just like he led Jesus, into this wilderness by his Spirit. He isn't surprised by our plight; he knows our needs. "He that planted the ear, shall he not hear? He that made the eye, shall he not see?" (Ps 94:9). God is our God: he will not desert us, and he does not tempt us to wickedness (Jas 1:13).[54]

With the word alone Pastor Martin addresses this crisis of doubt ("Is my life pleasing to God?"). Over the din of doubt and Satan's lies, Luther wants his hearers to hear God's merciful word. Do not believe Satan's lie that our material situation proves God's love or lack of love for us. No matter our office as clergy or layperson, our wealth or poverty, our peace or distress—our lives are pleasing to God because of his merciful word alone. In his word God is well pleased with you.

He has given us his word—it is near us in our hearts and in our mouths (Deut 30:14). Where the word remains, the one who believes the word remains too.[55] Even if we die, if we die with the word, we live—it is an eternal word.[56] "If you have the word of God, he feeds you like a sheep."[57] He is enough. His word is enough. Eat his word and live eternally.

FALLING FROM THE HEIGHTS: THE WORD AGAINST THE WORD

Satan is persistent. Thwarted once, he regroups and deploys a second offensive. This time he builds momentum by snatching Jesus's sole weapon: the word of God. "Oh, it's the word of God you want to have," Satan says. "I'll give it to you!"[58] "Now I will become a theologian and bring forth Scripture and make a beautiful sermon for the Lord."[59] This is a signature

53. *WA* 37:305.13–19; *WA* 52:173.
54. *WA* 37:310.31–34.
55. *LW* 57:258.
56. *LW* 57:259.
57. *WA* 17.1:65.36, 66.1.
58. *WA* 15:451.29. See also *WA* 27:62.26–28; *WA* 37:311.1–3; *WA* 45:34.1–3; *WA* 46:206.1; *WA* 52:174.22–23.
59. *WA* 36:120.5–7.

stratagem of Satan.⁶⁰ He grabs the sword of the word, even as you are holding it, and he thrusts it at you. Whether hilt or blade, he'll clobber you with whatever he can get his hands on.⁶¹

But the devil doesn't confront us as an enemy combatant. He appears as a comrade in arms—as a bright and beautiful, holy and mighty angel (2 Cor 11:14).⁶² And he comes bearing what seems to be the gift of the word. It looks like the word. It sounds like the word. It is taught as the word. But the devil has hollowed it out and filled it with a lie, wheeling this Trojan horse to the gates of our conscience.⁶³ It is the greatest assault and temptation: to twist, distort, and hollow out the word for our own purposes.⁶⁴

Satan knows the power of faith in the word—God's word, which does what it says and cannot be overthrown. And so, he strives to subvert and falsify faith under the appearance of true faith and the word.⁶⁵ Faith is taught so that we would doubt the faith itself and love what God does not command and desire what he does not promise.⁶⁶ "This is true devilish art."⁶⁷ It is a fearsome spiritual test. "It's an assault no one understands but those who have experienced it."⁶⁸ In this battle, we are faced with what looks and sounds like God's mercy and grace, wisdom and word.⁶⁹ But to be led by appearances is to be led by Satan and to put God to the test.⁷⁰ To hold our ground in this trial, we need not just a sharp spirit but the Holy Spirit.⁷¹

Satan is a master of subtlety. Luther spots a small but strange addition and a small but strange omission. First, the addition: Satan leads Jesus not into the temple but above it. Humans are meant to dwell inside of buildings, not on top of them. In the same way, Satan abuses and distorts

---

60. *WA* 37:312.3–4.
61. *WA* 29:58.17–18, 59.5–7; *WA* 46:206.9; *LW* 57:260, 263.
62. *WA* 37:311.4; *WA* 45:31.1–3; *LW* 57:260.
63. *WA* 17.1:66.31–33; *WA* 29:58.6–9, 59.3, 61.4–6.
64. *WA* 15:451.26–39, 452.1–17; *WA* 17.1:66.19–40, 67.1–9; *WA* 37:306.12; *WA* 46:206.21, 207.1; *WA* 52:174.13–19.
65. *WA* 20:275.19–21, 276.1–7.
66. *WA* 37:311.24–25; *LW* 76:370–71.
67. *WA* 29:61.6.
68. *WA* 37:306.28–29.
69. *WA* 37:306.3; *WA* 52:174.13–19; *LW* 57:261.
70. *WA* 17.1:66.31–33.
71. *WA* 27:62.34–35.

Scripture, twisting it against its intended use.[72] This leads to the second diabolical subtlety. Satan omits part of Ps 91:11: the phrase "in all your ways."[73] God has promised to protect us in the places he has placed us. We have not been placed in the air, like doves and sparrows, nor have we been given feathers and wings. The stairs of the temple are the path God has given and promised to guard us on.[74]

These two subtleties set the scene for Satan's test of Jesus and us: make God prove his promises. Don't just have a little faith; have great faith and leap from the heights.[75] If you trust God's word so much, won't he keep his promise to send his angels lest even your foot touch a stone? "You'll float down as if on a bed," the devil purrs, "for God does not deny Scripture and his word."[76] Satan hides this game of doubt under the cloak of the word and seeks every opportunity to stoke these "What-Ifs." Does God really care for you? Put his promises to the test! Don't eat the bread in your cupboard—real faith is waiting for God to send manna.[77] Jump from the heights, place yourself in grave danger, do this work, and do that work.

Works—that's what Satan makes out of faith. "This is nothing other than to leap from the pinnacle of the temple: to have faith in our faith, which we ourselves have devised, not the faith Christ has formed."[78] Satan leads poor souls with their self-devised creeds and doctrines, and he tells them that their ideas are so holy and good. Jump and see if God accepts them.[79]

Every age has its example of faith made works. Luther, for instance, trotted out his opponents on the right and the left. On the right, the Papists and monks grab some dream of theirs and apply it to Scripture.[80] They baptize altars, stones, and bells instead of preaching the gospel for

---

72. *WA* 17.1:66.26–30; *WA* 36:120.10–11; *WA* 37:311.6–9; *WA* 45:35.1–2.

73. *WA* 15:451.33–37; *WA* 20:277.15–17; *WA* 27:63.5–10; *WA* 29:59; *WA* 37:306.10–11; *WA* 37:311.39; *WA* 45:35.3, 36.1–3; *LW* 76:371; *WA* 52:174.30–32.

74. *WA* 29:59.10; *WA* 37:306.15–16; *WA* 45:36.1–3; *WA* 52:175.1–4; *LW* 57:260; *LW* 76:370.

75. *WA* 27.63.23–26.

76. *WA* 37:311.13–14.

77. *LW* 76:371.

78. *WA* 20:278.8–10. See also *WA* 17.1:66.23–26, 67.1–3; *WA* 20:277.3–4.

79. *LW* 57:264.

80. *WA* 37:306.19–21.

the forgiveness, life, and salvation of dear souls.[81] They peddle indulgences for freedom from death.[82] You say that repentance and hearing the word makes holy? Oh, that's too easy! Real holiness is eating fish on Fridays and wearing a gray habit.[83] They make a word and way where no word and way are.[84]

On the left, the Radicals despise the ordinary and mundane means our Lord has mercifully given us. Creatures are of no help, they say. Water has no power to give forgiveness and life—it's just what cows drink. It's a dog's bath![85] And bread and wine can't bring God present—they're just symbols.[86] Baptism and the Sacrament of the Altar are nothing. The Radicals claw and fight to tear down the word and way God has commanded. In this way they, too, make their own way where there is no way—like an invisible stairway in the sky.[87]

In contrast, Pastor Martin applies the word to this crisis of works ("Can I be forgiven?"). He lays down this axiom: the word prepares our way. That's how God works in his good will and pleasure. He doesn't need our puny works to impress him or to achieve some status that he will deign to look upon.[88] He forgives us by his word and mercy not because of anything we have done or any status we have achieved. He saves sinners by his word. He has sent his word for our forgiveness, life, and salvation: "And they cried to the LORD in their trouble, and he helped them out of their distress. He sent his word and healed them, and he saved them that they would not die" (Ps 107:19–20). He has wonderfully combined his holy word with ordinary water.[89] Without the word, water can do

---

81. *WA* 36:122.5–11.
82. *WA* 29:60.5–7.
83. *WA* 37:306.35, 307.1–4.
84. *WA* 29:59.13.
85. *WA* 20:276.35–36; *WA* 29:61.10–11, 62.1–2; *WA* 36:121.16–18; *WA* 37:311.31–33.
86. *WA* 29:62.8–9; *WA* 37:311.19–24.
87. *WA* 29:59.13.

88. While our Lord doesn't need our works, our neighbor does! In his mercy and good humor, the Lord our God—maker of heaven and earth—uses us as masks of his word for the provision, comfort, and benefit of our neighbors. If we won't comply with God's word and command, he'll use another person or creature to bless our neighbor. He does not need us, for his are the cattle on a thousand hills (Ps 50:10–15). And yet blessed is the one who says, Let it be according to your word; "Establish the thing, O God, that you have wrought in us" (Ps 68:28). See the 1522 Invocavit sermons, *TAL* 4:14–45; *LW* 51:70–100.

89. *WA* 20:276.36–37; *WA* 29:61.10–11, 62.1–2.

nothing—not even quench our thirst, as the first temptation makes clear, let alone do such great things as forgive sins and save sinners. Likewise, eating and drinking alone do no such great thing as bring Jesus present. It's the words written here: "Given and shed for you for the forgiveness of sins."[90] His word wonderfully accomplishes what it says, even if we struggle to see it. Close your eyes and open your ears and believe the word: in Christ your sins are forgiven.

What our Lord unites must never be put asunder. "Faith and baptism, word and water must be together."[91] It's not enough to use the word.[92] The word must speak the Spirit. The Spirit is who we strain to hear in the heat and pain of this trial. "Now learn to sift Satan: what's true faith, what's false? What's Scripture, what's Scripture turned upside down?"[93]

Christ pioneers the way through this assault, interpreting Scripture according to Scripture.[94] This is the true art of the apostles and the fathers.[95] To hear the Holy Spirit is to hear the word according to the word. The word Jesus quotes unmasks Satan's true intention: "You shall not put God your LORD to the test." The devil is stoking Jesus to put God to the test, to ask that ancient serpent's favorite question: "Did God really say?" But the Bible is clear that God is faithful to his word. "He speaks, and it is done; he commands, and it stands fast" (Ps 33:9). He does not turn or change like creatures do. And so, it won't do to dictate terms and conditions for the Lord our God to fulfill. We must let God be God. We must walk in faith, following his word.[96] What he has united will stand.[97]

The only way through this assault is to follow the way Christ has trailblazed for us by his word and example. For our sake, he doesn't work the miracles and mighty deeds he well could. Instead, he suffers.[98] He hides his divinity under his humanity, and he clings to the word.[99] "God lets me

---

90. On the Sacrament of the Altar in the *Small Catechism* (1529), see *TAL* 4:235–36 (*WA* 30.1:314–19; *BoC* 1959, 351–52).

91. *WA* 52:175.20–21.

92. *WA* 45:35.23–37.

93. *WA* 20:276.28–30.

94. *WA* 27:63.1–5; *LW* 57:264.

95. *WA* 27:63.10–15; *WA* 15:452.15–17.

96. *WA* 15:452.5–8.

97. *WA* 37:312.4–6; *LW* 76:373.

98. *WA* 37:306.12–13; *LW* 57:260.

99. *WA* 37:306.6–7; *WA* 52:174.26–28.

be afflicted in this trial so that I would believe his word."[100] "God cannot be found except in the word."[101] The word brings God near along with all his gifts, in particular, faith by the Spirit. "True faith makes all miracles. As Christ says, 'To those who believe all things are possible.'"[102] And that includes fending off the flaming darts and barbed attacks of the devil.

We have no power in ourselves to help ourselves. We must receive the word and let the word do its work, for there is no health and salvation outside our Lord Jesus and his word.[103] And so, when Satan comes and tempts you—whether on the right like the Papists or on the left like the Radicals—with works to test how much God really loves you, plant your feet firmly in the word and in a clear voice cry out: "I have God's word. I am baptized. God has given me his word; there I abide."[104] "I believe that the Son of God died for me. Blab away in my heart if you want! If I am weak—that's nothing to me. I am Christ. My ears don't hear a single one of your imaginations."[105]

BOW DOWN AND WORSHIP ME: WORSHIP WITHOUT THE WORD

Satan's last assault seems odd. "All this I will give to you, if you fall down and worship me" (Matt 4:9). Power over all the nations of the world is certainly tempting for us, but for Jesus? He's God—all these nations are already his. And how tempting can it be for Jesus to worship his ancient enemy? "No one can understand this trial," Luther quipped at table. "If I could preach it, I'd gladly die."[106] It is the trial Luther says the least about on average, but he strives to picture the trial and understand its devilish logic.

The god of the belly is Satan's final weapon. What the sword and Scripture failed to do, Satan thinks, perhaps money, goods, and honor

---

100. WA 17.1:66.33–34.
101. WA 27:63.29–30.
102. WA 20:276.4–5; quoting Mark 9:23.
103. WA 20:277.19–21.
104. WA 46:207.1–2.
105. WA 46:206.26–29. Luther also recounts a favorite story of a nun who can't make any further headway against Satan's accusations, and so she cries out, "I am a Christian!" WA 46:206.31; WA 25:325.
106. WATR 1:350.25–26 (351.18–19), no. 724.

will accomplish.[107] The divine devil steps forward and offers spirituality as a route to power, honor, and recognition before the world.[108] "He appears perhaps as an angel of God."[109] "He must have presented himself magnificently."[110] Satan doesn't claim to be God. He wants Jesus (and us!) to connect the dots: surely whoever can show all earthly kingdoms and wealth in a single moment could only be divine.[111]

This assault is well known to all of us. We are bombarded with material riches and those who craft them, clamoring to be our gods—gods who will serve us. If we only let our passions loose and forget baptism and the gospel, these gods say, we will rule and command the world around us.[112] We will feel delight and pleasure always. This trial presses us to crave and claw for more and more—to never be satisfied. "Whoever lives life as a serf longs to become a freeman; in turn, the freeman dreams of ascending to the office of prince; the prince seeks to become emperor and always desires to reach ever greater heights. This trial roams the world seeking whom it will devour; it disturbs nearly every human heart."[113] This temptation is like the first: let material needs and goods consume us. The first is a trial of lack and anger, while this is a trial of abundance, prosperity, pleasure, and joy.[114]

What a mercy and kindness of our Lord Jesus that he experienced the flood and sore burden of this temptation. "For we do not have a high priest who is unable to sympathize with our weakness, but one who was tempted in every way, just as we are, and yet without sin" (Heb 4:15). As in the other trials, Jesus faces this trial with his divinity hidden. According to his eyes, Christ wasn't able to see Satan—he only saw glory.[115] Somehow the maker of heaven and earth stood before Satan and felt the howl of desire and the roar of lust. "I am God," this divine devil says, "and I want to give you all of this."[116] He bore the full weight of this temptation

---

107. *WA* 46:207.3–4.

108. *WA* 15:452.34–36; *WA* 17.1:67.9; *WA* 37:306.34–35; *WA* 37:312.7–15; *WA* 45:36.4–5, 37.1–5; *WA* 52:175.36–39; *LW* 76:373.

109. *WA* 20:279.28–29.

110. *WA* 20:279.1.

111. *WA* 27:62.6–12.

112. *WA* 36:121.37–38.

113. *WA* 29:57.33–36, 58.21–22, here 57.35–36, 58.21–22; quoting 1 Pet 5:8.

114. *WA* 20:279; *LW* 76:373.

115. *WA* 29:56, 57.18–27.

116. *WA* 37:312.10.

in his human flesh. And he did this for us! In his name and by his word we, too, can stand tall against the breakers, wind, and storm of riches, power, and pleasure.

This tactic—kingdoms, power, and glory—has worked very well for Satan.[117] Tired of warring over the word of God, we abandon it.[118] We welcome worldly peace and quiet along with their friends, worldly power, glory, and order.[119] "We are sleek, fat, and bored, and we crave something new."[120] Get those preachers and pastors away from us! They only bring arguments and resentments against our neighbor and look at the disaster of their churches—full of sinners! Sated but looking for nibbles and tidbits, we flee from the discipline of our flesh, and we trade God's word, gospel, and command for human imaginations and ideas.

With this trade the devil claims God's own office and worship and crafts a visible righteousness that impresses the world.[121] "Satan wants to raise up worship of God without the word of God."[122] "The devil wants me to serve our Lord God with any other thing than what he has commanded."[123] And so, uncommanded holiness spreads like an infection.[124] We seize the articles of faith and Scripture, and we test them against our opinions and distort them until they fit our own ideas.[125]

For Luther, this distortion was on display in monastic discipline and the forced Lenten fast. Uncommanded holiness, such as putting on a monk's habit and not eating meat, ranked higher than commanded holiness, such as simple obedience to father and mother and God's word. Out of butter and herring the devil makes righteousness.[126] And he doesn't stop there: he makes Jesus into an accuser and his mother into a mediator.[127]

The devil is a barterer. "All this I will give to you, if you fall down and worship me" (Matt 4:9). Look at all the shiny things I will give you,

---

117. *LW* 57:269.
118. *LW* 57:262.
119. *LW* 57:265–66.
120. *WA* 37:312.28.
121. *WA* 15:452.18–39, 453.1–4; *WA* 11:27.10–33.
122. *WA* 27:62.12–13.
123. *WA* 37:312.17–18.
124. *WA* 37:307.12; *WA* 52:176.15.
125. *LW* 57:262; *WA* 45:42.1.
126. *WA* 37:306.34–35, 307.1–4, 21–22.
127. *LW* 57:266.

he says, if you just do this one small thing for me. "Not only, he says, will I give you bread, but also truth and peace, riches, glory, honor, and might—and whatever else is high and greatly regarded in the world—if you abandon God and his word and instead follow and serve me."[128] So far the glimmering devil has kept his side of the bargain. "In the papacy we lack absolutely nothing. We are stuffed with riches, pleasure, honor—therefore we have not been able to come to the gospel, nor are the Papists able to today. For how can they forsake honor, goods, friends?"[129] Many know the truth, but they do not want to risk their security for the sake of the word!

All this haggling and these conditional promises have one goal in sight: to enslave souls. Slowly, bit by bit, crumb by crumb, pleasure by pleasure, Satan leads us away from God's word and worship. He'll even let God's word and worship remain, so long as it's not alone, so long as it's joined with some uncommanded work.[130] To do so isn't to serve God but the devil, because God's word isn't present![131] "If we don't serve God alone, we serve the devil."[132] Whenever worship is proposed other than what God has commanded, it's Satan speaking, not God.[133] "We cannot serve God, if we do not have his word and command."[134]

In contrast to the devil's economy of haggling and slavery, our Lord already gives us all we need even without our asking. His mercies are like the sun and rain: they shine on the good and evil alike, they water the just and unjust too (Matt 5:45). These mercies are to be received in faith, not by sight. "You must not pine and long to feel God's mercy, but instead shut your eyes and think: 'I will cling to the word and believe—just as he promised me! I must not strive to feel it.'"[135]

Luther applies the balm of vocation against the wiles of Satan and the sore disease of our flesh. The doctrine of vocation is nested within the doctrine of the word. Wherever God's name and word are, God's service and worship are established. This expands our puny view of worship as an hour or two in a designated building. For Luther, worship encompasses

---

128. *WA* 29:57.29–31.
129. *WA* 20:279.8–10.
130. *WA* 29:57.4.
131. *WA* 37:307.22–25.
132. *WA* 52:175.16–17.
133. *WA* 27:62.15–16.
134. *WA* 52:176.34–35.
135. *WA* 11:27.30–33.

all of life. We are all too tempted to see our day-to-day lives—as husband or wife, parent or child, magistrate or citizen—as something apart from the word. It's all just ethics and technique: read this or that book on marriage, parenting, and ruling. But the doctrine of vocation teaches us how the word interprets the world.

In his tender compassion God has hung his word over each of us according to the various places he has placed us. Over one's husband or wife he hangs the gleaming and golden words: "Bone of my bones and flesh of my flesh" (Gen 2:23) and "You shall not commit adultery" (Exod 20:14). Over one's parents he writes, "You shall honor your father and your mother" (Exod 20:12); over one's children, "You fathers, do not provoke your children to anger, but raise them up in the nurture and command of the Lord" (Eph 6:4).[136]

These words show us how to read our neighbor and the world around us. They lay bare the true nature of things. God calls us to devote ourselves to these words placed over us and our neighbor. This devotion is nothing other than to fear, love, and trust in God above all things. "For God has written his word over my neighbor's head and said: You shall love your neighbor and serve him."[137] "That's serving God and his word and not the person."[138] We earn nothing by this service. God justifies us by the free gift of his word—he doesn't need our works! Our service to the word in our daily vocations is for God's glory and the benefit of our neighbor.[139]

And so everything is worship. This is true of our whole life, not just our life of faith—the time we spend in the explicit spiritual service of prayer, praise, and thanksgiving, whether in public or in private. God's mighty, creating, and sustaining word is everywhere. He has written it into creation and hung it over our heads and our neighbor's head. Marked with God's word, all his creatures—seen and unseen—testify to his praise and pleasure:

> O praise the LORD, you angels of his, you mighty heroes,
> you that fulfill his commandment,
> that man hears the voice of his word.

---

136. The Table of Duties in Luther's *Small Catechism* lists the various words written over each office of church, family, and society; see *TAL* 4:239–41 (*WA* 30.1:326–39; *BoC* 1959, 354–56).

137. *WA* 52:176.26–28.

138. *WA* 52:176.23; see also *WA* 37:307.15–21.

139. *WA* 45:45.1, 46.1–2.

> O praise the Lord, all you his hosts,
>   you servants that do his will.
> O praise the Lord, all you works of his,
> in all places of his dominion;
>   praise the Lord, O my soul. (Ps 103:20–22)

By his word he has given everything we need—in body and soul. He gives everything and needs nothing from us. And he even mercifully ordains us to join this work, providing for our neighbor and blessing our neighbor. The word written over all creation directs our hearts and eyes to all that is good, and his word disciplines our flesh, so that in our vocations—in church and in family and in society—we praise God.

And our Lord Jesus has made himself lower than the angels to teach us how to be creatures of the word. That's what he does for us in this temptation. "If you see the word of God, embrace it; if not, flee!"[140] "Whoever wants to serve God—he does what God has commanded in his word."[141] "In God's name must everything take place."[142] True worship is to honor God alone.[143] God institutes and initiates his worship and work by his word. It is the touchstone of truth; test all things against it (1 Thess 5:21).[144] In the service of God's word and command alone is true freedom.

Everything must be established by his word. That's the remedy Pastor Martin applied to the crisis of the church's foundation ("What founds the church?"). In contrast, the papacy built a church on the frail foundation of works of butter and fish and offices of men—all shrouded under God's word. Luther saw the papacy as using the word of God against the Spirit of God to cover the rot and stench of devilish imaginations for temporal glory and might. Luther was willing to grant the papacy a place so long as it humbly acknowledged that it is nothing without the word. Only the word of God founds the church.

By his word—praise be to God—our Lord Jesus Christ has overcome even this trial for us and all believers.[145] He is our champion and hero; sin, death, and the devil can't bear to see him take the field. "He is the one Law-slayer, sin-bearer, death-devourer, and devil-murderer."[146]

---

140. *WA* 15:452.39. See also *WA* 27:62.19.
141. *WA* 52:175.18–19.
142. *WA* 15:452.20.
143. *WA* 27:62.15–16; *WA* 46:207.11.
144. *WA* 27:62.19, 64.5–12; *WA* 52:177.16–17.
145. *WA* 29:58.22–23.
146. *LW* 57:271–72.

Christ conquers and cuts to pieces everything that the devil stirs up against his word, work, and honor.[147] He does this, again, only by the word: "Get away from me, Satan, for it stands written, 'You shall worship God your LORD and serve him alone.'" Our Lord Jesus teaches us not to argue with the devil—that just energizes him. Instead, he sends him packing with some rude words and the word of God.[148]

The Lord slays by the breath of his mouth, and we send Satan scattering by that same word and breath of the Lord.[149] God's word, even in sinful human lips, lays bare the nakedness of the divine devil and the fools who worship him.[150] "Out of the mouth of toddlers and sucklings have you ordained strength because of your enemies, that you might root out the enemy and the avenger" (Ps 8:2). "For you have magnified your name above all things through your word" (Ps 138:2). Simple people open their mouths to speak God's name, word, and gospel, and Satan's kingdom crumbles.[151] "God, who has already conquered, give us strength, that we might be victorious too. Amen."[152]

THE WORD IS MORE THAN ENOUGH

Let the word alone do the work. God's word is the source and boundary of Luther's pastoral care. It is the word that really nourishes us, clothes us, and shelters us—not food, clothes, or houses. So, too, it is the word, and not our work, that makes our lives pleasing to God; it is the word, and not an indulgence, that forgives our sins; and it is the word, and not the pope, that establishes the church on earth. Luther knew that pastoral care without the word isn't just powerless—it's idolatrous. And so, he kept the pastoral office simple, investing pastors with the Bible and the question, "Where is it written?" In this way, he taught pastors and parishioners alike to read the word, the world, and our lives by God's word.

That was Luther's Reformation program. He set to work like a gardener in an untended garden. He rooted out and discarded the weeds of human works, pilgrimages, and payments. He pruned back overgrown

---

147. *WA* 37:312.26–27.
148. *WATR* 1:351.25–27, no. 724.
149. *LW* 57:272; citing 2 Thess 2:8.
150. *LW* 57:271.
151. *LW* 57:271.
152. *WA* 37:307.32–34.

and proud plants of church office and institution. And he trained others how to do this work and how to maintain the garden of the church. "This teaching you have often heard," he preached, "that we should especially see and be certain that God has commanded it, and that outside of his word God begins nothing."[153] The fence and cistern must only be God's command and promise, word and name.

Of course, this program of the word alone isn't unique to Luther. The Christian church—founded solely by God's word—has always done this. We don't need Luther to teach us this. We can learn it from other dear saints, great and humble alike. Nevertheless, Luther's contribution to the communion of saints is that he set forth the doctrine of the word with special clarity and force. God's word does what it says. It accomplishes the purpose for which it was sent. It creates and sustains, it forgives, and it blesses. It speaks reality. It births the church. And it cleanses the church.

The pastoral crisis of the medieval period did not end with the Reformation, nor is it unique to that age. Every age faces the same crisis: Will we let the word alone do the work, or will we try our hand at solving things?

We have big problems. We don't have enough food, enough material goods: we're faced with death. We're worried that God doesn't really love us and that we can't know if he does: we're faced with doubt. We want to be able to make a difference in the world. We want security and pleasure: we're faced with lust.

Our enemy Satan is a master tactician. He doesn't follow an order or algorithm in combat. He strikes where he senses the greatest weakness. "He likes to enter the garden where the fence is lowest."[154] He approaches us in an array of colors: dark, bright, and beautiful.[155] And he is practical: why put all your eggs in one basket? Maybe God's word will help, but maybe it won't. Have a backup plan! He offers medicine for our weakness and need, whether death, doubt, or lust: a cup in which the deadly dregs of our desire are mixed with the strong wine of God's word.

Can God's word really do anything in the face of death, doubt, and lust? It sure looks like ordinary words in an ordinary book. And in our mouths it sounds like ordinary human speech. Can one little word of God really cut the devil down? In contrast, the devil suggests practical

---

153. WA 52:172.16–18.
154. WA 37:308.21–27, here 24.
155. LW 57:256.

tools for the task at hand: stones, works, and power. Things we can see and hear, smell and touch—things we can wield.

Our Lord Jesus Christ understands how appealing and tempting these suggestions are. He sympathizes with our weakness. In his great humility and kindness our God and Savior has borne the full weight of these temptations. And he did so with his divinity hidden. With mouth parched, stomach empty, and limbs weary he stood before the devil and his pragmatic, reasonable solutions. He felt how pragmatic and reasonable all this was, but he didn't give in.

Nor did he defeat Satan as we might have if we had the full power and might of the maker of heaven and earth. Our Lord could have dispatched Satan in any number of ways: a great angelic host could surely have routed one demon; the maw of the earth could have swallowed Satan like rebellious Korah; one word could have drowned the devil in the sea like cast-out Legion in a herd of swine.

But for your sake and mine he did none of these things. Instead, he held to the word of God alone. The word—according to our eyes and reason—isn't even a weapon. But armed with the word alone, Jesus overcame the devil and his lies, so that we can do the same. For the devil is already bound and defeated by the word.

And the only hope for the church today is to let the word alone do the work.

In the name of the Father and of the Son and of the Holy Spirit. Amen.

> Man does not live by bread alone, but by each
> and every word that comes from the mouth of God.   *Matt 4:4*
> Today if you hear his voice, harden not your hearts
> as in the provocation and as in the day of temptation
> in the wilderness.   *Ps 95:8*
> My zeal has brought me to death's door,
> for my adversaries forget your word.
> Your word has been tried so purely,
> and your servant loves it.   *Ps 119:139–40*
> Though I walk in the midst of trouble,
> yet shall you refresh me;
> you shall stretch forth your hand
> upon the furiousness of my enemies,
> and your right hand shall save me.
> The Lord shall bring trouble to an end for my sake;

> O Lord, your goodness endures forever;
> despise not the works of your own hands. *Ps 138:7–8*
> O praise the Lord, all you works of his,
> in all places of his dominion;
> praise the Lord, O my soul. *Ps 103:22*

O Lord, mercifully hear our prayer and stretch forth the right hand of your majesty to defend us from those temptations that rise up against us; through your Son, Jesus Christ our Lord, who lives and reigns with you and the Holy Spirit, one God, now and forever. Amen.

BIBLIOGRAPHY

Clapton, Ernest, ed. *Our Prayer Book Psalter*. London: Society for Promoting Christian Knowledge, 1934.

Ewangeli und Epistel: Mit anfang Meß Psalmen und Collecten teütsch mit figuren und etlich schön Gloß über die Ewangeli. Augsburg: Ott, 1513.

Legg, J. Wickham, ed. *The Sarum Missal: Edited from Three Early Manuscripts*. Oxford: Clarendon, 1916.

Tentler, Thomas N. *Sin and Confession on the Eve of the Reformation*. Princeton, NJ: Princeton University Press, 1977.

2

Pastoral Care in the Swiss Reformation

AMY NELSON BURNETT

THE DEFINITION AND PRACTICE of pastoral care have changed significantly over time, and with the reformations of the sixteenth century, they acquired specific confessional characteristics. The cure of souls in the Reformed churches of the Swiss Confederation and the southwestern corner of the Holy Roman Empire took shape in contrast to both the late medieval *cura animarum* and the emphasis on the consolatory function of the sacraments that was so prominent in the writings of the Wittenberg reformers. For the Swiss reformers, pastoral care involved not only the proclamation of the gospel but also the sanctification of life. Preaching, catechization, and church discipline were therefore the central elements of pastoral care, although there were important differences between Zurich and Geneva in the way these elements were used. Reflecting the Reformed concern with instruction, the visitation of the sick in the Swiss churches also took a new approach to the consolation of those approaching death.

BACKGROUND

Medieval canon law defined the care of souls (*cura animarum*) as the responsibility of the parish priest for the instruction and sanctification, by means of the sacraments, of all who lived within the parish boundaries. Theological education was not a prerequisite for ordination, and so many parish priests were ill-prepared to instruct their parishioners. Through the later Middle Ages, a variety of handbooks were written by clerics to aid pastors in this task, but for the most part, the duties of the parish priest, especially in rural parishes, were largely restricted to celebrating the parish Mass and administering the sacrament of baptism at the beginning of life and last rites at its end. The rise of the mendicant orders in the thirteenth century further contributed to the separation of the two tasks of instruction and sanctification, with the mendicant orders assuming responsibility for preaching and teaching.

The one place where the tasks of instruction and sanctification overlapped was the sacrament of penance. The Fourth Lateran Council (1215) required all Christians who had reached the age of reason to confess their sins to their own parish priest at least once a year. Sacramental confession was also a component of the rituals performed for the dying, along with reception of the consecrated host and extreme unction, or anointing with consecrated oil. Although sacramental confession provided opportunity for instruction and consolation, its core was the priestly absolution of mortal sins that restored the sinner to favor with God.

Luther's rejection of the medieval sacramental system had significant consequences for the understanding of pastoral care. In his 1520 treatise *On the Babylonian Captivity of the Church*, Luther defined a sacrament as a divine promise accompanied by a physical sign to be received in faith. Like the rainbow given to Noah or the fleece given to Gideon, the sign was a pledge that confirmed God's promise. Luther argued that because priestly absolution lacked a physical sign, it could not be a sacrament, but he accorded it a quasi-sacramental status as the private application of God's word: in it the priest spoke the words of divine forgiveness directly to the individual and so consoled consciences burdened by sin.[1] For Luther, the essence of the care of souls was the communication of God's word, whether publicly through preaching or applied individually through the sacraments, which could be called efficacious in the sense

---

1. See especially his discussion of baptism and penance in *WA* 6:527–31, 543–44, 572; English translation in *LW* 36:57–64, 81–83, 123–24.

that they imparted grace where faith was present.² The priesthood was no longer a separate estate created by sacramental ordination but a ministry in which individuals were set apart to preach and administer the sacraments. Because they provided reassurance and consoled troubled consciences, the sacraments played a central role in pastoral care for Luther and his followers.

ZURICH

Luther's understanding of pastoral care would be challenged by others who disagreed with his sacramental theology. By 1524 his colleague Andreas Bodenstein von Karlstadt had rejected the view that the bread and wine in the Lord's Supper were a pledge or assurance of forgiveness. He argued that faith came from hearing and that assurance of that faith must be present before one received the sacrament.³ The ramifications of this understanding of the Lord's Supper for pastoral care can be seen more clearly in Ulrich Zwingli's discussions of the sacraments.

Like Karlstadt, Zwingli stressed that one was saved by faith in Christ, not by eating the sacramental bread and wine or believing that those elements were the body and blood of Christ. The Eucharist did not take away sin but was instead a symbol of Christ's death given to his followers.⁴ Zwingli also disagreed with Luther concerning the consolatory power of absolution. Although he could grant that there might be some benefit in seeking counsel from a priest, he argued that absolution by the priest had no special ability to comfort consciences. Human words could not give assurance of forgiveness, for only God gave faith, which also brought sure confidence.⁵ The sacraments of baptism and the Lord's Supper attested to one's membership in the church as the body of Christ, but they had no consolatory power and thus no particular relevance for

---

2. *WA* 6:533; *LW* 36:66–67.

3. See Karlstadt, "On the Anti-Christian Abuse of the Lord's Bread and Cup."

4. *Ad Matthaeum Alberum de coena dominica epistola*, Z 3:342–43, 351/*HZW* 2:136–37, 143. At the beginning of this work, written in November 1524, Zwingli said that the pamphlet on the abuse of the bread and cup was the only work of Karlstadt's that he had read; see Z 3:335/*HZW* 2:131.

5. *Auslegen und Gründe der Schlußreden*, Z 2:393/*HZW* 1:317; cf. his list of Luther's errors in *Das diese Worte* [. . .], Z 5:819–20; Roth, *Privatbeichte und Schlüsselgewalt*, 110–12, 125–28.

pastoral care. The Lord's Supper was therefore celebrated in Zurich only as a public ceremony held four times a year.

As a consequence of his understanding of the sacraments, Zwingli understood the chief component of pastoral care to be preaching. The Zurich reformer did not directly address the topic of pastoral care during his relatively brief career, but he did write two pamphlets on the ministry that provide some insight into his views. *The Shepherd*, published in the spring of 1524, was directed against his Roman Catholic opponents and contrasted the qualities and duties of true and false pastors.[6] *The Preaching Office*, published in the summer of 1525, responded to the spread of Anabaptist preachers.[7] Here Zwingli asserted that there was only one office in the church, even if its holder was called by many names: pastor, preacher, bishop, evangelist, watchman, or prophet. Although Zwingli cited examples from the New Testament, his understanding of the ministry was most strongly shaped by the Old Testament prophets, who were called to uproot and destroy as well as to plant and upbuild (Jer 1:10). As prophets, ministers were to speak God's word forthrightly, even to those in power, and as preachers, they were to instruct, encourage, admonish, and rebuke as necessary.[8]

In marked contrast to Luther, Zwingli paid little attention to the consolatory functions of the ministry or to supporting those with doubts or spiritual difficulties. This reflected his understanding of predestination, for confident faith was the work of the Spirit alone.[9] His concern was instead to chastise sin and incite his hearers to Christian conduct. Like the Old Testament prophets, this was done through preaching and teaching. One result was the disappearance of private confession from the Zurich church, while visitation of the sick was transformed from a series of liturgical acts and the use of physical elements that reassured the dying into a time for prayer and instruction that did not require the presence of a minister. Zwingli's understanding of the unity of the ecclesial

---

6. *Der Hirt*, Z 3:5–69/HZW 2:5–69. The pamphlet was a revised version of the sermon Zwingli preached at the first Zurich disputation in January 1523.

7. *Von dem Predigtamt*, Z 4:382–433/HZW 2:150–85. Both works are discussed briefly in Cornick, "Reformation Crisis in Pastoral Care," 223–51.

8. Büsser, "Prophet—Gedanken zu Zwinglis Theologie," 7–18; Pak, *Reformation of Prophecy*, 112–21.

9. In this context he frequently cited John 6:44; cf. *Der Hirt*, Z 3:41–42/HZW 2:106; *Amica Exegesis*, Z 5:583, 591, 663/HZW 2:251, 257–58, 309.

and civic community also meant that he left the punishment of sin to the Christian magistrate.¹⁰

More directly connected to Zwingli's understanding of the ministry was the creation of the *Prophezei*, the daily meeting of ministers and laity to hear the Bible read in its original languages and its meaning explained.¹¹ Zwingli saw the interpretation of languages as the second function of the prophetic office, linked to the duty of teaching scripture.¹² Under the leadership of Zwingli's successor, Heinrich Bullinger, the *Prophezei* would be transformed into a Reformed academy and imitated in the other Reformed cities of the Swiss Confederation.

Bullinger both built on and modified Zwingli's understanding of the ministry, in the process paying more attention to its pastoral and pedagogical function. By the later 1530s his model for the ministry was not only the Old Testament prophet but also the New Testament bishop.¹³ Like Zwingli, he rejected the priestly absolution given in sacramental confession and held that confession of sin should be made directly to God and more generally within public worship.¹⁴ Although he did not discuss his understanding of pastoral care explicitly in his published works, it is clear, especially from his correspondence, that he understood pastoral care as helping individuals apply to their own lives what they have heard preached publicly.¹⁵

Bullinger's pastoral and pedagogical concerns can be seen most clearly in his short *Instruction for the Sick* (1535), which he wrote to fill the vacuum left by the abolition of the traditional rites surrounding death. It was intended not just for those present at the deathbed but for every Christian, whose entire life should be a preparation for death. Bullinger explained that the sick should interpret their illness as God's testing and consider death to be a departure from the miseries of human existence for the eternal joys of heaven. He also rejected the practices that had developed from belief in purgatory and provided a new understanding of

---

10. Lavater, "Regnum Christi etiam externum," 338–81; Baker, "Church Discipline or Civil Punishment," 3–18.

11. Büsser, "Reformierte Erziehung in Theorie und Praxis," 199–216.

12. *Von dem Predigtamt*, Z 4:398, 416–18/HZW 2:161, 172–74.

13. Bolliger, "Bullinger on Church Authority," 159–77; Pak, *Reformation of Prophecy*, 133–42; Timmerman, *Prophecy and the Prophetic Office*, 301–8.

14. See his letter to Johannes Honter, 28 Aug. 1543, Bullinger, *Briefwechsel* 13:236–48, discussed in Roth, *Privatbeichte und Schlüsselgewalt*, 102–7.

15. Zsindely, "Bullinger als Seelsorger," 21–32; Mühling, "Bullinger als Seelsorger im Spiegel seiner Korrespondenz," 271–87.

traditional deathbed rituals. Thus, confession was a genuine admission of sinfulness to God, not an enumeration of sins in the ear of a priest, and the dying should be satisfied with the knowledge that they had shared in the Lord's Supper as a communal remembrance of Christ's death. Instead of being anointed with oil, the sick should be given medication and everything that strengthened their faith. All comfort and consolation came from a proper understanding of the gospel of forgiveness of sins through faith in Christ.[16]

Bullinger understood pastoral care as pedagogy and persuasion, and he did not grant to the clergy the independent right to exercise church discipline. Following Zwingli, he held that the Christian magistrate had the sole right to punish those who lived dishonorably. Because the purpose of the Lord's Supper was to console sinners, it was not to be linked with excommunication.[17] In effect, pastoral care in the Zurich tradition was limited to preaching and instruction, both public and private, whereas supervision of conduct was the responsibility of a morals court accountable to the magistrate.

BASEL

The understanding of pastoral care developed in a different direction in Basel, due to distinct views of both the sacraments and church discipline. Although Johannes Oecolampadius agreed with Zwingli that the bread and wine did not become Christ's body and blood in the Lord's Supper, he did believe that the Holy Spirit could use the sacrament as a vehicle to convey grace and strengthen faith.[18] This had implications for the celebration of the Lord's Supper. The church ordinance issued in 1529 provided that the sacrament was celebrated in one of the city's four parish churches in rotation each week, and it specified that ministers

---

16. Bullinger, "Unterweisung der Kranken 1535," in *Schriften*, 1:111–69; Mühling, "Welchen Tod sterben wir?," 55–68. The Zurich pastor Otto Werdmüller provided a brief liturgy to be used at the deathbed in his pamphlet *Der Tod: wie sich ein Christ in seinen und anderer todsnoeten halten* (1549); Baschera, "Preparation for Death," 313–28. Significantly, Bullinger and Werdmüller were writing not just for ministers but also for the laity.

17. Baker, "Church Discipline or Civil Punishment," 13–15; Baker, "Christian Discipline, Church and State, and Toleration."

18. On the development of Oecolampadius's eucharistic theology in debate with the Wittenberg reformers, see Burnett, *Debating the Sacraments*, 139–57.

could give the sacrament to the sick and dying who desired it.[19] The city's first agenda, published in 1526, contained a liturgy to be followed when visiting the sick that included the administration of the Eucharist. The instructions emphasized that reception of the bread and wine testified to the unity of Christ's body, but the practice implicitly acknowledged that the sacrament also had a consolatory function.[20]

More importantly, Oecolampadius disagreed with Zwingli about the relationship between the civil and ecclesial communities. The Basel reformer believed that excommunication was necessary both to act against sinful conduct and to preserve the purity of eucharistic fellowship. He held that the church, not the magistrate, was responsible for disciplining sinners, and in 1530 he argued that excommunication ought to be administered by the pastors and two leading laymen in each parish. Basel's council modified this proposal by giving the responsibility for excommunication to a committee of three laymen within each parish and reducing the minister's role to that of advisor.[21] After Oecolampadius's death at the end of 1531, a conflict broke out among the city's ministers over the excommunication of Catholics and Lutherans who voluntarily abstained from receiving the Lord's Supper in Basel. The conflict was resolved only through the intervention of the Strasbourg pastors Martin Bucer and Wolfgang Capito, who emphasized the importance of personal admonition and held that excommunication should be used only as a last resort against those who had committed grave sin but refused to heed admonition.[22] The precise relationship between magistrate and ministers, and especially the right of the latter to denounce sin from the pulpit and exercise church discipline, continued to be a cause of conflict within Basel's church.[23]

STRASBOURG

In the meantime, however, Martin Bucer had been won over to Oecolampadius's vision of a system of church discipline exercised independently of magisterial control. Bucer's views on the ministry and its responsibility

19. Dürr and Roth, *Aktensammlung*, 3:395.

20. Burnett, *Teaching the Reformation*, 50–52; Reinis, *Reforming the Art of Dying*, 164–69.

21. Kuhr, "Calvin and Basel," 19–33; Kuhr, "Macht des Bannes und der Buße"; Burnett, *Yoke of Christ*, 56–62.

22. Burnett, *Yoke of Christ*, 62–65; Friedrich, "Kirchenzucht und -bann," 193–202.

23. Burnett, "'Kilchen ist uff dem Radthus'?," 49–65.

for pastoral care evolved significantly over his career, reflecting both the many influences on his theology and his own experiences in Strasbourg. An ardent admirer of Erasmus, he was won to Luther's views after attending the Heidelberg disputation in 1518. With the outbreak of the eucharistic controversy at the end of 1524, he sided with the Swiss reformers, and ultimately it was Oecolampadius rather than Zwingli who would have the greatest impact on him. Both his efforts to end the eucharistic controversy and his conflicts with Anabaptists and spiritualists in Strasbourg made him more receptive to Wittenberg theology, especially the instrumental role of the ministry and the efficacious nature of the sacraments when they were received in faith.[24]

Bucer would be the first of the reformers to devote an entire treatise to the topic of pastoral care. Published in 1538, *Concerning the True Care of Souls* opened with a discussion of the nature and ministries of the church. Bucer distinguished between the deacons who helped meet the physical needs of the congregation and those who cared for souls. He argued that the demands of the pastoral ministry were so great and varied that it was necessary to have lay elders in each church to assist the ministers.[25] In an extended discussion of Ezek 34:16, Bucer identified the tasks of pastoral care as seeking the lost, returning strays to the fold, healing the sick and injured, strengthening the weak, and tending the strong.[26] The longest chapter of the treatise, concerning the "hurt and wounded sheep," described a system of church discipline that included exclusion from the Lord's Supper and imposition of public penance on those who had committed grave sin. The excommunication of contumacious sinners was also necessary to protect the "strong sheep" from contagion.[27] The weak were to be encouraged to attend worship, receive the sacraments, and participate in the other practices of the church.[28]

---

24. Bucer acknowledged these changes in the retraction that he incorporated into the third edition of his commentary on the Synoptic Gospels, published in 1536; see Burnett, *Yoke of Christ*, 87–90.

25. *Von der waren Seelsorge*, MBDS 7:112–22; Bucer, *Concerning the True Care*, 25–39.

26. Bucer defined the stray sheep as those who have been turned away from true faith by false doctrine and led to the "bondage of the law" and "the heresies of false apostles"; by this he meant especially the Anabaptists who had withdrawn from Strasbourg's church; see MBDS 7:154–57; Bucer, *Concerning the True Care*, 91–95.

27. MBDS 7:157–206, 219–24; Bucer, *Concerning the True Care*, 97–162, 183–89.

28. MBDS 7:209–10, 222–24; Bucer, *Concerning the True Care*, 167–68, 181–83.

Although Bucer devoted most of *Concerning the True Care of Souls* to the exercise of church discipline, his view of pastoral care was much broader, as can be seen from his 1536 commentary on the Gospels. In his discussion of Matt 16:18-19, he defined the power of the keys as "the duty and power of administering the church of God," which included governing God's people through "teaching, exhortation, admonition, correction, rebuke, punishment, the practice of prayer, the distribution of the sacraments, and the entire administration of the pastoral office." It also included the power to exclude those who refused to accept such admonition and live a God-pleasing life and to readmit them when they sought pardon for their sin.[29] Through the last years of his life, Bucer identified discipline, along with preaching and the administration of the sacraments, as an essential part of the church's ministry.[30]

Bucer did not restrict the proclamation of the gospel to public gatherings; it was also to be taught in homes and to individuals.[31] Catechization played a central role in Bucer's understanding of pastoral care. Through the 1530s, he and his colleagues repeatedly asked the Strasbourg council to make attendance at catechism instruction mandatory for all of the city's children and servants (many of whom were teenagers). They also asked for the authority to examine young people before they were admitted to the Lord's Supper for the first time, and in 1534 Bucer proposed the introduction of a confirmation ceremony in which children professed their faith publicly. The council expressed its general sympathy for the pastors' requests, but it consistently refused to mandate anything.[32]

GENEVA

The fullest development of the ideas present in Bucer's pastoral theology would occur in Geneva. John Calvin spent the years 1538-41 in

---

29. In *Sacra Qvatvor Evangelia, Enarrationes Perpetuae* (Basel: Herwagen, 1536), 353B-54C, cited in Burnett, *Yoke of Christ*, 91.

30. Bucer is sometimes identified as one of the first to make discipline a mark of the church, but this overlooks the context in which discipline was discussed. Debate concerning the marks of the church occurred chiefly against Roman Catholics, who insisted on the need for a visible hierarchy. Bucer's discussion of preaching, sacraments, and discipline occurred instead in the context of the responsibility of ministers toward their pastoral charges; see especially his works written in England; Burnett, *Yoke of Christ*, 208-16.

31. The Strasbourg pastors petitioned the city council for the right to visit householders periodically already in 1531; Burnett, *Yoke of Christ*, 66.

32. Burnett, "Church Discipline and Moral Reformation," 439-56.

Strasbourg, where he became familiar with Bucer's vision for the role of lay elders and the understanding of church discipline as pastoral care. For Calvin, as for Bucer, discipline was intended to bring sinners to repentance and emendation of life and to protect both the faithful and the purity of eucharistic fellowship from unrepentant sinners. Calvin also believed that ministers and lay elders were to take an active role in directing and shaping the religious life of their spiritual charges. Pastoral care in Geneva comprised a blend of church discipline, catechetical instruction, and household visitation.

After Calvin returned to Geneva in the fall of 1541, he drafted a church ordinance that created four offices within the church: ministers, teachers, deacons, and lay elders, the last of whom assisted the ministers in their oversight of the laity. The ministers and elders together formed the consistory, which met weekly to deal with the religious and moral failings of the Genevan populace. The elders were chosen from the city's governing councils, which gave the magistrate an indirect say in its decisions. The consistory became the institutionalized means of exercising pastoral care in the city and its territory. Those reported to the consistory were summoned to its weekly meetings, where they were questioned, rebuked and instructed, and admonished to reform, with the threat of exclusion from the Lord's Supper if they refused to do so.[33]

The consistory was regarded by earlier generations of scholars as a repressive and punitive institution, akin to the Catholic Inquisition. However, the publication of the consistory's records has significantly changed our perceptions of its role in providing pastoral care. Consistorial discipline certainly had a punitive aspect, but the consistory also encouraged the acceptance of Reformed doctrine and worship, suppressed behavior considered superstitious or "papist," settled disputes between neighbors, reconciled husbands and wives or parents and children, enforced new standards of sexual conduct, and promoted a way of living that they thought pleased God.[34]

Geneva's quarterly communion services provided a more focused opportunity for the pastoral tasks of instruction and admonition. In the

---

33. On the origins of the consistory and the historiography concerning it, see Watt, *Consistory and Social Discipline*, 5–11, and the works cited there.

34. There is a growing body of research on the Genevan consistory; for a shorter overview, see Manetsch, *Calvin's Company of Pastors*, 182–220; for concrete examples of these activities, see Kingdon, *Reforming Geneva* and Watt, *Consistory and Social Discipline*. On the consistory's functioning under the leadership of Theodore Beza, see Manetsch, "Pastoral Care East of Eden," 274–313.

weeks before the Supper was celebrated, the ministers preached on the catechism, and a catechetical review session—especially for children—was held on Sunday afternoon. Children old enough to receive their first communion were publicly examined concerning their knowledge of the catechism. The consistory also met more frequently in the weeks before the Lord's Supper was celebrated, to reconcile those who had earlier been told to abstain from communion and to exclude those who were deemed not properly prepared to receive it. In the 1550s the ministers were also given the right to visit each household in the weeks before the communion service to examine the catechetical knowledge and conduct of servants and those from outside Geneva. In 1561 this practice was codified as an annual household visitation, made by pastor, elder, and *dizenier* (the civic official who oversaw one of the districts into which the city was divided) so that they could examine and instruct all household members in the weeks leading up to the Easter communion service.[35]

The Genevan church ordinance also required pastors to visit the sick and dying. The 1542 liturgical agenda provided guidelines for carrying out this task, stressing the minister's duty to instruct, console, and pray with the sufferers.[36] As in Zurich, words rather than ritual actions or physical objects brought comfort and assurance to the dying.

In their approach to pastoral care, Zurich and Geneva functioned as the two poles, with the former restricting the ministers' pastoral authority to preaching and teaching, and the latter creating institutional and liturgical structures for church discipline and pastoral accompaniment of the laity. The church of Bern was most strongly influenced by Zurich and, like Zurich, it made supervision of conduct the responsibility of a secular morals court.[37] This led to tensions concerning the relationship between the church and the secular government in Bern's Francophone territories in the Vaud, where the clergy looked to Geneva for guidance.[38] The disagreement had implications not only for church discipline but also for other practices such as deathbed visitation. To some extent the differences concerning pastoral care were smoothed over by the Consensus

---

35. Carbonnier-Burkard, "Temps de la cène," 57–73; Manetsch, *Calvin's Company of Pastors*, 265–83; Grosse, *Rituels de la Cène*, 466–70.

36. Manetsch, *Calvin's Company of Pastors*, 284; McKee, *Pastoral Ministry and Worship*, 604–10.

37. Schmidt, "'Gemeinde-Reformation,'" 85–121.

38. The conflict in the Vaud is examined in detail by Bruening, *Calvinism's First Battleground*.

Tigurinus of 1549, which established a common understanding of the Lord's Supper. The Consensus acknowledged that the sacraments were incitements to gratitude and that they testified, represented, and sealed God's grace to believers, but it stopped short of saying that they conveyed grace.[39] This position undermined the role of the sacraments as a form of pastoral care and moved Zurich and Geneva closer together in their pastoral praxis.

This development was aided by the maturation of a new generation raised within the Reformed tradition and as a consequence did not accept the consolatory function of the sacraments taught by both Roman Catholics and Lutherans. In all of the Swiss Reformed churches, the sanctifying role of the sacraments in medieval pastoral care was replaced by oversight of conduct, whether by the consistory or by a secular morals court. The chief forms of pastoral care were public and private instruction as well as prayer with and for those in need of consolation. These tasks were primarily the responsibility of the ministers, but they could also be carried out by laymen and women who had learned to apply the gospel message to their own lives.

BIBLIOGRAPHY

Baker, J. Wayne. "Christian Discipline, Church and State, and Toleration: Bullinger, Calvin, and Basel, 1530–1555." In *Reformiertes Erbe: Festschrift für Gottfried W. Locher*, edited by Heiko A. Oberman et al. Zwingliana 19 (1992) 35–48.

———. "Church Discipline or Civil Punishment: On the Origins of the Reformed Schism, 1528–1531." *Andrews University Seminary Studies* 23 (Spring 1985) 3–18.

———. "Church, State, and Dissent: The Crisis of the Swiss Reformation, 1531–1536." *Church History* 57 (June 1988) 135–52.

Baschera, Luca. "Preparation for Death in Sixteenth-Century Zurich: Heinrich Bullinger and Otto Werdmüller." In *Preparing for Death, Remembering the Dead*, edited by Jon Øygarden Flaeten and Tarald Rasmussen, 313–28. Refo500 Academic Studies 22. Göttingen: Vandenhoeck & Ruprecht, 2015.

Bolliger, Daniel. "Bullinger on Church Authority: The Transformation of the Prophetic Role in Christian Ministry." In *Architect of Reformation: An Introduction to Heinrich Bullinger, 1504–1575*, edited by Bruce Gordon and Emidio Campi, 159–77. Texts and Studies in Reformation and Post-Reformation Thought. Grand Rapids: Baker, 2004.

Bruening, Michael W. *Calvinism's First Battleground: Conflict and Reform in the Pays de Vaud, 1528–1559*. Studies in Early Modern Religious Reforms 4. Dordrecht: Springer, 2005.

---

39. Campi and Reich, *Consensus Tigurinus (1549)*, 129/261.

Bucer, Martin. *Concerning the True Care of Souls*. Translated by Peter Beale. Edinburgh: Banner of Truth, 2009.
Bullinger, Heinrich. *Briefwechsel. Werke*. Abteilung 2. Edited by Ulrich Gäbler et al. 21 vols. Zurich: Theologischer Verlag, 1973–.
———. *Schriften*. Edited by Emidio Campi et al. 9 vols. Zurich: Theologischer Verlag, 2004–.
Burnett, Amy Nelson. "Church Discipline and Moral Reformation in the Thought of Martin Bucer." *Sixteenth Century Journal* 22 (Autumn 1991) 439–56.
———. *Debating the Sacraments: Print and Authority in the Early Reformation*. New York: Oxford University Press, 2019.
———. "'Kilchen ist uff dem Radthus'? Conflicting Views of Magistrate and Ministry in Early Reformation Basel." In *Debatten über die Legitimation von Herrschaft: Politische Sprachen in der Frühen Neuzeit*, edited by Luise Schorn-Schütte and Sven Tode, 49–65. Berlin: Akademie Verlag, 2006.
———. *Teaching the Reformation: Ministers and Their Message in Basel, 1529–1629*. Oxford Studies in Historical Theology. New York: Oxford University Press, 2006.
———. *The Yoke of Christ: Martin Bucer and Christian Discipline*. Sixteenth Century Essays and Studies 26. Kirksville, MO: Sixteenth Century Journal, 1994.
Büsser, Fritz. "Der Prophet—Gedanken zu Zwinglis Theologie." *Zwingliana* 13 (1969) 7–18.
———. "Reformierte Erziehung in Theorie und Praxis." In *Wurzeln der Reformation in Zürich. Zum 500. Geburtstag des Reformators Huldrych Zwingli*, edited by Fritz Büsser, 199–216. Leiden: Brill, 1985.
Campi, Emidio, and Ruedi Reich, eds. *Consensus Tigurinus (1549): Die Einigung zwischen Heinrich Bullinger und Johannes Calvin über das Abendmahl. Werden—Wertung—Bedeutung*. Zurich: TVZ, 2009.
Carbonnier-Burkard, Marianne. "Le temps de la cène chez les réformés français." In *Édifier ou instruire? Les avatars de la liturgie réformée du XVIe au XVIIIe siècle*, edited by Maria-Cristina Pitassi, 57–73. Paris: Champion, 2000.
Cornick, David. "The Reformation Crisis in Pastoral Care." In *A History of Pastoral Care*, edited by G. R. Evans, 223–51. London: Cassell, 2000.
Dürr, Emil, and Paul Roth. *Aktensammlung zur Geschichte der Basler Reformation in den Jahren 1519 bis Anfang 1534*. 6 vols. Basel: Historische und antiquarische Gesellschaft, 1921–50.
Friedrich, Reinhold. "Kirchenzucht und -bann vor dem Hintergrund des Briefwechsels Bucers mit den Basler Predigern im Jahr 1532." In *Basel als Zentrum des geistigen Austauschs in der frühen Reformationszeit*, edited by Christine Christ-von Wedel, Sven Grosse, and Berndt Hamm, 193–202. Spätmittelalter, Humanismus, Reformation 81. Tübingen: Mohr Siebeck, 2014.
Grosse, Christian. *Les Rituels de la Cène. Le culte eucharistique réformé à Genève (XVIe–XVIIe siècles)*. Travaux d'humanisme et renaissance 443. Geneva: Droz, 2008.
Karlstadt, Andreas Bodenstein von. "On the Anti-Christian Abuse of the Lord's Bread and Cup." In *The Eucharistic Pamphlets of Andreas Bodenstein von Karlstadt*, edited by Amy Nelson Burnett, 205–18. Early Modern Studies 6. Kirksville, MO: Truman State University Press, 2011.
Kingdon, Robert M. *Reforming Geneva: Discipline, Faith and Anger in Calvin's Geneva*. Cahiers d'humanisme et renaissance 103. Geneva: Droz, 2012.

Kuhr, Olaf. "Calvin and Basel: The Significance of Oecolampadius and the Basel Discipline Ordinance for the Institution of Ecclesiastical Discipline in Geneva." *Scottish Bulletin of Evangelical Theology* 16 (Spring 1998) 19–33.

———. *"Die Macht des Bannes und der Buße." Kirchenzucht und Erneuerung der Kirche bei Johannes Oekolampad (1482–1531)*. Basler und Berner Studien zur historischen und systematischen Theologie 68. Bern: Peter Lang, 1999.

Lavater, Hans Rudolf. "Regnum Christi etiam externum: Huldrych Zwinglis Brief vom 4. Mai 1528 an Ambrosius Blarer in Konstanz." *Zwingliana* 15 (1981) 338–81.

Manetsch, Scott M. *Calvin's Company of Pastors: Pastoral Care and the Emerging Reformed Church, 1536–1609*. Oxford Studies in Historical Theology. New York: Oxford University Press, 2013.

———. "Pastoral Care East of Eden: The Consistory of Geneva, 1568–1582." *Church History* 75 (June 2006) 274–313.

McKee, Elsie. *The Pastoral Ministry and Worship in Calvin's Geneva*. Travaux d'humanisme et renaissance 556. Geneva: Droz, 2016.

Mühling, Andreas. "Bullinger als Seelsorger im Spiegel seiner Korrespondenz." In *Heinrich Bullinger: Life, Thought, Influence. Zurich, Aug. 25–29 2004. International Congress Heinrich Bullinger (1504–1575)*, edited by Emidio Campi and Peter Opitz, 1:271–87. Zürcher Beiträge zur Reformationsgeschichte 24. Zurich: Theologischer Verlag Zürich, 2007.

———. "Welchen Tod sterben wir? Heinrich Bullingers 'Bericht der Kranken' (1535)." *Zwingliana* 29 (2002) 55–68.

Pak, G. Sujin. *The Reformation of Prophecy: Early Modern Interpretations of the Prophet and Old Testament Prophecy*. Oxford Studies in Historical Theology. New York: Oxford University Press, 2018.

Reinis, Austra. *Reforming the Art of Dying: The* Ars Moriendi *in the German Reformation (1519–1528)*. St Andrews Studies in Reformation History. Aldershot: Ashgate, 2006.

Roth, Erich. *Die Privatbeichte und Schlüsselgewalt in der Theologie der Reformatoren*. Gütersloh: Bertelsmann, 1952.

Schmidt, Heinrich Richard. "'Gemeinde-Reformation.' Das bernische Sittengericht zwischen Sozialdisziplinierung und kommunaler Selbstregulation." In *Bäuerliche Frömmigkeit und kommunale Reformation*, edited by Hans von Rütte, 85–121. Itinera 8. Basel: Schwabe, 1988.

Timmerman, Daniël. *Heinrich Bullinger on Prophecy and the Prophetic Office (1523–1538)*. Reformed Historical Theology 33. Göttingen: Vandenhoeck & Ruprecht, 2015.

Watt, Jeffrey R. *The Consistory and Social Discipline in Calvin's Geneva*. Changing Perspectives on Early Modern Europe 22. Rochester, NY: University of Rochester Press, 2020.

Zsindely, Endre. "Bullinger als Seelsorger." In *Bullinger-Tagung 1975: Vorträge gehalten aus Anlass von Heinrich Bullingers 400 Todestag*, edited by Ulrich Gäbler and Endre Zsindely, 21–32. Zurich: Institut für Schweizerische Reformationsgeschichte, 1977.

3

Pastoral Care in the French Reformation

MARTIN I. KLAUBER

One of the most challenging responsibilities for a pastor, regardless of time or place, is managing tragic circumstances. Ministers encounter these situations occasionally, often more frequently than they would like. In the aftermath of unspeakable tragedies such as shootings, floods, or tornadoes, thoughts and prayers usually feel insufficient. During these moments, compassion and empathy are essential traits for any pastor. Unfortunately, these qualities are often in short supply.

Nevertheless, one can sometimes turn to historical examples for guidance. This chapter highlights the large French Reformed church just outside of Paris. With a seating capacity of about four thousand people, this church had a total congregation of approximately fifteen thousand. The church frequently faced tragedies, and in many of these instances, the community responded through prayer and fasting.[1]

The Charenton Temple was located approximately eight kilometers from Notre-Dame Cathedral in Paris, at the confluence of the Seine and Marne Rivers. It was a long trip to attend services. While some could walk

---

1. See De Félice, *Protestants d'autrefois*, 3; Douen, "Quatorze Mille Places du Temple de Charenton."

to the temple, this journey was particularly difficult during the winter months. Wealthier individuals often used horse-drawn carriages, while others utilized boats for transportation. The boats, however, required towing upstream, which was typically performed by horses or individuals navigating along the towpath. There were three designated boarding points for Huguenots intending to embark on these vessels: the first was located near Notre-Dame Cathedral, the second at the Tournelle Bridge, and the third on the opposite bank of the Seine near the Marie Bridge. Navigating these waterways was not without challenges, particularly during inclement weather, which could result in rough conditions—most notably where the Seine and Marne Rivers converge. Consequently, maritime accidents were not uncommon. One of the most tragic incidents occurred on January 18, 1654, when a large boat capsized, resulting in the death of fifty-seven parishioners returning to Paris from Charenton. In the aftermath, many of the deceased were interred at the Protestant cemetery in Charenton on January 19, although not all the bodies had been recovered by that date. Given the magnitude of this tragedy, one might reasonably expect the Reformed congregation at Charenton to declare a day of fasting in response to such a profound loss.[2]

Fasting played an important role in the life of the Parisian congregation, as it did for all the French Reformed churches. Advice for fasting was included in the Discipline that was approved at the first national synod, held in 1559 in Paris. It was revised several times in subsequent synods and spelled out the rules, regulations, and structure of the French Reformed churches. This document specified the following:

> In times after persecution or plague, or war, or famine or another great calamity; when one elects new ministers of the Word of God, or when a new Synod is about to meet, one could, if necessity requires it, to name a certain day or several days to require public and special prayers accompanied by a fast, unscrupulously and without superstition, but with careful due diligence. And the churches will be admonished to celebrate the fast together as far as it would be possible, according to the circumstances of the place and the time.[3]

The Reformed approach to fasting significantly differed from that of Roman Catholicism. Protestants criticized the obligatory fasts mandated

---

2. Read, "Catastrophe arrivée, le 18 janvier 1654 à Charenton-Saint-Maurice."

3. Cited in De Félice, *Protestants d'autrefois*, 157; see also Sunshine, "French Protestantism on the Eve of St-Bartholomew," 340–77.

by the church calendar, particularly those associated with the liturgical seasons of Advent and Lent. They did not reject fasting altogether but opposed the idea that it could play a role in an individual's salvation. This view developed from their commitment to the doctrine of *sola fide*, according to which they opposed fasting as part of a works-based form of justification. Ulrich Zwingli critiqued obligatory Lenten fasting during the infamous "sausage affair" in Zurich, highlighting the tension between ecclesiastical mandates and individual conviction. While fasting within the Reformed tradition was generally practiced collectively, John Calvin permitted personal fasting for spiritual fortification. Protestant fasting in France typically went beyond abstaining from food and drink; it also included extended services featuring psalm-singing, prayer, and preaching. These community-wide fasts were primarily designed to elicit repentance for both personal and communal sins.[4]

Raymond Mentzer observes that communal fasting was generally not observed on Sundays and was predominantly conducted during the weekdays. On these fast days, Sunday Sabbath rules were upheld, resulting in the closure of stores and the prohibition of various forms of entertainment. One was expected to prepare at home by reciting specific prayers, both before attending services and upon returning from them. The congregation would meet early in the morning, typically at 7 or 8 a.m. The fasting observances were lengthy, usually extending until approximately 5 or 6 p.m., and involved three distinct, lengthy sermons, each lasting around two hours. Services were held at 9 a.m., 1 p.m., and 3 p.m. Given that the Charenton congregation employed multiple pastors simultaneously, it was common for three different preachers to deliver the sermons for a single day. Scripture readings during these services were also long, often encompassing entire books of the Bible, with some services featuring the reading of at least thirty complete chapters. Most parishioners attended at least two services, with many participating in all three. On occasion, attendance was so high that services were necessitated in the courtyard, employing canvas coverings in inclement weather.[5]

The connection between the tragic incident on the Seine and the practice of fasting provides insight into how the congregation reacted.

Notably, the subsequent sermon was not delivered until the following Sunday, January 25, 1654. My research yielded no evidence of a fast

---

4. Mentzer, "Fasting," 335–40.

5. De Félice, "Temple de Charenton," 360–61; Mentzer, "Fasting," 345–46; De Félice, *Protestants d'autrefois*, 166–67.

day being proclaimed after the tragedy. This absence of a fast may suggest that the congregation was in a state of shock; additionally, given that many of the bodies had yet to be recovered, there may not have been sufficient time to organize a midweek fast day. Traditionally, fasting days were announced from the pulpit at least two weeks before the observance, reinforcing that the community was not prepared for immediate introspection through fasting. Mentzer highlights that while conducting a fast on a Sunday was atypical, such occurrences were not without precedent. Notably, on February 1, two weeks following the tragic accident, Pastor Jean Daillé, who served at Charenton, continued his sermon series on the New Testament book of Titus. He focused on Titus 3:8, "This is a trustworthy saying. And I want you to stress these things, so that those who have trusted in God may be careful to devote themselves to doing what is good. These things are excellent and profitable for everyone." Intriguingly, Daillé did not refer to the tragedy that had transpired just two weeks prior, raising questions about the socioreligious dynamics at play in the wake of such a significant event.[6]

Ironically, there was only one sermon addressing the tragedy, the message delivered on January 25 by Pastor Charles Drelincourt, who stands out among his contemporaries due to his unique qualifications and background. Hailing from Sedan—a principality governed by Henri-Robert de la Marck, who embraced Protestantism in 1563—Drelincourt's lineage was impressive. His father, Antoine Drelincourt, who was from Normandy, fled to Sedan during the French Wars of Religion, subsequently serving as the secretary to the prince. This position allowed Antoine the means to secure a solid education for his son, who attended the highly regarded Reformed Academy in Sedan. There, he was instructed by distinguished figures such as the renowned Hebraist Jacques Cappel, the Scottish theologian John Cameron, and Daniel Tilenus, who became an Arminian and a vocal critic of the Synod of Dort.

Upon his ordination, Drelincourt was appointed to lead the Protestant congregation in Langres, situated in northeastern France. However, once there, he encountered significant challenges: the municipal authorities denied the congregation permission to construct a dedicated temple despite allowing Protestant worship in the nearby chateau at Pressigny. In response, Drelincourt began prioritizing personal visits to his congregants. This approach would characterize his ministry throughout his

---

6. Daillé, *Sermon*.

career, highlighting his steadfast commitment to his congregation. The stress Drelincourt experienced probably contributed to a severe illness that lasted for three months. Finally, since constructing a new church building was deemed impossible, Drelincourt accepted an invitation to serve as one of the pastors at Charenton, a role in which he would serve for nearly the final fifty years of his life.[7]

One of Drelincourt's most famous publications was his *The Christian's Defence Against the Fears of Death* (1651).[8] This treatise went through forty-two editions from 1651 to 1699 and another fifteen from 1700 to 1792, more than any other work of Reformed piety written during the era of the Edict of Nantes.[9] He also composed a massive five-volume work with about eight hundred pages each, *Les visites charitables ou les consolations chrétiennes pour toutes sortes de personnes affligées* (1667–69). *Les visites charitables* is a recitation of the personal calls that Drelincourt had made to those in need over a lifetime of ministry. The work offers practical guidance for pastoral care. By omitting the names of those involved, Drelincourt encouraged parishioners to share their stories with him. As a celebrated bestseller, the work equipped pastors with essential tools for visitation across many challenging circumstances, complete with thoughtfully suggested prayers to be recited in the presence of those in distress. The situations included in the book are comprehensive, ranging from the loss of a spouse or child to the struggles of financial hardship, severe illness, and persecution. It even provides advice on the conversion of a loved one to Roman Catholicism and the profound courage required in the face of impending martyrdom for one's faith. This work is a comprehensive resource for pastors navigating virtually every conceivable challenge they may encounter on their sacred journey of support and healing.[10]

Drelincourt's January 25 sermon at Charenton was based on Luke 13:1–5:

> Now there were some present at that time who told Jesus about the Galileans whose blood Pilate had mixed with their sacrifices. Jesus answered, "Do you think that these Galileans were worse sinners than all the other Galileans because they suffered

---

7. McKee, "Pastoral and Polemical Theology," 277.
8. Drelincourt, *Christian's Defence*.
9. Carbonnier-Burkard, "Pasteurs français auteurs d'une littérature d'édification," 42.
10. Drelincourt, *Visites charitables ou les consolations chrétiennes*. For a discussion of this work see Carbonnier-Burkard, "Visiter les malades."

this way? I tell you, no! But unless you repent, you too will all perish. Or those eighteen who died when the tower in Siloam fell on them—do you think they were more guilty than all the others living in Jerusalem? I tell you, no! But unless you repent, you too will all perish."

The sermon was published and, in a dedicatory letter to the Marquis de Pardaillan, who lost a son in the accident, Drelincourt wrote:

> The disastrous accident which happened to this church was nothing compared to the irreparable loss of your son, of most happy memory. We have considered it as a public loss and there is nothing so damaging to the heart than the bitter tears over this tragedy. God knows my emotions and my tears when I learned of this horrible news, so I decided to write to you. I tried to overcome my sadness to comfort you even though my soul was incredibly damaged to write to a father who has been so horribly afflicted. But, besides these consolations, I believe sir that it is my particular duty to include you in the grace that has been shown to our congregation. I have been busy all week along with my colleagues in visiting the families who have lost loved ones. So that if I had all the skills that I am lacking, I still would not have enough time to do everything that I need to do to respond adequately to such a horrible thing. Nevertheless, sir, I will try and will not make any excuses for my defects. For as the habits of sorrow are without ornament or trappings, a sermon amid these tears and groanings and in a sadness that cannot be described has no need of eloquence or flowery language. An afflicted heart such as yours does not require such words. It only needs balm to cure its wound. And the earth does not produce anything that can serve as a cure unless if by miracle, so I pray that God would extend his hand of grace to you. The only true balm comes from heaven which flows from the tree of life so that in this very life where pain abounds so strongly, only the Lord can soothe your soul.[11]

The sermon presents an exhortation to repentance in the face of profound tragedy. The biblical narrative on which it is based refers to two unfortunate events. The first involves the actions of Pilate, who mingled the blood of certain Galileans with their sacrifices. The second event refers to the catastrophic collapse of a tower, which resulted in the deaths

---

11. Drelincourt, *Sermon*, i–iv. See also Read, "Catastrophe arrivée, le 18 janvier 1654 à Charenton-Saint-Maurice," 480–81.

of eighteen people in Jerusalem. Jesus explained that those who perished were not any more sinful than others, challenging the idea that sin and suffering are typically connected. By employing these two historical illustrations, Jesus urged his audience to recognize the vagaries of life and the need for repentance.

Drelincourt expressed the idea of divine sovereignty, arguing that God has complete authority over the natural order, even during times of great hardship. He contended that the suffering individuals face within the church resonates throughout the entire body of Christ. This sorrow includes a powerful reminder for people to reflect on their actions and seek repentance for their sins, which could help them avoid a similar calamity. Additionally, Drelincourt referred to the earlier chapter of the Gospel of Luke, particularly Luke 12:13–21, which recounts the parable of the rich fool. In this story, the rich man is focused solely on hoarding his plentiful harvest and decides to build larger barns to ensure financial security. Yet, he is unaware that he would die that very night. The central lesson of this story displays the unpredictability of life and the necessity of being ready for death, as we cannot know when our time will come. This was also a major theme of *The Christian's Defence Against the Fears of Death*.[12]

In examining the historical context surrounding the account of Pontius Pilate allegedly intermingling the blood of Galileans with their sacrificial offerings, Drelincourt undertook a critical analysis, referencing Acts 5:37. In this passage, Gamaliel recounts the insurrection led by Judas the Galilean, an event subsequently detailed in Josephus's *Antiquities of the Jews*. According to the story, Judas discouraged his followers from paying tribute to Caesar, leading Pilate to deploy military forces to quell the uprising. According to one interpretation, Pilate's troops may have surprised the rebels while they were offering their sacrifices, resulting in the mixture of the blood of those killed with that of the sacrificial offerings. However, a significant chronological discrepancy emerges, suggesting that this incident could not have occurred during Pilate's governance but approximately thirty years prior. Josephus indeed recounts a separate, calamitous occurrence involving Pilate, which transpired after he controversially requisitioned funds from the temple treasury to build an aqueduct stretching from the pools of Solomon to Jerusalem. This act was perceived as a gross indignity by the Jewish populace, prompting

---

12. Drelincourt, *Sermon*, 2–3.

Pilate to send undercover soldiers disguised as civilians. The soldiers then started attacking the crowd, resulting in chaos. Nonetheless, the details of this event do not align with the biblical account, making it challenging to identify the specific biblical episode. Drelincourt speculated that the Galileans referenced in the biblical account may be identified as Samaritans, considering that the Galileans were beyond Pilate's jurisdiction, making direct persecution unlikely. He noted that the Samaritans conducted their sacrifices on Mount Gerizim, suggesting that Pilate's potential aggression would have been directed there. Drelincourt further questioned the nomenclature of "Galileans," positing that during the first century, it was not uncommon for individuals to be identified by broader geographical labels—akin to modern references to people from Holland despite their actual provincial origins. Moreover, he highlighted the negative views of the Jewish community toward both Galileans and Samaritans, referring to Philip's negative attitude in John 1:46 regarding the reputation of Nazareth, situated in Galilee, and to Mark 14:70, where Peter's accent is associated with his identification as a Galilean. Such references display an unfortunate sense of satisfaction from the misfortunes of others, combined with a predisposition to attribute blame to those who suffer. In contrast, Jesus asserts that the people who experienced suffering were no more guilty than those who had not faced similar tribulations.[13]

In this part of the sermon, the scholarly abilities of Drelincourt are particularly noteworthy, as he goes to considerable lengths to explain a seemingly straightforward point. His reference to the works of the historian Josephus, specifically regarding the incident in which Pilate mingled the blood of those he executed with their sacrifices, is quite unusual for the contemporary reader. Indeed, it is uncommon to encounter a preacher today referring to Josephus in a sermon. Drelincourt was committed to academic integrity and accuracy in his homiletics, even when such depth may not be necessary. This approach suggests a high caliber of preaching that the Parisian congregation had come to expect.

Furthermore, the practical applications presented in Drelincourt's sermon are particularly significant. He emphasized Christians' need to remain constantly aware of God's providence and care. The appropriate response for the believer is to follow God's commandments. Drelincourt

---

13. Drelincourt, *Sermon*, 5–15.

also cautioned that the Lord might discipline believers in order to lead them on the right path.[14]

Drelincourt went on to discuss God's meticulous providence, using as an example the passage from Matt 10 where Jesus said, "Are not two sparrows sold for a penny? Yet not one of them will fall to the ground outside your Father's care. And even the very hairs of your head are all numbered. So don't be afraid; you are worth more than many sparrows" (vv. 29–31). If God pays attention to such small matters, he must be attentive to more significant affairs such as the tragedy on the Seine—and even more importantly, these affairs would be part of God's overall plan. We do not necessarily know why God allows these things to take place, but we should rest in the confidence that he is in control. Here Drelincourt cited Job 14:5: "A person's days are determined; you have decreed the number of his months and have set limits he cannot exceed." He also cited Matt 24:39–41: "That is how it will be at the coming of the Son of Man. Two men will be in the field; one will be taken and the other left. Two women will be grinding with a hand mill; one will be taken and the other left."

The reason some will be taken, and others not, belongs to the mysterious will of God. Drelincourt chastised his congregation, saying they knew well that God did not love those who perished less than those who survived. God wanted some to go to eternal glory and others to continue to serve him in this life. Further, he distinguished between those who die in the faith and those who do not. There is a certain comfort for those who are left behind, knowing that their loved ones are with the Lord; on this point Drelincourt referred to Ps 116:15: "Precious in the sight of the Lord is the death of his faithful servants."[15]

The speaker drew an insightful parallel between the deaths of the parishioners and the biblical narrative of the Israelites crossing the Jordan River into the promised land. This analogy posits that, in their demise, these individuals are not merely departing from earthly existence but entering a celestial realm—the heavenly Canaan. They are portrayed as gathering "celestial manna," which symbolizes the divine nourishment derived from the gospel. Drelincourt elaborated on the notion that these departed souls join the ranks of angels within the "church of the firstborn," where their names are inscribed in the annals of heaven. This assembly is characterized by singing exalted praises within the heavenly choir.

---

14. Drelincourt, *Sermon*, 19.
15. Drelincourt, *Sermon*, 31–34.

Drelincourt also acknowledged the profound sorrow experienced by those who remain on earth, as well as the emotional weight of their grief. He concluded with a contemplative observation: when believers are allowed to witness the heavens opened to them and to behold divine glory, their overwhelming sorrows will be transformed into expressions of praise and gratitude. This vision of the Lord, welcoming them with open arms while they contemplate his glory, serves as a source of immense hope. Drelincourt recognizes that such grief is too intense for immediate comfort and that while time is necessary for healing, God does not leave his people in despair; instead, he offers them solace amid extreme sorrow.[16]

While Drelincourt did seek to console, he did not miss the opportunity to exhort. He stressed that Christians should recognize their true citizenship in heaven and forsake the vanities of this world. One should be ready at any moment to surrender one's soul to the Lord. Christians should, therefore, take a deep look at their own sinfulness. One could die in a similar way at any time, and the believer should be ready to give their account before God.

At this point, Drelincourt's sermon took a gruesome turn. Anyone could die suddenly in any number of ways, such as drowning, being burned alive, or being torn to pieces and eaten by wild animals. The earth could swallow people up, as happened to Korah and his followers in Num 16. Angels could come and destroy entire cities. One could even be eaten by worms. Drelincourt also pointed to the example of Achan, who hid the forbidden items stolen from Jericho, and the punishment that fell upon him and his family. The Bible, after all, describes God as a consuming fire (Deut 4:23–24).

Drelincourt explained that some people, even in his congregation, had performed worse deeds than Pilate. Instead of mixing the blood of the innocent with the blood of their sacrifices, many have mingled the works of Satan with those of heaven. He said that many have come to church out of habit or custom and never really taken to heart the message of the gospel. Many diminish the value of the Lord's Supper by making such loud noises that the pastor could not even hear himself preaching the word. Some leave the Eucharistic service early for no reason and miss the blessings of communing with the Lord. God has given us, he said, six days to do our work and take care of our affairs, but the Christian Sabbath should be reserved for God. Many possess horses or expensive

---

16. Drelincourt, *Sermon*, 36–37.

carriages to make the trip to Charenton easier but do not bother to come. Some even leave early before the benediction. Many feel that nobody notices such disrespectful behavior, but God knows everything and is not pleased.

Furthermore, these actions reflect what is in one's heart, and God knows that too. As one repents in heart, mind, and actions before the almighty God, he will hear us and forgive. The Lord anxiously waits for us to come to him with a humble spirit. He will guide believers through life and lead them into eternal bliss, that they may join the church triumphant when the day of death comes. The time of separation from loved ones who have gone before us will be very short compared to eternity, and one can look forward to a joyful reunion.[17]

Drelincourt seized the opportunity to offer solace and encouragement to his congregation both through this sermon and through his poignant communication with the Marquis de Pardaillan. This letter has parallels with the famous correspondence from Abraham Lincoln to Lydia Parker Bixby, a widow grieving the loss of five sons during the American Civil War. The sermon exemplifies the height of Drelincourt's contributions, showcasing his profound commitment to pastoral care—an area in which he arguably surpassed his colleagues at Charenton. His work stands as a seminal text on the subject. Moreover, the enduring relevance of his message is noteworthy; calamities persist across generations, and contemporary pastors are still confronted with the age-old question concerning theodicy: why does God permit such tragedies to unfold?

BIBLIOGRAPHY

Carbonnier-Burkard, Marianne. "Les pasteurs français auteurs d'une littérature d'édification, au XVIIe siècle." *Bulletin de la Société de l'Histoire du Protestantisme Français* 156 (Janvier-Février-Mars 2010) 37–48.

———. "Visiter les malades: une oeuvre de charité en version réformée selon le pasteur Charles Drelincourt (1595–1669)." In *Les Oeuvres protestantes en Europe*, edited by Céline Borello, 43–59. Rennes: Presses Universitaires de Rennes, 2013.

Daillé, Jean. *Sermon sur l'espitre de St. Paul à Tite, chapitre 3 verset 8*. Paris: Samuel Perier, 1654.

de Félice, Paul. *Les protestants d'autrefois: Vie intérieure des églises, moeurs et usages*. Paris: Librairie Fischbacher, 1899.

———. "Le Temple de Charenton—Les services religieux." *Bulletin de la Société de l'Histoire du Protestantisme Français* 55 (Juillet-Aout 1906) 348–61.

---

17. Drelincourt, *Sermon*, 39–52.

Douen, O. "Les Quatorze Mille Places du Temple de Charenton." *Bulletin historique et littéraire* 25 (1876) 381–84.

Drelincourt, Charles. *The Christian's Defence Against the Fears of Death*. Translated by Marius D'Assigny. Liverpool: Nuttall, Fisher, and Dixon, 1810.

———. *Sermon sur Saint Luc 13. versets, 1. 2. 3. 4. & 5, Prononcé à Charenton le 25 janvier, 1654*. Paris: Samuel Perier, 1654.

———. *Les visites charitables ou les consolations chrétiennes pour toutes sortes de personnes affligées*. 5 vols. Genève: Jean Antoine et Samuël De Tournes, 1666–69.

McKee, R. Jane. "The Pastoral and Polemical Theology of Charles Drelincourt (1595–1669)." In *The Theology of the French Reformed Churches: From Henri IV to the Revocation of the Edict of Nantes*, edited by Martin I. Klauber, 276–95. Grand Rapids: Reformation Heritage, 2014.

Mentzer, Raymond A. "Fasting, Piety, and Political Anxiety Among French Reformed Protestants." *Church History* 76 (June 2007) 330–62.

Read, Charles. "La catastrophe arrivée, le 18 janvier 1654 à Charenton-Saint-Maurice." *Bulletin historique et littéraire* 38 (1889) 479–86.

Sunshine, Glenn S. "French Protestantism on the Eve of St-Bartholomew: The Ecclesiastical Discipline of the French Reformed Churches, 1571–1572." *French History* 4 (Sept. 1990) 340–77.

4

"Committed by Us to Their Spiritual Charge"

The Pastoral Theology of the Tudor Royal Ecclesiastical Injunctions

ANDRE A. GAZAL

INTRODUCTION

THE FRONTISPIECE OF THE Great Bible (1539) vividly depicts Henry VIII enthroned, committing the English Bible to Archbishop Thomas Cranmer (1489-1556) and Thomas Cromwell (1485-1540), who in turn distributes it to the subjects throughout the realm. This striking image portrays not merely the general concept of royal supremacy, that the monarch is the "Supreme Head," or "Supreme Governor," of the national church, and as such exercises divinely invested authority over it. Rather, the frontispiece presents a theological aspect of royal supremacy that is not directly addressed in the scholarly literature on the subject: its relationship to pastoral ministry.

While many narratives of the English Reformation describe the exercise of royal supremacy directly over bishops and archbishops like Cranmer, Matthew Parker (1504-75), Edwin Sandys (1519-88), Edmund Grindal (1519-83), etc., they do not consider the extent to which royal supremacy bears on pastoral ministry in the primary sources. In keeping with the theme of this Festschrift for my beloved *Doktorvater*, colleague, and friend, Scott Manetsch, the present essay will explore this subject in the Tudor royal ecclesiastical injunctions. However, for a moment, let us return to the frontispiece of the Great Bible.

As we mentioned above, the frontispiece shows Henry conferring the English Bible upon Cranmer and Cromwell, two principal figures in his government, with Cranmer as the highest primate in the realm and Cromwell as Keeper of the Seal and Vicegerent of Spiritualities. Yet, throughout the rest of the picture, one can see below the central image of Henry, Cranmer, and Cromwell a portrayal of a priest preaching to a congregation, which is a consequence of the Bible having been widely distributed. The implication is clear: the priest can preach because the king initially issued the Bible. The source of the priest's Bible, as well as the function of the preaching that he performs, has been delegated to him by the king (through the archbishop, in this case). Because of royal supremacy, pastoral authority within the realm ultimately resides in the king as "Supreme Head."

What the frontispiece portrays visually, other sources state clearly, even directing specific areas of pastoral ministry within the context of the parish. This is the case with the Tudor royal ecclesiastical injunctions issued during the reigns of the Tudor monarchs concerning the implementation of the reformations they initiated in local parishes through various royal visitations conducted by groups of royal commissioners. This essay will argue that the royal ecclesiastical injunctions issued from the reign of Henry VIII to that of Elizabeth I specifically regard pastoral authority as being derived from royal supremacy. The injunctions were orders drafted and issued under the auspices of the monarchs to direct specific pastoral activities within the local parish. Royal commissions would be dispatched on visitations to parishes to deliver the injunctions to the parish priests. Bishops would also be charged with enforcing these injunctions.

We will support the above thesis by closely examining the content of the injunctions, not only to show where they clearly locate pastoral ministry within royal supremacy but also to explore how pastoral ministry was conducted, being sourced institutionally within royal supremacy. The above thesis will also be supported by a secondary argument: pastoral ministry in England during the Reformation focused on catechesis. By "catechesis," we mean an overall program of teaching the Christian faith to parishioners that comprises many aspects. Taking as their point of departure the traditional catechesis, which entails instruction principally in the Apostles' Creed, the Lord's Prayer, and the Decalogue,[1] the royal ecclesiastical injunctions use this traditional scheme as a central feature of the monarchs' reformist agendas. The first of these injunctions—those issued by Henry VIII in 1536 and 1538, respectively—provide the basis for this radical transformation of pastoral ministry while simultaneously maintaining continuity with key aspects of traditional catechesis.

ROYAL SUPREMACY AS THE SOURCE OF PASTORAL CARE: THE HENRICIAN INJUNCTIONS

In declaring the monarch to be the "Supreme Head of the Church of England," the Act of Supremacy (1534) established the legal basis for a national church severed from Roman obedience. As "Supreme Head," Henry actively sought to define the character of this national church. Indeed, "for increase of virtue in Christ's Religion," he intended to exercise his full authority "to visit, repress, redress, reform, order, correct, restrain, and amend all such errors, heresies, abuses, offences, contempts, and enormities, whatsoever they be."[2] According to G. W. Bernard, Henry sought to reform the church according to his understanding of Erasmus's vision for ecclesiastical reform.[3]

Among other things, Henry's reformist agenda entailed abolishing papal pardons, indulgences, pilgrimages, and, very significantly, monasteries—things that "Erasmus and other like-minded theologians and churchmen severely criticized."[4] Moreover, the exercise of royal supremacy also included the regulation of pastoral practice. This means that the

---

1. This program of catechesis was largely based on that drafted by Archbishop John Peckham (1230–92) of Canterbury at his provincial council at Lambeth in 1281. This system of instruction, *De informatione simplicium*, or *Ignorantia Sacerdotum* (the opening words of the document) entailed teaching the Lord's Prayer, the Apostles' Creed, the Hail Mary, the Ten Commandments, the Seven Works of Mercy, the Seven Virtues, the Seven Deadly Sins, and the Seven Sacraments. Moreover, the clergy were to instruct their parishioners in these essential formularies of the faith four times a year in the vernacular. See Duffy, *Stripping of the Altars*, 53.

2. Act of Supremacy (1534), in Bray, *Documents of the English Reformation*, 114.

3. Bernard, *King's Reformation*, 236–37.

4. Bernard, *King's Reformation*, 236–37.

exertion of royal supremacy amounted to an indirect employment of pastoral authority as it extended into matters of catechesis.

The first attempt at theologically defining the English Church was the Ten Articles (1536). This document was drafted after Henry's delegation returned from Wittenberg, where it was negotiating a possible alliance between Henry and the Schmalkaldic League. The preface of the Ten Articles declares the general jurisdiction of royal authority over pastoral practice:

> Among other cures appertaining unto our princely office, whereunto it hath pleased Almighty God of his infinite mercy and goodness to call us, we have always esteemed and thought, like as we also yet esteem and think, that it most chiefly belongeth unto our said charge diligently to foresee and cause, that not only the Word and commandments of God should most sincerely be believed, and most reverently be observed and kept of our subjects, but also that unity and concord of opinion, namely in such things as doth concern our religion, may increase and go forthward, and all occasion of dissent and discord touching the same be repressed and utterly extinguished.[5]

Among the principal duties of the Christian monarch is not simply to expect but to *cause*, or induce both belief and obedience to, the word of God. Next, the king is to ensure unity among his subjects around this common faith and obedience—a unity that he has the right to maintain by force, as the preface asserts. This preservation of doctrinal unity is essential to preventing the "dangers of souls," and so the specific pastoral aim of royal supremacy is to protect the spiritual well-being of Christian subjects through the clarification of truth. Thus, royal supremacy entailed fostering a common, national faith that would manifest itself in national obedience to divine commands.

The preface then distinguishes two categories for the proceeding articles: those "commanded expressly by God and necessary for salvation," and those that "containeth such things as have been of long continuance for a decent order and honest policy, prudently instituted and used in the churches of our realm, and be for that same purpose and end to be observed and kept accordingly."[6] The articles necessary for salvation are those concerning the ecumenical creeds, baptism, penance, the Eucharist, and justification.

5. Preface, "Ten Articles," in Bray, *Documents of the English Reformation*, 163.
6. Preface, "Ten Articles," in Bray, *Documents of the English Reformation*, 164.

The first article maintains continuity with traditional catechesis in that it mandates the clergy to instruct the faithful in the Scriptures as well as the Apostles' Creed, the Nicene Creed, and the Athanasian Creed. Notably, each article alleges that the clergy teaches the people on behalf of the king, thereby discharging *his* pastoral role:

> First, as touching the chief and principal articles of our faith, since it is thus agreed that as hereafter followeth, by the whole clergy of this realm, we will that the bishops and preachers shall instruct and teach our people, by us committed to their spiritual charge, that they ought and must most constantly believe and defend all those things to be true, which be comprehended in the whole body of and canon of the Bible, and also in the three creeds, or symbols.[7]

This and each subsequent article throughout the document employs the same formula: "We will that the bishops and preachers shall instruct and teach our people, *by us committed to their spiritual charge.*" Even though the clergy teach, the king commends those to be taught to their spiritual oversight. In entrusting his subjects to the clergy's instruction, the king provides pastoral care for them. Thus, within the parameters of the Henrician Supremacy, the clergy function as the spiritual agency of the monarch, who is the ultimate pastor within the realm. Though conducted indirectly through clerical agency, pastoral care, especially in the form of catechesis, is a duty delegated by the monarch.

Following the directives regarding the proper instruction that the clergy are to impart concerning baptism is an evangelical cast on the traditional sacrament of penance, which they are also required to teach. While the article on penance affirms all three parts of the sacrament (i.e., contrition, confession, and absolution), it reinterprets them by way of faith in Christ's sacrifice. In this regard, the article identifies two parts of contrition: first, acknowledgment of "the filthiness and abomination" of one's own sin; and second, "faith, trust, and confidence of the mercy and goodness of God, whereby the penitent must conceive certain hope and faith that God will forgive him his sins, and repute him justified, and of the number of his elect children, not for the worthiness of any merit or work done by the penitent, but only for the merits of the blood and passion of our Lord Jesus Christ."[8] Although the article affirms the

---

7. Bray, *Documents of the English Reformation*, 164.
8. Bray, *Documents of the English Reformation*, 167.

necessity of auricular confession, it omits any further comment regarding the penitent's act of confession and instead emphasizes that the priest's absolution is the reason for the confession. Moreover, the article defines this third part of penance as an application of "the promises of God's grace and favour to the penitent."[9] However, absolution still includes works of satisfaction such as prayers, fasting, and alms, "which must make restitution or satisfaction in will and deed to [one's] neighbours in such things as they have done them wrong and injury in, and must do all other good works of mercy and charity, and express their obedient will in executing and fulfilling of God's commandment outwardly."[10] Such works of satisfaction necessarily accompany true faith.

After requiring the clergy to teach the faithful about the real physical presence of Christ in the Eucharist, the document continues with the fifth article, concerning justification. Reflecting the convictions of Henry and the traditionalists, this article asserts that good works accompany faith in justification: "Sinners attain this justification by contrition and faith joined with charity."[11] God "requireth us and commandeth us, that after we be justified, we must also have good works of charity and obedience toward God, in the observing and fulfilling outwardly of his laws and commandments."[12]

The remaining five articles—those that are not necessary for salvation—pertain to the use of images, the veneration of saints, the performance of other rites and ceremonies, and the doctrine of purgatory. Images represent various virtues embodied by the saints they portray and thus serve as "kindlers and stirrers of men's minds and make oft to remember and lament their sins and offences."[13] This exemplary role of the saints also serves as the basis for honoring them as among the elect in heaven who continuously worship Christ. As part of their worship, the saints pray for and with the faithful on earth, and for this reason, the clergy are to encourage parishioners to pray to them.

Various traditional rites and ceremonies—such as sprinkling oneself with water in remembrance of one's baptism, bearing candles on Candlemas, receiving ashes on Ash Wednesday, carrying palms on Palm Sunday, and creeping to the cross on Good Friday—are to be retained as

9. Bray, *Documents of the English Reformation*, 167.
10. Bray, *Documents of the English Reformation*, 168.
11. Bray, *Documents of the English Reformation*, 170.
12. Bray, *Documents of the English Reformation*, 170.
13. Bray, *Documents of the English Reformation*, 171.

things "good and laudable, to put us in remembrance of those spiritual things that they do signify"; moreover, "none of these ceremonies have the power to remit sin, but only to stir up and lift up our minds unto God, by whom only our sins be forgiven."[14]

In keeping with the mediatory tone of the Ten Articles, the article on purgatory is tentative. It directs the clergy to impress upon the faithful the importance of praying for departed souls, especially through Masses. Also, while acknowledging support for the doctrine of purgatory from 2 Maccabees and various ancient Christian authors, the article, however, asserts that the Scriptures generally are uncertain about the alleged pains suffered in purgatory.[15] For this reason, it encourages the faithful to commit those departed souls to God's mercy. At the same time, the reformist nature of the document manifests itself in the instructions to abolish the alleged papal abuses associated with purgatory, such as indulgences.[16]

In addition to defining the doctrinal distinctives of the Church of England after the passage of the Act of Supremacy, the Ten Articles also defined the pastoral theology of this national church. First, in keeping with the late medieval English Church, the Ten Articles still portray pastoral care as catechesis in which the clergy are charged with teaching the faithful the essentials of the Christian faith as expressed in the creeds—all within the larger context of parish life. Second, the Ten Articles locate the sources of pastoral care and practice in royal ecclesiastical authority. Pastoral care is now a function delegated by the king as "Supreme Head." On behalf of the "Supreme Head," the clergy were to instruct the people whom he has committed to their charge in the essentials of the Christian faith and the doctrines behind traditional ceremonies and rites, according to a reformist interpretation. The goal of pastoral care for both Henry and his Vicegerent of Spiritualities, Thomas Cromwell, was to ensure the obedience of the faithful in a Christian society being defined by the new national church. The Ten Articles set forth the theology of this church with this specific pastoral aim in mind. Further, accompanying the Ten Articles are the directives for their practical implementation within the context of the parish. These are the Henrician injunctions (1536, 1538). The injunctions intended to translate the Ten Articles directly into the discharge of pastoral ministry, and in turn they directly extended into matters of parishioners' devotional life.

14. Bray, *Documents of the English Reformation*, 173.
15. Bray, *Documents of the English Reformation*, 173.
16. Bray, *Documents of the English Reformation*, 174.

The first injunctions drawn up by Cromwell commanded the enforcement of the various laws enacted by Parliament that abolished papal authority throughout the realm. Next, the Ten Articles were to be taught regularly in sermons. This also required the clergy to inform people in their spiritual charge concerning the discontinuation of certain holy days that heretofore were part of the traditional calendar. A radical feature of the injunction that purported to transform traditional devotional life was its indirect attack on the cult of the saints, along with the practice of pilgrimages associated with it. The stated pastoral goal of this article was that "all superstition and hypocrisy [that has] crept into divers men's hearts may vanish away."[17] Reflecting Henry's own antagonism to the cult of the saints, the injunction undermines devotion to the saints first by admonishing the faithful to regard them in no other way than that which is urged by the Ten Articles referenced above. Moreover, the injunction urges the faithful to seek what they need directly from God himself, who is "the very author of the same."[18] Second, the injunction discourages one of the central aspects of such veneration: pilgrimages to the shrines of the saints. In this regard, the injunction directs the clergy to encourage the faithful to prioritize deeds that foster godliness over pilgrimages, deeds such as "the keeping of God's commandments and fulfilling of his works of charity." Further, the clergy are to persuade them that "they shall please God more by the true exercising of their bodily labour, travail, or occupation, and providing for their families than if they went about to the same pilgrimages."[19] Living obediently to God's commands as Christian subjects far exceeds the vain reverence of saints in the pursuit of holiness.

As per the Ten Articles, the injunctions order the clergy to instruct their parishioners in the major components of traditional catechesis, consisting of the Lord's Prayer, the Apostles' Creed, and the Decalogue. Not only were the clergy to teach the content of these formularies to the people in their cures, but they were also to equip parents and masters to teach the same to their children and servants, respectively.[20] A particularly notable feature of this catechesis is the requirement of parents and masters to teach their charges a trade or occupation that will provide

---

17. Bray, *Documents of the English Reformation*, 176.
18. Bray, *Documents of the English Reformation*, 176.
19. Bray, *Documents of the English Reformation*, 176.
20. Bray, *Documents of the English Reformation*, 177.

them with a living so they will not need to beg.[21] This alteration of traditional catechesis demonstrates that instruction in the faith entails both understanding and application to one's life in the Christian commonwealth. Further, living the faith via a productive occupation in society effectively displaces the monastic estate as the holiest spiritual vocation. This aspect of the injunction coincides with the government's campaign to dissolve the monasteries during the same year that it was issued. Thus, it appears that, among other things, this vocational extension of catechesis served to justify the regime's attack on monasticism. Pastoral care, as prescribed in this injunction, involves the exertion of royal ecclesiastical authority through the structure of traditional catechesis—which, in turn, will radically alter the devotional life of the parish.

The Henrician injunctions of 1538 continued to implement the agenda of parochial reform via altered catechesis. Probably the most conspicuous feature of this mandated program of catechesis was the requirement for the faithful to have full access to the Bible in the vernacular. "You shall provide on this side the feast [of] Easter next coming (06 April 1539) one book of the whole Bible of the largest volume, in English, and the same set up in some convenient place within the said church that you have cure of, whereas your parishioners may most commodiously resort to the same and read it."[22] To meet this requirement, the Great Bible completed by Miles Coverdale (1488–1569) would be displayed from the chancels of individual churches.

The third injunction then expressly forbade the discouragement of anyone from reading or hearing the Bible: "you shall discourage no man privily or apertly from the reading or hearing of the same Bible, but shall expressly provoke, stir and exhort every person to read the same as that which is the very lively Word of God, that every Christian man is bound to embrace, believe and follow if he looked to be saved."[23] However, the same injunction cautioned against allowing disputes among parishioners concerning the interpretation of difficult passages by requiring them to refer to those qualified to interpret them, such as the clergy, for an explanation.[24] While all should be free to read and hear the word of God for faith and life, not all were free to interpret! Biblical interpretation must

---

21. Bray, *Documents of the English Reformation*, 177.

22. Bray, *Documents of the English Reformation*, 179. It should also be noted that not all copies of the injunctions contained this order. See Bernard, *King's Reformation*, 524.

23. Bray, *Documents of the English Reformation*, 179–80.

24. Bray, *Documents of the English Reformation*, 180.

necessarily be mediated through the instruction of the clergy, who are learned in the Scriptures.

Some important pastoral implications emerge from this injunction: first, equal access to Scripture does not result in equal understanding; second, unrestrained individual interpretation of the Scriptures simultaneously disrupts the stability of the church and endangers people's souls, because it can too easily lead to heresy; third, biblical exposition is the essential—and thus central—component of catechesis, and it is therefore the principal task of the clergy in their care of souls.

The injunctions stressed the role of traditional catechesis. They required the clergy to instruct the faithful in either the Lord's Prayer or the Creed in English every Sunday and holy day, "to the intent that they may learn the same by heart, and so from day to day to give them one like lesson or sentence of the same, till they have learned the whole Lord's Prayer or Creed, in English by rote."[25] This instruction, furthermore, was to include a sustained, detailed exposition of these formularies, as well as the Ten Commandments. The clergy were also to prepare parents and masters to teach the same to their children and their entire households.[26] In keeping with traditional practice, priests were to teach parishioners the Creed and the Lord's Prayer within the context of confession during Lent, similar to late medieval practice.[27] Parishioners, moreover, were to demonstrate proficiency in the Creed and Lord's Prayer before partaking of the Eucharist.

Preaching occupies a central place in this catechesis. The sixth injunction requires a sermon at least every quarter throughout the year "wherein you shall purely and sincerely declare the very gospel of Christ, and in the same exhort your hearers to the works of charity, mercy, and faith specially prescribed and commanded in Scripture, and not to repose their trust or affiance in any other works devised by men's fantasies beside Scripture."[28] In general, such works supposedly created by human imagination are linked to the veneration of saints, such as pilgrimages to their shrines and honoring their images. Thus, scriptural preaching, as

---

25. Bray, *Documents of the English Reformation*, 180.

26. Bray, *Documents of the English Reformation*, 180.

27. Bray, *Documents of the English Reformation*, 180. Late medieval English cleric John Mirk (active ca. 1380–1420) especially emphasized the importance of individual instruction in these formularies with penitents during confession in his *Instructions for Parish Priests*. See Mirk, *Instructions*, 7–21.

28. Bray, *Documents of the English Reformation*, 180.

a principal means of catechesis, bolsters an understanding of the gospel while fostering a Christian life that actively cultivates charity, mercy, and faith. At the same time, it subverts sundry traditional practices by emphasizing that they have no ground in Scripture, rendering them not only invalid but also superstitious and blasphemous.

Because of the significant place preaching occupies in the overall program of catechesis, the injunctions require absent priests to make provision for suitable substitutes who are capable of preaching and teaching. The injunctions furthermore guard the function of preaching by restricting it only to those properly licensed by a diocesan bishop, the archbishop of Canterbury, or the king himself.[29] Finally, the injunctions require every parish to keep registers.[30]

The injunctions of 1536 and 1538 endeavored to translate the doctrine of the Ten Articles into parish life by way of an amended traditional catechesis. Despite its largely traditional structure, this catechesis promoted a predominantly humanistic and reformist biblical piety by utilizing orthodox formularies, while simultaneously undermining and marginalizing key aspects of late medieval devotional life, such as the practices linked to the cult of the saints. These injunctions also emphasized to the faithful that pastoral authority was now a function of the Supreme Head, who delegated it to the clergy as the spiritual shepherds of the realm.

Despite the contention of some scholars that religious policy under Henry took a "reactionary" turn beginning in 1539 with the passage of the Six Articles Act, it essentially remained consistent.[31] In fact, there was no contradiction between the Six Articles and the injunctions above as well as the Ten Articles and the later *Bishops' Book*. Instead, the Six Articles represent a clarification of specific issues, especially those related to pastoral life and ministry.

After the first article affirms Christ's real presence in the Eucharist, the following five declare, respectively, that receiving communion in both kinds—that is, both the bread and the wine—is not for salvation "by the law of God";[32] that priests are to continue practicing celibacy "by the law of God";[33] that those in other religious vocations are also to keep their

---

29. Bray, *Documents of the English Reformation*, 181.
30. Bray, *Documents of the English Reformation*, 182.
31. Bernard, *King's Reformation*, 500.
32. Bray, *Documents of the English Reformation*, 224.
33. Bray, *Documents of the English Reformation*, 224.

vows of chastity; that it is "meet and necessary" that private Masses "be continued and admitted *in this the King's English Church and Congregation* as whereby good Christian people, ordering themselves accordingly, do receive both godly and goodly consolations and benefits, and is agreeable to God's law";[34] and finally, that auricular confession is to be retained as "expedient and necessary."[35] Very notably, the Six Articles strongly emphasize that the national church is the "King's," underscoring the fact that his ecclesiastical authority directs the spiritual lives of his subjects through the clergy. It is his church under God, and the national congregation is his divinely commissioned charge that has been placed in the care of the clergy under his auspices.

Some of the injunctions' requirements had to be modified due to unanticipated circumstances. For instance, public access to the vernacular Bible encouraged various parties to disrupt services by debating the meaning of Scripture with priests in the middle of their sermons. These and other such disturbances prompted Parliament to restrict Bible reading to those of noble status. According to Diarmaid MacCulloch, this "restriction of Bible reading reflects Henry's concern about its abuse . . . since the first authorization of the Bible in 1538."[36] Furthermore, while other modifications were made to the injunctions, the new statement of doctrine produced in 1543, *The King's Book*, generally confirmed a reformist version of traditional church life, including the Seven Sacraments, even though it raises doubts concerning purgatory and—as had been the case since the passage of the Act of Supremacy—attacks various alleged papal abuses.[37]

By the time Henry VIII died on January 28, 1547, the English Church maintained the general structure of traditional catechesis. However, this catechesis was very *untraditional*: while it aimed to instruct parishioners in the traditional formularies of the faith, this same teaching undermined some key aspects of late medieval church life. Most significant was the movement of the locus and source of pastoral authority from the pope to the king as the shepherd of the national church, with the clergy discharging pastoral care at his behest. When Henry's young son, Edward VI (r. 1547–53), succeeded him, pastoral care via catechesis acquired a more decidedly evangelical character, as the official and

---

34. Bray, *Documents of the English Reformation*, 224. Emphasis added.
35. Bray, *Documents of the English Reformation*, 224.
36. MacCulloch, *Thomas Cranmer*, 311.
37. Bernard, *King's Reformation*, 588.

evangelical reformations would converge in the person of the precocious monarch under the principal leadership of Henry's archbishop of Canterbury, Thomas Cranmer.

PASTORAL CARE AS EVANGELICAL CATECHESIS ACCORDING TO THE EDWARDIAN INJUNCTIONS

When Henry VIII's son by Jane Seymour ascended the throne of England as Edward VI, he was already under the tutelage of evangelical mentors such as Hugh Latimer (1487–1555), Nicholas Ridley (1500–1555), Thomas Goodrich (1494–1554), John Cheke (1514–57), Richard Cox (1500–1581), and, of course, Archbishop Cranmer himself. The Reformation—now effectively directed by Cranmer and Edward Seymour (1500–1552), the duke of Somerset, who acted as Lord Protector (and who would later be displaced and succeeded by John Dudley (1504–53), the duke of Northumberland)—would be nothing less than what MacCulloch describes as a "revolutionary act."[38] Such a religious revolution entailed bringing the Church of England directly into the orbit of the larger Protestant movements that had been developing on the Continent. This endeavor involved aggressive, official, evangelical reformation striking at the very heart of traditional devotion—public worship and, with it, pastoral practice. The evangelical reformation of pastoral practice through a radical appropriation of traditional catechesis was the subject of the royal injunctions drafted on behalf of Edward in 1547.

Drafted by Cranmer and Somerset, these injunctions were published on July 31, 1547. They reaffirmed most of the prescriptions stipulated by the Henrician injunctions of 1536 and 1538 but added new provisions that effected further evangelical reform of pastoral ministry. The preamble of these injunctions avers the pastoral role of the king and his government: he and the protector, who leads the government in his stead, "minister these godly injunctions" to suppress "idolatry and superstition throughout all his realms and dominions and to plant true religion."[39] Royal ecclesiastical authority still serves as the source of pastoral authority, and with it, pastoral care. For this reason, the program of catechesis included regular, quarterly instruction in the doctrine of royal

---

38. MacCulloch, *Boy King*, 9.
39. Bray, *Documents of the English Reformation*, 247.

supremacy, "that the King's power within his realms and dominions is the highest power under God, to whom all men within the same realms and dominions, by God's laws owe most loyalty and obedience, afore and above all other powers and potentates on earth."[40] Specifically, the clergy were to preach on this doctrine as part of their sermon cycle at least four times per year.[41]

Like their Henrician predecessors, these injunctions openly discourage participation in the cult of the saints. To quell superstition in the hearts of the faithful, the clergy were to emphasize the performance of charitable works based on Scriptural exposition.[42] Furthermore, as in the previous injunctions, the saints and their images only serve the pedagogical purpose of illustrating the virtues exemplified by their lives. To reinforce this attitude toward the saints, the clergy are now ordered to remove any torches, candles, tapers, or wax images placed in front of any statue or picture of a saint. Instead, only two candles are to be placed on the high altar, which signifies "that Christ is the very true light of the world."[43] Additionally, the clergy are instructed to preach against pilgrimages, relics, images, and other such "superstitions" as being opposed to the word of God, and they are to recant those instances when they advocated the same.[44]

Moreover, the Edwardian injunctions expand on the use of traditional catechesis. On those holy days when there is no sermon, the clergy are to instruct the faithful in the Lord's Prayer, the Apostles' Creed, and the Ten Commandments.[45] They are also to prepare parents, masters, and other heads of households to teach these formularies to their children, servants, and anyone committed to their charge. As with their predecessors, these injunctions incorporate occupational training into the larger program of catechesis so as to discourage people from monasticism.[46]

Once again, the central feature of this catechetical program is lay access to the vernacular Bible, but this time, Scripture would be accompanied by an English translation of Erasmus's *Paraphrases of the*

---

40. Bray, *Documents of the English Reformation*, 248.
41. Bray, *Documents of the English Reformation*, 248.
42. Bray, *Documents of the English Reformation*, 248.
43. Bray, *Documents of the English Reformation*, 249.
44. Bray, *Documents of the English Reformation*, 251.
45. Bray, *Documents of the English Reformation*, 249.
46. Bray, *Documents of the English Reformation*, 251.

Four Gospels.[47] With the Bible and a means of understanding it openly available, the clergy are to "exhort every person to read the same, as the very lively Word of God, and the special food of man's soul, that all Christian persons are bound to embrace, believe, and follow, if they look to be saved; whereby they may the better know their duties to God, their Sovereign Lord the King and their neighbour."[48] The pastoral aim of widespread but mediated exposure of the laity to Scripture is clear: that they would live obediently and faithfully as citizens of a Christian society, but now as a result of an evangelical faith. Furthermore, the clergy are to ensure that people did not provoke arguments during the reading of Scripture; instead, they should encourage them to listen quietly to the reader.[49]

The injunctions next address matters of clerical conduct. They prohibit the clergy from frequenting taverns and alehouses and then instruct them that "after their dinner and supper, they shall not give themselves to drinking or riot, spending their time idly, by day or by night at dice, cards, or tables playing, or any other unlawful game, but at all times as they shall have leisure, they shall hear or read somewhat of Holy Scripture, or shall occupy themselves with some other honest exercise, and that they always do the things which appertain to honesty, with endeavor to profit the common weal, having always in mind that they ought to excel all others in purity of life and should be examples to the people to live well and Christianly."[50] As traditionally affirmed, pastoral care through catechesis entails not only teaching the Scriptures and sound doctrine but also exemplifying the Christian life before parishioners, such that living according to scriptural and orthodox teaching might strengthen the Christian commonwealth. This point reaffirms the operative principle of these injunctions as well as those issued under the young king's father: under the divinely appointed oversight of the king, the clergy care for the faithful of the nation with their whole lives.

Further, in accord with traditional pastoral practice, the Edwardian injunctions direct the clergy to incorporate basic instruction in the faith via the Lord's Prayer, the Apostles' Creed, and the Ten Commandments

---

47. Bray, *Documents of the English Reformation*, 252.
48. Bray, *Documents of the English Reformation*, 250.
49. Bray, *Documents of the English Reformation*, 250.
50. Bray, *Documents of the English Reformation*, 250. The priest's instruction of the people in the Christian faith by his own example was something heavily stressed in late medieval pastoral theology. See Mirk, *Instructions*, 2.

into confession during Lent before partaking of the Eucharist. Priests are to carefully examine parishioners in each of these essentials of the Christian faith. Should a penitent not show sufficient knowledge of these formularies, the priest is to discourage that person from "God's board."[51] To proceed to the Eucharist bereft of understanding concerning the central tenets of the faith will incur "great peril of their souls."[52] Here, the connection is established between knowledge as preparation for right practice and spiritual health. The source of spiritual health is an ever-increasing understanding of the contents of the faith.

Since preaching is the central means of conveying an understanding of the Scriptures and the faith, the injunctions strictly regulate it. As with the Henrician injunctions, only those licensed by the king, the protector, the diocesan bishop, or the archbishop of Canterbury may preach.[53]

The injunctions now turn to worship according to the prescribed liturgy, along with various other pastoral matters. Appointed fasts are to be observed. Common prayer is to be followed in its assigned order. Insisting on the clergy's increased understanding of Scripture, the injunction requires "every parson, vicar, curate, chantry priest, and stipendiary" who does not have a bachelor of divinity to own English and Latin copies of the New Testament as well as Erasmus's *Paraphrases*.[54] These same clergy are to demonstrate their understanding of the Scriptures before all commissioners sent by the government on ecclesiastical visitations, whose purpose is to ensure parish compliance with the injunctions.[55] During every celebration of the Eucharist, one chapter from the Epistles and one from the Gospels is to be read. At Evensong (i.e., evening prayer), one chapter from the Old Testament and one from the New Testament are to be read in English.[56] Following this are directions for ministering to the dying.

The Edwardian injunctions readily acknowledge the point of death as the time when the faithful are most vulnerable: "Those persons which be sick or in peril of death be oftentimes put in despair by the craft and subtlety of the devil who is then most busy, and specially with them that lack the knowledge, sure persuasion, and steadfast belief that they may be

---

51. Bray, *Documents of the English Reformation*, 251.
52. Bray, *Documents of the English Reformation*, 251.
53. Bray, *Documents of the English Reformation*, 251.
54. Bray, *Documents of the English Reformation*, 253.
55. Bray, *Documents of the English Reformation*, 253.
56. Bray, *Documents of the English Reformation*, 253.

made partakers of the great and infinite mercy which Almighty God of his most bountiful goodness and mere liberality, without our deserving, hath offered freely to all persons that put their full trust and confidence in him."[57] It is indeed at the point of death when temptation is most intense, since this is the time when Satan attempts most assiduously to undermine the dying's faith in God's grace and mercy, thereby securing their eternal condemnation. The injunctions at this point give explicit direction for ministering to people in this indescribably desolate state:

> Therefore, that this damnable device of despair may be clearly taken away and firm belief and steadfast hope surely conceived of all their parishioners, being in any danger, they shall learn, and have always in readiness, such comfortable places and sentences of Scripture as do set forth the mercy, benefits and goodness of Almighty God, towards all penitent and believing persons, that they may at all times, when necessity shall require, promptly comfort their flock with the lively Word of God, which is the only stay of man's conscience.[58]

One of the most crucial acts of pastoral care is ministering to the spiritual needs of those who have taken ill or lie at the threshold of death. It is at this time when guilt regarding one's sins viciously assaults the conscience, hastening one's descent into despair. The priest must be prepared to simultaneously arrest such despair and fortify the believer's faith and hope by proclaiming the promises of God's grace contained in the gospel as the only cure for the troubled conscience. This approach to consoling the sick and dying brings an evangelical dimension to extreme unction (which was no longer regarded as a sacrament but as a traditional rite of the church) as well as the overall "art of dying." Evangelical scriptural catechesis became the central component of this vital pastoral work.

Additionally, the injunctions prohibit the continuation of certain late medieval devotional practices, including processionals around churches and through churchyards. Instead, "immediately before high mass the priest, with others of the choir, shall kneel in the midst of the church and sing or say, plainly and distinctly, the Litany, which is set forth in English,[59] with all the suffrages following, and none other procession or litany to be had or used but the said Litany in English, adding nothing

---

57. Bray, *Documents of the English Reformation*, 253.
58. Bray, *Documents of the English Reformation*, 253.
59. That is, Thomas Cranmer's 1544 English Litany.

thereto but as the King's grace shall hereafter appoint."[60] Furthermore, once the service started, parishioners were not allowed to leave.[61]

The injunctions also greatly alter the rhythm of traditional religious practice that defined local community life throughout England. First, they confirm a significant reduction in the number of holy days. While the excess holy days, the injunctions contend, were instituted with the admirable intention "that the people should that day give themselves wholly to God,"[62] over time, these holy days became occasions for laziness and self-indulgence, resulting in decreased productivity.[63] Second, even if people bother to attend Mass, they learn absolutely nothing—which again disregards what the injunctions' authors see as the central pastoral function of catechesis. Parishioners are thus to observe those holy days that have been retained:

> Therefore, all the King's loving and faithful subjects shall from henceforth celebrate and keep their holy date, according to God's word and pleasure, that is, in hearing the Word of God read and taught in private and public prayers, in acknowledging their offences to God, and amendment of the same; in reconciling themselves charitably to their neighbours, where displeasure hath been; in oftentimes receiving the communion of the very body and blood of Christ; in visiting of the poor and sick; in using all soberness and godly conversation.[64]

Additionally, the clergy are told to teach their parishioners that they may, out of necessity, reap the harvest or labor on appointed holy and festival days with clear consciences before God.[65]

Next, the injunctions employ the Eucharist as an instrument of church discipline. Proceeding from the principle that the Eucharist is the sacrament of unity, the injunctions aver that "variance and contention is a thing that displeaseth God and is most contrary to the blessed communion of the body and blood of our Lord Jesus Christ."[66] Dissension and conflict among the faithful shatter the unity of the parish and therefore impugn the very nature and function of the Eucharist itself. For this

60. Bray, *Documents of the English Reformation*, 253–54.
61. Bray, *Documents of the English Reformation*, 254.
62. Bray, *Documents of the English Reformation*, 254.
63. Bray, *Documents of the English Reformation*, 254.
64. Bray, *Documents of the English Reformation*, 254.
65. Bray, *Documents of the English Reformation*, 254.
66. Bray, *Documents of the English Reformation*, 254.

reason, the injunctions command that the clergy under no circumstances admit any in their charge to the Eucharist "who hath maliciously and openly contended with his neighbour, unless the same do first charitably and openly reconcile himself again, remitting all rancour and malice, whatsoever controversy hath been between them."[67] Parishioners in conflict with one another must be lovingly and publicly reconciled before they can partake of the Eucharist, as it is the sacrament that confirms and strengthens the unity of the church. These same instructions are provided in greater detail in both the 1549 and 1552 editions of the *Book of Common Prayer*, in the section immediately preceding the Service of Holy Communion.

Those entrusted with the care of souls are responsible for preaching regularly. Every priest, whether "a dean, archdeacon, master of collegiate church, master of hospital [or] prebendary," is to preach at least twice a year, either at the church directly under his care or at another.[68] This injunction seeks to mitigate what its authors consider one of the most detrimental consequences of absenteeism: the significant lack of preaching, resulting in the spiritual neglect of the people in the parish. Moreover, as has been the case throughout the injunctions, this directive confirms the greater goal of making scriptural preaching the central aspect of evangelical catechesis.

The clergy are to teach their parishioners to faithfully observe all "the laudable ceremonies of the Church which the King commanded to be observed, and as yet not abrogated."[69] Thus, worship and devotional observance are immediately tied to royal supremacy. The king, in whom ultimately resides pastoral authority, shapes and reinforces the spiritual lives of those he rules by determining how this worship and devotion are to take place through the ministrations of the clergy. The king once again shows that spiritual care for the people is committed to him by God.

Immediately following the order to observe all rites ordered by the king is a prohibition of religious practices considered "superstitious," which greatly imperil the soul. Such practices include abusing holy water by casting it onto one's bed, images, or other inanimate objects; keeping consecrated bread on one's person; carrying around the Gospel of John;

---

67. Bray, *Documents of the English Reformation*, 254.
68. Bray, *Documents of the English Reformation*, 254.
69. Bray, *Documents of the English Reformation*, 255.

making wooden crosses for Palm Sunday; ringing bells; and blessing with a holy candle to drive away demons, fantasies, and dreams.[70]

The foregoing prohibitions transition into orders to remove all things related to the veneration of saints. Priests, with the assistance of their wardens, are to eradicate all shrines, tables, candlesticks, pictures, monuments, murals, stained glass windows, and other accessories that depict "feigned miracles, pilgrimages, idolatry, and superstition."[71] Additionally, the clergy are to exhort parishioners to remove the same kinds of objects from their houses.[72] The wardens are then to replace such instruments of superstition with "a comely and honest pulpit to be set in a convenient place . . . for the preaching of God's Word."[73] These measures seem to constitute a graphic, visual aspect of evangelical catechesis, one that is evidenced by the stated pedagogical reason for the injunction: "so that there remain no memory of the same."[74] The elimination of objects relating to the veneration of the saints forces parishioners to unlearn the "superstition" inculcated by the late medieval church. Conversely, the replacement of those objects with a pulpit visually prepares the faithful within the sacred space to learn evangelical truth. The placement of the pulpit in a prominent location also compels congregants to remember that the preached word is central to worship. The sacred space is now transformed into a holy house of evangelical scriptural catechesis.

Dismantling the cult of the saints redirects the use of the parish's finances, which is the subject of the next injunction. Within three months following a visitation by royal commissioners, every parish is to acquire a chest with a hole on top. There are to be three keys to this chest, each of which is to be kept by the priest and two wardens. The chest is to be placed by the altar, "to the intent the parishioners should put into it their oblation and alms for their poor neighbours."[75] The priest is to counsel his parishioners to give to this chest rather than expend those resources on "pardons, pilgrimages, trentals, decking of images, offering of candles, giving to friars, and upon other like blind devotions."[76] Giving to the poor and needy represents "a true worshipping of God, required earnestly

---

70. Bray, *Documents of the English Reformation*, 255.
71. Bray, *Documents of the English Reformation*, 255.
72. Bray, *Documents of the English Reformation*, 255.
73. Bray, *Documents of the English Reformation*, 255.
74. Bray, *Documents of the English Reformation*, 255.
75. Bray, *Documents of the English Reformation*, 255.
76. Bray, *Documents of the English Reformation*, 255.

upon pain of everlasting damnation . . . also, whatsoever is given for their comfort is given to Christ himself and is so accepted of him, that he will mercifully reward the same with everlasting life."[77] The diversion of alms from the veneration of the saints to relieving the poor functions as a practical component of catechesis. The chest is to be located near the altar, which suggests very vividly that giving alms to the poor is a necessary part of worship. Moreover, alluding to Jesus's commendation of the sheep in Matt 25, the injunction presents giving to the poor as the highest act of piety, because it is giving directly to Christ himself. The proceeds are to be distributed among the poorest in the presence of the entire parish. Any remaining funds are to be used to repair nearby roads. Furthermore, money given by various fraternities and guilds as well as income from rents, the sale of cattle, and bequests would be spent on any needed church repairs.[78] Evangelical pastoral care via catechesis sought to cultivate a piety that would manifest itself in aiding the poor, the commonwealth, and the local church as the center of the parish.

The remaining injunctions address matters of clerical conduct, long a concern of church authorities since the late Middle Ages. Priests are to give themselves wholly to the administration of their parishes. The clergy are also to abstain from visiting women who are about to give birth, except when they are sick. Furthermore, priests are not to retrieve corpses but are to wait until they are brought to the churchyard.[79] Following these instructions are the prohibitions and penalties for simony.

In keeping with the injunctions' consistent emphasis on preaching, the next injunction acknowledges the significant shortage of preachers in the realm and therefore requires the clergy to read one of the appointed homilies prepared by Cranmer. This *Book of Homilies*, along with the *Book of Common Prayer*, would serve as the two principal means of evangelical scriptural catechesis, with the former instructing the faithful in living out a justifying faith in a Christian society, and the latter teaching them evangelical truth by the way they worship.[80]

After this comes an injunction that acknowledges the regular harassment of more traditional priests by parishioners who, because of their "small learning," "have for a long time favored fantasies rather than

---

77. Bray, *Documents of the English Reformation*, 255–56.
78. Bray, *Documents of the English Reformation*, 256.
79. Bray, *Documents of the English Reformation*, 256.
80. See Hicks, *Worship by Faith Alone*.

God's truth."[81] To mitigate this brazen disrespect toward the clerical office, the injunction expresses the king's charge for his subjects to reverence the priesthood with all charity because it is "appointed of God" to teach God's word.[82]

Finally, the last injunctions prescribe a program of catechesis for the youth. Those who teach the youth are to use the English primer authorized by Henry VIII.[83] The Latin primer and grammar he authorized are to be used for those learning Latin.[84] Since private Masses were abolished, chantry priests would now devote their time to teaching the youth with these resources.

The Edwardian injunctions represent the consolidation of the official reformation initiated by Henry VIII and the evangelical one that ran parallel to it. As with their Henrician predecessors, these injunctions located pastoral authority in royal supremacy. The monarch—or Protectors Somerset and Northumberland, in the case of Edward—delegated this authority through the bishops to the rest of the clergy. Driving the evangelical reformation of the national church on behalf of the young king, Archbishop Cranmer significantly enhanced the catechesis that remained the essence of pastoral care. Central to this enhancement was Cranmer's evangelical reform of worship through the *Book of Common Prayer* and the *Book of Homilies*, which together would train the faithful in a biblical piety. At the same time, Cranmer and his colleagues utilized the framework of traditional catechesis for evangelical ends. However, the implementation of this ambitious program of reform, which entailed the transformation of pastoral ministry, came to an abrupt halt with the unexpected passing of the zealous evangelical "Josiah."

REVERSAL AND RENEWAL: THE PASTORAL THEOLOGY OF THE MARIAN AND ELIZABETHAN INJUNCTIONS

After the death of Edward VI in 1553, his half-sister, Mary (r. 1553–58), eventually came to the throne, determined to return England to papal

---

81. Bray, *Documents of the English Reformation*, 256.
82. Bray, *Documents of the English Reformation*, 256.
83. *King Henry's Primer*, 1545. See Burton, *Three Primers*, 436–612.
84. Bray, *Documents of the English Reformation*, 257.

obedience.⁸⁵ Toward this end, Mary's first Parliament repealed the ecclesiastical legislation enacted during the reigns of Henry VIII and Edward VI in 1554. Later that year, on November 29, Parliament formally reconciled the Church of England to Rome. Though Mary repudiated royal supremacy, she did, however, exercise royal ecclesiastical authority long enough to issue injunctions that reversed those promulgated by her two predecessors.

The injunctions issued by Mary ordered bishops—led by her cousin, the new archbishop of Canterbury, Reginald Pole (1500–1558)—to restore the ceremonies of the old church. The bishops were also to remove all married clergymen from their parishes while showing leniency toward priests who were widowed at the time the injunctions took effect.⁸⁶ Furthermore, married clergymen could remain in their benefices as long as they would undergo penance and vow to abstain from relations with their wives.⁸⁷ Bishops were directed to secure qualified curates for vacant parishes. Finally, in keeping with their Edwardian predecessors, these injunctions required prelates to provide a book of homilies as a source of regular preaching for the faithful. This book of homilies was most likely prepared by Marian Bishop of London Edmund Bonner (1500–1569). These injunctions reflect the larger aim of the Marian regime to restore traditional religion in the various parishes throughout the realm, as well as several of the practical reforms advocated by Pole and some higher churchmen at the Council of Trent.⁸⁸ However, Mary's legislative reunion with Rome and its translation into pastoral ministry would be short-lived following the deaths of both Mary and Pole on November 17, 1558, and the accession of Henry's second daughter, Elizabeth I.

Following Elizabeth's coronation in January 1559—and after considerable political maneuvering, intrigues, and compromise—a modified but evangelical reformation of the national church resumed with Parliament's passage of two acts. The first was the Act of Supremacy of 1559, which restored royal ecclesiastical authority. However, it now declared the monarch "Supreme Governor" of the Church of England.⁸⁹ The sec-

---

85. For the events that occurred between the death of Edward VI and Mary Tudor's accession, see Dickens, *English Reformation*, 283–86.

86. Bray, *Documents of the English Reformation*, 316.

87. Bray, *Documents of the English Reformation*, 316.

88. For Pole's career, see Mayer, *Reginald Pole*; and Edwards, *Archbishop Pole*. For the reform agenda of the Council of Trent, see O'Malley, *Trent*.

89. The change of title represented a compromise within Parliament due to the

ond was the Act of Uniformity, which reinstated a revised version of the 1552 *Book of Common Prayer*. With royal supremacy officially restored, Elizabeth's government—aided by an evangelical episcopal bench consisting of figures like Matthew Parker (1504–75) of Canterbury, Edmund Grindal (1519–83) of London, Edwin Sandys (1519–88) of Worcester, John Jewel (1522–71) of Salisbury, and Richard Cox (1500–1581) of Ely—now endeavored to translate this church settlement into pastoral ministry through a new set of injunctions.

The injunctions issued under Elizabeth mostly mirror those of Edward but entail new provisions for establishing a definitively evangelical ministry in the parishes. Because these injunctions served the purpose of implementing the reforms prescribed chiefly in the Acts of Supremacy and Uniformity as settled law for the national church, "they came to be regarded as a bulwark of conservative orthodoxy" against the rising Puritan movement later in Elizabeth's reign.[90] Even though the Act of Supremacy identifies the queen as "Supreme Governor," instead of "Supreme Head," of the English Church, it did not in any way diminish the ecclesiastical authority possessed and exercised by either Henry or Edward. The Act still portrays the monarch, even the queen, as the ultimate constitutional source of pastoral authority in the preface to the injunctions:

> The Queen's most royal Majesty, by the advice of her most honourable council, intending the advancement of the true honour of Almighty God, the suppression of superstition throughout all her Highness' realms and dominions, and to plant the true religion to the extirpation of all hypocrisy, enormities and abuses as to her duty appertaineth, doth minister unto her loving subjects these godly injunctions hereafter following. All which injunctions, her Highness willeth and commandeth her said loving subjects obediently to receive and truly to observe and keep, every man in their offices, degrees, and states, as they will avoid her Highness' displeasure and the pains of the same hereafter expressed.[91]

---

controversial notion of a woman functioning as "Supreme Head." See Jones, *Faith by Statute*, 89–144.

90. Bray, *Documents of the English Reformation*, 335. It should be noted that in the following century, Charles I (r. 1625–49) sought to use them as authoritative grounds for conformity in the Church of England. Furthermore, the binding authority of the Elizabethan injunctions was the subject of intense debate among conformists themselves. For this discussion, see Milton, *England's Second Reformation*, 41–51.

91. Bray, *Documents of the English Reformation*, 335.

As "Supreme Governor," the monarch's chief duty before God is to establish true religion (i.e., evangelical religion) throughout the realm and, in so doing, to remove all hindrances to it. The spiritual impediments that must be removed to foster "true religion" are those associated with Rome, which the previous regime sought to restore. Such "superstition" breeds hypocrisy. It is with the intent of fostering the spiritual welfare of her subjects that the queen ministers to them by issuing these injunctions, which the clergy in turn would implement at the direction of various royal commissions and bishops. Thus, like Edward and Henry, Elizabeth, as "Supreme Governor," maintains true religion in the realm by assigning pastoral care to the clergy through the bishops. Royal supremacy still makes the monarch the chief pastor of the realm.

The injunctions prescribe a regular program of preaching by requiring the clergy to read a sermon from the *Second Book of Homilies*, which would be produced and edited by Elizabeth's bishops every quarter.[92] These injunctions retain the Edwardian directive to utilize traditional catechesis as a vehicle for evangelical doctrine, along with lay access to the English Bible and Erasmus's *Paraphrases of the Four Gospels*.[93] Yet the injunctions incorporate many new directives concerning pastoral ministry and parish life.

The Elizabethan injunctions remove the penitential strictures against clerical marriage promulgated by their Marian predecessors.[94] They also prescribe specific dress for those serving in parishes and universities.[95] They prohibit parishioners from advocating heresy and using "charms, sorcery, enchantments, witchcrafts, soothsaying, or any like devilish device."[96] Implied here is the allegedly close relationship between witchcraft and heresy. Both corrupt and destroy the spiritual life of the parish and the nation, and so faithful pastoral care through catechesis will continuously weaken such deleterious forces.

Logically following these prohibitions are orders for parishioners to attend church regularly for common prayer and preaching; these orders strongly reinforce the evangelical conviction that worship consisting of common prayer and Scriptural preaching is altogether catechesis. The centrality of common prayer for catechesis serves as the basis for

---

92. Bray, *Documents of the English Reformation*, 336.
93. Bray, *Documents of the English Reformation*, 336.
94. Bray, *Documents of the English Reformation*, 342.
95. Bray, *Documents of the English Reformation*, 343.
96. Bray, *Documents of the English Reformation*, 343.

prohibitions of parishioners provoking disputes with their rectors and disrupting services. Mitigating such tendencies requires consistent, regular teaching, which arguably accounts for the significant emphasis on teaching that is evident in the requirement for the clergy to teach the youth in the Creed, the Ten Commandments, and the Lord's Prayer every Sunday before Evening Prayer and holy days.[97] Because the spiritual well-being of the faithful vitally depends on sound catechesis in all its aspects, only those approved and licensed by the bishop could teach.[98]

Just as the clergy are responsible for teaching and preaching, so the laity are equally obligated to learn from said preaching and teaching: "No man, woman, nor child shall be otherwise in the time of service than in quiet attendance, to hear, mark, and understand that [which] is read, preached, or ministered."[99] To ensure that parishioners will attend church so that they may receive the instruction necessary for their spiritual well-being, the injunctions require the bishops to appoint in every parish "three or four discreet men which tender God's glory and his true religion" and who will diligently see "that all parishioners duly resort to their church upon all Sundays and holy days, and there to continue the whole time of the godly service."[100] These individuals charged by the priest to fulfill this task are to admonish parishioners who have been "found to be slack or negligent in resorting to the church" and who have "no great nor urgent cause of absence."[101] If the errant parishioners fail to amend their ways after these warnings, those who initially reproved them are to report them to the bishop.[102]

Finally, the injunctions clearly state the goal of pastoral ministry through this overall program of evangelical catechesis. Those teaching the youth as mentioned above are to "stir and move them to the love and due reverence of God's true religion, now truly set forth by public authority."[103] Instruction in the truth shapes the affections of the learners to the point where they love the "true religion" as defined by the queen and Parliament in conjunction with the church, and through the same love the object of this religion, God himself. By "stirring" this love for God

97. Bray, *Documents of the English Reformation*, 344.
98. Bray, *Documents of the English Reformation*, 343–44.
99. Bray, *Documents of the English Reformation*, 343.
100. Bray, *Documents of the English Reformation*, 344.
101. Bray, *Documents of the English Reformation*, 344.
102. Bray, *Documents of the English Reformation*, 344.
103. Bray, *Documents of the English Reformation*, 344.

through true, evangelical religion, the clergy will "enduce" those whom they instruct "to all godliness."[104] Such godliness produces not only better Christians but, very importantly, a stronger Christian society whose definitive virtue is charity, which is the bond of the commonwealth.

Thus, the chief aim of pastoral ministry through evangelical catechesis is to produce true Christians who, out of a genuine love for God and his truth, will form a genuinely Christian society by strengthening the bond of love. The injunctions authorized by Elizabeth state this aim clearly in relation to the queen's own spiritual authority to maintain and promote such a society by strengthening its bond of love. The injunctions highlight this aspect of royal authority when addressing the divisions within Christian society concerning the rites prescribed by Parliament via the *Book of Common Prayer*:

> Because in all alterations and specially rites and ceremonies, there happeneth discord among the people, and thereupon slanderous words and railings whereby charity, the knot of all Christian society, is loosed. The Queen's Majesty being most desirous of all other earthly things, that her people should live in charity both towards God and man, and therein abound in good works, willeth and straightly commandeth all manner of her subjects to forbear all vain and contentious disputations in matters of religion, and not use in despite or rebuke of any person, these convicious words: "Papist," or "Papistical heretic," "schismatic" or "sacramentary," or any such like words of reproach. But if any manner of person shall deserve the accusation of such, that first he be charitably admonished thereof. And if that shall not amend him, then to denounce the offenders to the ordinary or some higher power having authority to correct the same.[105]

Strident division within England over the liturgical reforms enacted by Parliament evinced the dissolution of love as the unitive virtue of society. The queen's stated desire, and thus pastoral aim, is for her Christian subjects to live according to the law of love as declared in the two greatest commandments. Living in love toward God and neighbor manifests itself in good works. Yet this does not happen when, in a Christian society, people slander one another on account of liturgical and eucharistic differences (not to mention the fact that such division within the realm could prove politically dangerous to the queen, as would be confirmed

---

104. Bray, *Documents of the English Reformation*, 344.
105. Bray, *Documents of the English Reformation*, 345.

in the later part of her reign). While the injunction commands abstention from such conflicts, it also makes provision for those instances in which an accusation of aberrant belief might be true by applying Jesus's directions recorded in Matt 18. If the accused is guilty of one of the alleged "heresies" listed above, the accuser is to confront and admonish him or her privately. Should such admonition fail to effect change in the guilty party, the accuser must inform either the bishop or a magistrate authorized to act.

Tellingly, the injunction seems to link societal dissension resulting from the dissolution of the bond of charity to the sin of contumacy. Since contumacy, stemming from pride, disrupts the public Christian order, it becomes subject to magisterial as well as episcopal correction, which means that the civil magistrate is an equal partner with the bishop in the spiritual care of the Christian society. Indeed, the correction of sin for the sake of preserving Christian society according to the law of love is now a joint civil-ecclesiastical function empowered by royal authority, meaning that the queen serves as both prince and shepherd under the Great Shepherd.

CONCLUSION

The withdrawal of the English Church from papal obedience under Henry VIII drastically altered its traditional devotional life. This disruption largely resulted from the Act of Supremacy of 1534, in which Parliament declared the monarch to be "Supreme Head of the Church of England." As we have argued above, the doctrine of royal supremacy effectively transferred ultimate pastoral authority from the pope to the monarch, which meant that even though the monarch himself did not exercise the clerical functions of preaching, administering the sacraments, etc., he delegated pastoral authority to those who would. The royal ecclesiastical injunctions depict this radical change in ecclesiology as well as Henry's attempt through Thomas Cromwell and various royal commissions to translate it into parish life and pastoral ministry. Yet pastoral care as catechesis continued, as the injunctions required the clergy to teach parishioners the faith through an exposition of the Apostles' Creed, the Decalogue, and the Lord's Prayer—even within the context of confession, in keeping with previous late medieval practice. The only difference now was that the clergy were engaging in pastoral care as catechesis on behalf of the monarch, to whom was committed the spiritual as well as temporal charge of his subjects. Another way in which the practice of pastoral care as catechesis differed from that of the late medieval church was that it undermined those practices associated with the cult of the saints.

The injunctions issued under Edward VI represent the transformation of the official reformation initiated by Henry into one that was decidedly evangelical, as directed by Archbishop Cranmer. Though they do not state the doctrine of royal supremacy as explicitly as their Henrician predecessors, these injunctions still generally regard pastoral authority as being derived from the monarch and delegated to the clergy. Pastoral care is still portrayed as catechesis. The Edwardian injunctions maintain the structure of traditional catechesis, consisting of instruction in the Creed, the Decalogue, and the Lord's Prayer, but this instruction is explicitly evangelical, highlighting themes such as justification by grace through faith alone. Moreover, a central feature of this evangelical catechesis was the expanded educational program promulgated by Archbishop Cranmer, consisting of the *Book of Common Prayer* and the *Book of Homilies*. These two books served the larger purpose of evangelical catechesis by inculcating into the faithful a biblical piety through the way they worship as well as a regular rotation of preaching that sought to practically apply evangelical doctrine to the lives of the faithful.

Following Mary's attempts through her injunctions to reverse the implementation of evangelical reforms, especially within the ministry, the government of her successor, Elizabeth I, resumed but moderated the evangelical reformation of Edward. The injunctions issued under Elizabeth were mostly identical to those of Edward but added features that stressed biblical instruction as an essential component of pastoral care as catechesis. Furthermore, even though the 1559 Act of Supremacy declared the monarch "Supreme Governor" of the Church of England, it affirmed the queen's possession and exercise of ecclesiastical authority. The Elizabethan injunctions not only confirm royal supremacy as the institutional source of pastoral authority but also expand on it at certain salient points, most significant of which is their portrayal of the queen's pastoral aim for her subjects in a Christian society—namely, that they would function according to the law of love as expressed by the two great commandments, with both the clergy and the magistracy acting on her behalf toward this end. Thus, the Reformation in England simultaneously retained the practice of pastoral ministry as catechesis while sourcing it in the sacred authority of Christ's Royal Vicar.

BIBLIOGRAPHY

Bernard, G. W. *The King's Reformation: Henry VIII and the Remaking of the English Church*. New Haven: Yale University Press, 2005.

Bray, Gerald, ed. *Documents of the English Reformation*. Minneapolis: Fortress, 1994.

Burton, Edward, ed. *Three Primers Put Forth in the Reign of Henry VIII: A Goodly Primer, 1535; The Manual of Prayers, or the Primer in English, 1539; King Henry's Primer, 1545*. Oxford: Oxford University Press, 1834.

Dickens, A. G. *The English Reformation*. 3rd ed. University Park: Pennsylvania State University Press, 1989.

Duffy, Eamon. *The Stripping of the Altars: Traditional Religion in England, 1400–1580*. New ed. New Haven: Yale University Press, 2022.

Edwards, John. *Archbishop Pole*. Archbishops of Canterbury Series. New York: Routledge, 2016.

Hicks, Zac. *Worship by Faith Alone: Thomas Cranmer, The Book of Common Prayer, and the Reformation of Liturgy*. Downers Grove, IL: IVP Academic, 2023.

Jones, Norman L. *Faith by Statute: Parliament and the Settlement of Religion, 1559*. London: Royal Historical Society, 1982.

MacCulloch, Diarmaid. *The Boy King: Edward VI and the Protestant Reformation*. New York: Palgrave, 2001.

———. *Thomas Cranmer*. Rev. ed. New Haven: Yale University Press, 2017.

Mayer, Thomas F. *Reginald Pole: Prince and Prophet*. Cambridge: Cambridge University Press, 2000.

Milton, Anthony. *England's Second Reformation: The Battle for the Church of England, 1625–1662*. Cambridge Studies in Early Modern British History. Cambridge: Cambridge University Press, 2021.

Mirk, John. *Instructions for Parish Priests*. Edited by Edward Peacock. London: Trubner, 1868.

O'Malley, John W. *Trent: What Happened at the Council*. Cambridge, MA: Belknap, 2013.

5

Bénédict Pictet (1655–1724)
A Case Study in Pastoral Care[1]

JONATHON BEEKE

Upon hearing of Bénédict Pictet's death in 1724, the well-known French pastor Antoine Court (1696–1760)—dubbed by some as the "Restorer of Protestantism in France"—wrote this: "I was told you speak to me of the most sad and the most overwhelming thing that could ever happen to me—of the death of the famous Pictet, of this great man, of this incomparable man, of this man so tender and good that he had for me so much kindness that he treated me as if I were one of his children. Ha, what a blow my dear friends. It is so distressing for me that I have neither the strength nor the words to speak about it."[2] Court's estimation of Pictet was based on his two-year stay in Geneva, in which he had extensive interaction with the Genevan professor and theologian. Otto Selles even suggests that Pictet, who cared well for the younger French pastor, became to Court "the spiritual and even natural father he had never known."[3]

---

1. This chapter is an expanded version of a paper presented under the same title at the Evangelical Theological Society annual meeting, November 20, 2024.

2. As quoted by Selles, "Case of Hidden Identity," 93. See also Duley-Haour, "Correspondance d'Antoine Court, une Correspondance Pastorale?" Duley-Haour argues that Court's massive "pastoral correspondence" was more diplomatic in nature than pastoral; when it did contain pastoral instructions, these largely stemmed from Pictet.

3. Selles, "Case of Hidden Identity," 99.

What are we today to make of "this great man," "this incomparable man," "this man so tender and good"? Reflecting on the scholarship and symposiums of 2024, it appears that the tricentennial year of Pictet's death came and went without much mention of the Genevan professor; if he was indeed such a "great man," an "incomparable man," should there not have been a greater tricentennial recognition of his life and ministry?[4] While Court's depiction of his mentor certainly borders on hagiography, arguably a fresh examination of Pictet's life, ministry, and writings is warranted. Largely an overlooked figure of Reformed orthodoxy, Pictet is most often remembered as the one who delivered the funeral oration for his uncle and theological instructor, Francis Turretin (1623–87). And yet, considered in his own right, Pictet was an influential and important theologian and pastor within the early-modern context. Not only did Pictet take over the professorship of theology at the Genevan Academy from his uncle, and then hold this position for nearly forty years, but he was also a prolific writer, most notably composing his *Theologia Christiana* (1696)—expanded to three volumes in its French edition of 1721—and what came to be an eight-volume work on Christian morality (*La morale chrétienne ou l'art de bien vivre* [1693; 1696; 1700; 1709]).[5]

Contrary to those who believe the Reformed orthodox were cold, sterile, and dispassionate in their theology,[6] this essay argues that Pictet's writings evidence a sensitive and caring pastoral theology that was attuned to the needs of his local congregation. It is impossible in the space here to conclusively demonstrate this argument throughout Pictet's writings; therefore, the argument remains selective and invites further

---

4. Apart from one self-published translation of Pictet's *The Marrow of Christian Ethics*, the year 2024 did not evidence any other interest in Pictet studies; see Pictet, *Marrow of Christian Ethics*. In comparison, during 2005, a year that marked the four hundredth anniversary of Theodore Beza's death, at least two symposiums were dedicated to Beza. This comparison does not suggest that the two were of equal importance to the Reformation cause; rather, the simple point made here is that one is remembered but the other often overlooked.

5. While the aim here is not to provide a biography of Pictet's life, it is significant to note that his professorship at the Genevan Academy overlapped with Turretin's for one year. For more on Pictet, see especially the only full-length biography devoted to him: De Budé, *Vie de Bénédict Pictet*. More concise treatments can be found in these sources: Klauber, "Family Loyalty and Theological Transition"; Klauber, "Reformed Orthodoxy in Transition"; Van Asselt, "Scholasticism in the Time of Late Orthodoxy," 184–89; Rouwendal, "Late Orthodoxy—Benedict Pictet," 249–54; Wolfe, "Bénédict Pictet"; DeYoung, *Religious Formation of John Witherspoon*, 36–38.

6. For an overview of this debate and its literature, see Muller, "Calvin and the 'Calvinists'"; Van Asselt and Rouwendal, "State of Scholarship."

corroborative study. Acknowledging that selectivity is necessary, this essay focuses on three neglected French works from Pictet: his unique *Fivefold Catechism* (*Cinq catéchismes* [1707; 1715]), *Pious Conversations of a Believer and His Pastor* (*Entretiens pieux d'un fidèle avec son Pasteur* [1710]), and a collection of prayers entitled *Prayers for Each Day of the Week and Various Occasions* (*Prières pour tous les jours de la semaine, et sur divers sujets* [1712; 1746; 1822; 1827]). In addition to teaching theology, preaching, and the administration of the sacraments, the selection of these three pieces will show that Pictet used a variety of other methods (i.e., catechetical instruction for young and old, an imagined counseling dialogue between an inquiring congregant and his pastor, and models of prayer for various occasions) to disciple and care for his flock, thus demonstrating a pastoral heart that cared for and addressed his parishioners' spiritual needs and concerns. Before examining each of these three works in turn, however, it is necessary first to situate Pictet's ministry contextually.

HISTORICAL CONTEXT OF PICTET'S MINISTRY

As indicated above, Pictet followed in the footsteps of his uncle, teacher, and mentor, Francis Turretin, by becoming a student at the Genevan Academy and then, later, a professor of theology. One month after turning twenty-three, Pictet was received into the Genevan Company of Pastors with the following commendation: "Who having made known the profit he made in his studies and the fine gifts that divine providence had departed on him for the future edification of the church, [Pictet] will be consecrated on June 29, 1678."[7] For nearly fifty years following his consecration, alongside his professorial duties of teaching and writing, Pictet labored in this capacity as pastor. According to Jean Gaberel, the nineteenth-century historian of Geneva, Pictet was able to simultaneously wear these two hats (pastor and theologian) exceptionally well, largely because he devoted himself to his work, committing his morning hours to his theological work and his afternoon hours to pastoral care and visitation.[8]

---

7. Gaberel, *Histoire de L'Église de Genève*, 3:102. "Lequel ayant fait paraître le profit qu'il a fait dans ses études et les beaux dons que la Providence divine lui a départis pour l'édification future de l'Église, il sera consacré le 29 juin 1678." Cf. De Budé, *Vie de Bénédict Pictet*, 12. All French translations are my own.

8. Gaberel, *Histoire de L'Église de Genève*, 3:102.

Pastoral concerns and duties were especially challenging in late seventeenth-century Geneva. With the revocation of the Edict of Nantes in 1685 (after which French Protestants lost many of their religious liberties), Geneva witnessed a large influx of refugees. While estimates of the exact number vary, waves of Protestants fled France; although anyone who was caught trying to leave was severely punished, Myriam Yardeni has estimated the number of emigrants to be between two hundred thousand and three hundred thousand.[9] A natural stopping point for many of those who fled was Geneva. According to Gaberel, some three thousand of these refugees were offered asylum in Geneva near the end of the seventeenth century.[10] The three churches of Geneva (Saint Pierre Cathedral, Temple Saint-Gervais, and Temple de la Madeleine) could not adequately handle the increasing population. As Matthew Miller notes, even finding a seat in one of the three churches on a Sunday morning became increasingly difficult, prompting the building of a new church—the Temple Neuf—which began construction in 1713.[11] Given his prominence in Geneva at that time, Pictet preached the inaugural sermon in this fourth church on December 15, 1715.[12]

As the many French refugees were displaced from their homes, without employment, and frequently separated from family, the amount and level of required pastoral care in late seventeenth-century Geneva were significantly elevated. Didier Boisson remarks quite pointedly, "Families were torn apart. A couple might leave without their children, a wife without her husband, and children without their parents."[13] Alongside his other pastoral duties, Pictet was committed to providing spiritual and physical care to all who came to Geneva. According to Eugène de Budé, the nineteenth-century biographer of the Genevan pastor, Pictet tirelessly gave himself to this work: "Pictet is there, always on duty, this

---

9. As cited by Olsen, "Edict of Nantes and Its Revocation," 23. Cf. Yardeni, *Réfuge protestant*, 17. Didier Boisson puts the number of Protestants who fled from 1680–1750 at 150,000–180,000. See his chapter "Revocation of the Edict of Nantes and the *Désert*," 232. Boisson notes that the most significant wave occurred between 1685 and 1688.

10. Gaberel, *Histoire de L'Église de Genève*, 3:89.

11. Miller, "Geneva's First New Church," 225–26. As Miller notes, the Temple Neuf was designed for "Calvinistic worship" and was patterned after the Parisian Temple de Charenton (which was destroyed due to the revocation of the Edict of Nantes in 1685). As such, the Temple Neuf would have been especially favored by Huguenot refugees, who saw in this church a reflection of their former place of worship.

12. Pictet, *Sermon fait le Jour de la Dedicace du Nouveau Temple, le XV*; cf. De Budé, *Vie de Bénédict Pictet*, 112–14; Miller, "Geneva's First New Church," 228–32.

13. Boisson, "Revocation of the Edict of Nantes and the *Désert*," 233.

worthy supporter of the unfortunate, lifting them up, comforting without ever tiring, whether they were distinguished people, ladies of high birth, or those innumerable bands of poor unknown who rushed to our land after having resisted the French guards at the risk of their lives."[14]

In addition to the influx of refugees increasing the demand for pastoral care in Geneva, the variety and extent of duties required of a Genevan pastor were also challenging. Scott Manetsch's significant work *Calvin's Company of Pastors* has been especially helpful in more deeply understanding the role of the Genevan pastor. Manetsch has noted that one of the most succinct descriptions of the Genevan pastoral office comes from Theodore Beza's *Confession of the Christian Faith*. Written more than a century before Pictet's ordination, Beza's apology outlines the many responsibilities of a pastor. These duties are summarized by Manetsch as follows: "[The pastors] preach, they pray, they administer the Lord's Supper, they baptize children, they officiate at weddings, they perform household visitations, they provide spiritual counsel, and they exercise church discipline."[15] In other words, pastoral care was intense, multiform, and enduring; at no point could a pastor claim he had come to the end of his labors.[16]

Many of the pastoral duties established by Calvin and Beza—and formalized in the *Ecclesiastical Ordinances* of 1561—carried over into the seventeenth century. Thus, before Easter each year, it was expected that every pastor would visit all households in his parish and meet with the parents, children, and servants at length.[17] This was a significant undertaking, for, as Gaberel notes, each parish in Geneva contained no fewer than two thousand souls.[18] Linked to this schedule of pastoral visitation, the pastor was to monitor the schooling of small children and examine catechumens at least four times per year to determine if they could

---

14. "Pictet est là, toujours au devoir, ce digne soutien des malheureux, relevant, consolant sans se lasser jamais, que ce fussent des personnes de distinction, des dames de haute naissance, ou ces bandes innombrables de pauvres inconnus qui se ruaient sur notre sol après avoir, au péril de leurs jours, résisté aux gardes françaises." De Budé, *Vie de Bénédict Pictet*, 130.

15. Manetsch, *Calvin's Company of Pastors*, 74. Cf. Beza, *Confession de la Foy Chrestienne*, 194–96.

16. Manetsch records the story of a young pastor in the late summer of 1576 who wanted to abscond his duties; this ultimately led to the pastor's resignation, as the Company of Pastors disallowed his desired four-month leave of absence. See Manetsch, *Calvin's Company of Pastors*, 68–69.

17. Cf. Manetsch, *Calvin's Company of Pastors*, 281–82.

18. Gaberel, *Histoire de L'Église de Genève*, 3:94.

partake of the Lord's Supper. Furthermore, the Genevan pastor was to meet with those who desired to marry and then to perform the marriage ceremony when asked. Pastors were responsible for the poor in the parish and thus required to attend the weekly charity fund meetings. The pastor was constantly called on to visit the sick, a heavy task especially in the winter. The pastors were to take turns visiting those in the city prison;[19] they were to give monthly reports to the Geneva consistory regarding the moral status of their parishioners; they were to reduce as much as possible the number of moral offenses handled by the consistory; they were to mediate any household quarrels or conflict; and, high on the list for the Genevan pastorate, they were to preach approximately seventy-five sermons per year[20] and deliver an additional seventy-five addresses or expositions from the pulpit (for an average of 150 speaking engagements per year).[21]

Much of what was expected of pastors in Calvin's Geneva carried over into the seventeenth and eighteenth centuries.[22] In his *Marrow of Christian Ethics*, Pictet included a chapter in which he addressed the duties of a pastor to his flock, the duties of the flock to their pastor, and then the duties of elders and deacons. Pictet listed fifteen obligations for the pastor, but for the other three groups he only listed nine. While Pictet's list of pastoral duties includes items such as teaching accurate doctrine, providing comfort and consolation, constant prayer, refutation of error, and diligent attention to the morals of the flock, it focuses more on the *manner* and *motive* in which the pastor fulfills his vocation. Thus, according to Pictet, the pastor must not claim for himself lordship in the church;

---

19. Manetsch, *Calvin's Company of Pastors*, 283.

20. Gaberel comments how Pictet, often criticized for being cold in his preaching style, was completely other than this. According to Gaberel, Pictet's preaching possessed a perfect clarity; it was a simple and natural style, and he could draw his audience in by presenting "grand ideas in forms so true that everyone finds in the words of the preacher the image of his own thoughts." Gaberel, *Histoire de L'Église de Genève*, 3:90–91.

21. Manetsch notes that by the time of the 1561 *Ordinances*, "a [weekly] total of thirty-three services had been established in the city's three parish churches: eleven worship services on Sunday, and twenty-two preaching services during the rest of the week (including four 'sunrise' services at 4 a.m. or 5 a.m.)." See *Calvin's Company of Pastors*, 149.

22. Apparently, the annual estimate of 150 sermons or speaking engagements per pastor remained consistent until the Revocation, as Jacob Vernet complained how taxing it was that fourteen pastors had to cover 1,800 pulpit appearances per year. See Gaberel, *Histoire de L'Église de Genève*, 3:94–96 (from where much of the preceding paragraph's list of pastoral duties is also drawn).

he must in his labor *only* have the glory of God in mind; he must not be a respecter of persons, favoring the rich and severely treating the poor; he ought to care for and love everyone; he must be socially aware and considerate of "circumstances, place, time, and persons"; he must practice what he preaches, being a stranger to the vices he preaches against; and he must be absolutely loyal to his flock, not abandoning them in times of persecution unless it is deemed necessary for their good.[23] Pictet echoed this in his *Christian Theology*, stressing that pastors are an instrument of God to be used for the care of souls and that the aim of their ministry is the sanctification and eternal salvation of the people entrusted to their care.[24] In short, the pastor must be one who, having himself been transformed by the gospel, is motivated to love and serve his flock with excellence, all for the glory of God alone. This involves sacrifice, determination, and long hours of hard work.[25]

PICTET'S *FIVEFOLD CATECHISM*

Having to some degree considered the pastoral office within the late seventeenth-century Genevan context, and with an understanding of Pictet's

---

23. See Pictet, *Marrow of Christian Ethics*, 317–19.

24. Pictet writes, "I do not want to focus on showing the usefulness and excellence of the ministry; we cannot doubt it when we consider: 1) that God is the author of this ministry; 2) that ministers are the organs that God uses for the assembly of the saints; 3) that the care of souls is committed to them; 4) that they deal with the most sublime mysteries of religion; 5) that Jesus Christ, the prophets, and the apostles exercised the ministry; and 6) that the aim of the ministry is to bring men to sanctification and eternal salvation." Pictet, *Théologie Chretiene*, 2:448 (book XIV, ch. XX). The original French reads as follows: "Je ne veux pas m'attacher à faire voir *l'utilité & l'excellence du Ministére*; On n'en sauroit douter quand on confidérera, 1. Que Dieu est l'Autheur de ce Ministére. 2. Que les Ministres sont les organs, dont Dieu se sert, pour l'affemblage des Saints. 3. Que le soin des ames leur est commis. 4. Qu'ils traittent des Mystéres les plus sublimes de la Religion. 5. Que J. Christ, les Prophétes, & les Apôtres ont éxercé le Ministére. 6. Que le but du Ministére eft d'amener les hommes à la sanctification, & au salut éternel."

25. The story is told of how a certain professor from Basel tried to visit Pictet to inquire about his son, who was apparently studying at the Genevan Academy. Arriving at nine o'clock in the morning, the man was told that Pictet was not available (as he was out visiting the sick), but that the man could come back the next morning between four and five o'clock. After arriving early the next day, he found Pictet at work. When the man asked about his son, Pictet replied that he was a "mediocre student" since he would not work more than thirteen hours a day; as Pictet instructed the student's father, the scholar's lamp should be lit earlier than the lamp of the craftsman. See the story as recounted by Gaberel, *Histoire de L'Église de Genève*, 3:103.

expectation for not only *what* the pastor must do but also *how* and *why*, it is necessary next to examine the Genevan pastor's writings to determine if his ideal of pastoral care is evident. As already noted, the focus here is on three of his works (each representing a different genre); these will be considered chronologically.

It appears that Pictet first wrote his *Fivefold Catechism* in 1707 and then revised and expanded it in a later 1715 edition.[26] Just under 140 pages of text in its final form, the *Fivefold Catechism* is a shorter work presented in question-and-answer format that, as its name implies, is divided into five distinct catechisms: (1) a catechism on the main events, figures, and historical data of the Bible; (2) a catechism on what Pictet considered to be the primary biblical doctrines; (3) a moral catechism explaining the Ten Commandments and the Lord's Prayer; (4) a polemical catechism refuting the doctrine and practices of the Roman Catholic Church; and (5) a brief catechism titled *Pour les petits enfans* (that is, one designed for small children who have not yet had any religious education).[27] Pictet's goal, as the preface makes clear, was to instruct the youth of Geneva in the fundamentals of the Reformed religion through catechesis.

As De Budé notes, catechetical instruction was an "important branch" of Pictet's pastoral work.[28] Evidently, Pictet believed that grounding the Genevan children in religious truths was crucial to pastoral care. It is worth noting the methodological approach that Pictet chose to accomplish this, something that is especially reflected in the ordering of his fivefold catechism. The first and largest catechism (nearly 45 percent of the entire work) is devoted to providing a scriptural foundation; this catechism works through hundreds of questions that test Bible knowledge

---

26. I'm grateful to Matthew Miller for alerting me to and providing access to this earlier 1707 edition: Pictet, *Cinq Catechimes* [sic] (1707); Pictet, *Cinq Catechismes* (1715). Unless indicated otherwise, references will be to the 1715 edition. In the preface to this later edition, Pictet acknowledges that "several years ago" he gave to the public this fivefold catechism but that he purposed to update and expand this work with the 1715 publication; he notes it is here "greatly increased for those who are more advanced in age" ("Avis au Lecteur," 3). While Pictet suggests that this edition is "greatly increased," the changes are relatively minor (for example, whereas the 1707 edition only lists what God created on the first and sixth days of the creation week, the 1715 edition spells out what God created on each of the six days). In total, the 1715 edition is approximately twenty pages longer than the 1707 edition.

27. This is the (incorrect) order as listed on the title page of the 1715 edition, whereas the catechism itself follows a slightly different order, placing the doctrinal catechism fourth in the order (rather than second). A 1729 version corrects the order of the table of contents to match the content of the catechism. Cf. Pictet, *Cinq Catechismes* (1729).

28. De Budé, *Vie de Bénédict Pictet*, 147.

(the equivalent of a giant modern-day Bible trivia quiz). The questions are divided into forty chapters, and they evaluate knowledge of both Old and New Testaments, beginning with creation in the first chapter and working through successive chapters on the patriarchs, the exodus, the giving of the law, the conquest of Canaan, the judges and kings of Israel, the prophets, the birth and ministry of Jesus Christ, and the apostolic church. Details small and great are covered. Students were expected to know, for example, the name of Abraham's second wife, the names of Jacob's thirteen children, the year of Joseph's death, the particulars and significance of the Passover, how long the Israelites stayed in Egypt, and the names of every king of Judah and Israel since Rehoboam. Following this first catechism's many questions and answers, Pictet concludes with this brief exhortation: "I pray to God that he will give you the grace to meditate well on these Sacred Books with profit. Amen."[29]

Pictet's second catechism—twenty-four chapters that work through questions related to the Decalogue and the Lord's Prayer—particularly highlights his approach to pastoral care. He is concerned to show that mere assent to the biblical truths and data of the first catechism, while important, is not sufficient for salvation. According to Pictet, the objective, historical realities (and especially those as expressed in the Apostles' Creed) have their personal subjective uses; in other words, trusting in the death and resurrection of Jesus Christ *necessarily* effects the believer's death to sin and resurrection to a new life of obedience in Christ. The guide for this, as Pictet continues to unfold, is the perfect law of God (i.e., the Ten Commandments). Because believers fail in this duty, they must repent daily, confessing their sin and resolving to walk in newness of life.[30] As those who continually fail in measuring up to God's standard, believers must recognize their dependence upon God; this naturally leads to Pictet's examination of the quintessential Christian prayer: the Lord's Prayer.

With pastoral care and insight, Pictet's next catechism—consisting of thirteen polemical chapters treating the "principal controversies" the Reformed had with the Roman Catholics—warns against theological errors that the second catechism's emphasis on morality may lead to. While good works are necessary, and even demonstrate the believer's love for

---

29. "Je prie Dieu qu'il vous fasse la grace de bien méditer ces Livres Sacrez, et d'en profiter. Amen." Pictet, *Cinq Catechismes*, 63.

30. See Pictet, *Cinq Catechismes*, 81–82.

God, Pictet's third catechism teaches that good works do not merit eternal life, as this is a gift of God's free grace.[31]

With the fourth catechism and its emphasis on doctrine, Pictet next moves to a succinct survey of what he considered to be all the major points of religious instruction. This catechism moves at a brisk pace through the primary *loci* of theology: prolegomena (chs. 1–2); theology proper (ch. 3); anthropology (chs. 4–6); Christology (chs. 7–11); soteriology (chs. 12–14); ecclesiology (chs. 15–17); and eschatology (chs. 18–19).

Pictet's fifth and final catechism is especially noteworthy, as it illustrates well his pastoral sensitivity. This last catechism—only four pages long in the original—was designed to reach and educate the youngest children. From the preface, it is understood that Pictet intended the first four catechisms to be for children up to nine or ten years old; the expanded 1715 edition could reach children even a bit older than this group.[32] However, Pictet clarified that the fifth catechism remained unaltered and that its target audience was the very youngest age group, presumably children who were three to five years old. The questions and answers are short, pithy recitations. Many of the answers range from one to five words. Consider the following exchange between the teacher and student: "Who is your Savior? Jesus Christ. Who is Jesus Christ? The only Son of God. Jesus Christ, is he God or man? He is true God and true man. Why was Jesus Christ made man? To die. Why did he have to die? To save us. What do we deserve? We deserve death. How do we deserve this? By our sin."[33] In eight brief, accessible chapters, young children are instructed in what they are to believe concerning God, Jesus Christ, sin, the way of salvation, the need for good works, prayer, the two sacraments, and the hope of resurrection after death. Pictet's fifth catechism demonstrates that he was committed to pastoring all ages within the Genevan church; not only was this eminent professor concerned about the theological training of future pastors and ecclesiastical leaders, but he evidenced a pastoral desire that

---

31. Pictet, *Cinq Catechismes*, 98–99.

32. Pictet writes in the preface, "I have put [in the catechisms] the foundational elements [*prémiers élemens*] of religion, and I believe that this can suffice for the small children, up to the age of nine or ten years old. Today, I give again these same catechisms, but greatly augmented for those who are more advanced in age. I have not added anything to the fifth. I believe, that after having taught the fifth to the very youngest [*plus petits*], we could teach them the first four which have already been printed, so as not to burden their memory too much, and then follow with these." Pictet, *Cinq Catechismes* ("Avis au Lecteur"), 3–4.

33. Pictet, *Cinq Catechismes* ("Avis au Lecteur"), 130–31.

even the youngest of children in Geneva would know Jesus as Lord and Savior. With remarkable simplicity and acuity, Pictet distilled the fundamental teaching of Christianity, offering this to the Genevan toddlers in accessible, bite-size portions. True to his ideal, Pictet's pastoral sensitivities and concerns were not limited by age or intellectual maturity.

PIOUS CONVERSATIONS

A second example from Pictet's corpus that illustrates his pastoral care comes from a work entitled *Pious Conversations of a Believer and His Pastor*.[34] A different genre than his catechisms, this larger work—exactly five hundred pages—is a collection of eight hypothetical conversations between a believing congregant and his pastor. As signaled by the subtitle and the work's preface, the imagined conversations are far-reaching. While the subtitle suggests that the conversations center on advice promoting the believer's holiness, it further indicates that, scattered throughout the conversations, the author will adjudicate several cases of conscience, exposit relevant passages of Scripture, and even provide a historical account of various saints who were martyred for their faith. Near the end of the preface, Pictet envisioned that he would provide more such volumes, depending on the success of this first volume.[35]

Given the conversational nature of the work, it is difficult to neatly categorize the eight dialogues. While a table of contents is included at the end, the eight conversations are not divided into distinct or easily recognizable topics, nor is there an exact linear direction to them; rather, the conversations are somewhat free-flowing and overlap with one another. The overarching theme, however—something to which the work repeatedly returns, and from multiple angles—is assurance of faith. Throughout *Pious Conversations*, the hypothetical pastor encourages, counsels, admonishes, and instructs, pointing the struggling believer to the finished work of Jesus Christ. While this is acknowledged to be the believer's foundation of assurance, at the same time, the doubting congregant is challenged to live a life of holiness. The pastor works through the believer's numerous questions, skillfully and patiently addressing his

---

34. See Pictet, *Entretiens Pieux*.

35. According to De Budé, Pictet followed this with a second volume in 1713 entitled *Conversations d'un chrétien qui désire travailler à son salut avec son Pasteur*. This was apparently published in Rotterdam. I have not yet been able to locate a copy of this work. See De Budé, *Vie de Bénédict Pictet*, 101.

doubts and fears. As each conversation unfolds, it becomes evident that Pictet's imaginary conversations were an accurate representation of the deep-seated, inward struggles that doubting Christians—presumably those under his pastoral care—wrestle with. Pictet made this more explicit within the work's preface, stating that his aim was "to answer many frequently asked questions that have been posed to me many times."[36]

In the first conversation, Pictet stresses the surpassing excellency of Christianity over all other sciences and therefore insists on the necessity of striving after Christian perfection. The imagined pastor does not cheapen Scripture's demands but, referencing Matt 5:48, instructs his disciple: "Everyone is obligated to work toward being perfect, as Jesus Christ commands us: 'Be perfect, as your [heavenly] Father is perfect.'"[37] While he realizes that perfection is impossible in this life, the Christian must nevertheless strive after it. At the beginning of the second conversation, the "faithful student" summarizes the ten principles, or pieces of counsel, the pastor gave him concerning this pursuit: the Christian must (1) ardently desire perfection; (2) pray for it with fervor; (3) set God before his eyes at all times; (4) not forsake corporate worship; (5) study and know his own particular sins and temptations; (6) think often of death and the coming judgment; (7) guard his senses against the entrance of sin; (8) oppose even the smallest beginnings of sin; (9) continuously fight against sinful passions; and, finally, (10) never commit an action without asking if it would displease God.[38] As this second conversation makes clear, the standard of our actions is not our conscience, nor our good intentions, but the righteous demands of God's law.[39]

In the third conversation, the young believer asks whether all sins are equal, and if even small sins are damning. The diligent pastor carefully works through this question, contrasting the dreadful effects of sin with the necessity of good works and what they accomplish. The fourth conversation considers whether it is necessary to gather for public worship and, if so, what this entails. But the heart of the work—and thus the focus of this section—is especially found in the fifth conversation; here, Pictet carefully lays out the necessary characteristics of a true Christian.[40]

36. Pictet, preface to *Entretiens Pieux*: "... d'y répondre à plusieurs questions qu'on fait souvent et qu'on m'a fait plusieurs fois."
37. Pictet, *Entretiens Pieux*, 14.
38. Pictet, *Entretiens Pieux*, 62–63.
39. Pictet, *Entretiens Pieux*, 64–74.
40. Apparently, Pictet envisioned a shift in the work as the fifth conversation began;

The entire conversation works through the young believer's struggle with assurance of faith. As this conversation opens, the congregant confesses, "In the first conversation that I had with you, I asked of you advice that would tend towards Christian perfection because I believed I was a Christian; but, having since made many reflections, I fear that I am not what I thought I was. So, I would be very obliged to you if you would give me a portrait of a true Christian, so that by examining myself in this portrait, I can know for certain what I am."[41]

In answer to this request, the pastor begins by stressing that a true Christian must have a correct knowledge of Jesus Christ. And yet, as he continues, mere knowledge is not sufficient; there are many who will say "Lord, Lord who will not enter the kingdom of heaven."[42] Furthermore, there also those who zealously perform the outward duties of religion and are yet not true Christians; some, he says, are "very assiduous in all the exercises of piety, who sing the praises of God with elevations of the eyes ... who take communion as often as they can, who speak continuously about God, who make beautiful prayers ... who visit hospitals, who regulate well their devotional hours," and yet they do so only for "human reasons."[43] Thus, the pastor warns against relying on knowledge or the performance of religious duties as the ground of assurance.

If bare knowledge or performance is not the indicator of a true Christian, the remainder of the fifth conversation makes clear that a true Christian is one who imitates Christ. While the pastor repeatedly acknowledges that exact Christlikeness will never be fully realized in this life, someone who has never experienced a transformation of the heart cannot be assured of their salvation.[44] A true Christian is one who hates

---

at the end of the fourth conversation, the text signals the conclusion of the first part ("*Fin de la premiére Partie*"). It is not immediately apparent why this division is made (i.e., it is not referenced either in the preface or the table of contents, nor is it obvious from the conversation itself).

41. Pictet, *Entretiens Pieux*, 194. The young believer echoes this request again, saying, "I am waiting for you to be so kind as to paint me a portrait of a true Christian" (197).

42. Pictet, *Entretiens Pieux*, 203. The reference is to Matt 7:21.

43. Pictet, *Entretiens Pieux*, 206–7.

44. The pastor affirms that right knowledge of Jesus Christ is essential to Christianity, and yet he is not content with only this: "This knowledge," he continues, "must penetrate our hearts; it must make deep impressions; it must fill us with admiration for God, for his virtues, for his wisdom, for his grandeur, for his justice, for his mercy, and it must inflame us with love for this Supreme Being and for our Divine Redeemer; it must make us well aware of our nothingness, our corruption, it must excite in us ardent desires to please him, it must purify our heart, and it must give us horror for vice." Pictet, *Entretiens Pieux*, 201–2.

sin—not simply the consequences of sin—and earnestly desires to live a life of obedience. The questioning believer is instructed to test whether he has genuine faith not by examining his intellectual abilities or external actions but by examining his heart—testing his affections and desires. Pictet, through the hypothetical pastor, succinctly and solemnly states, "We can be Christians and be sinners, but one cannot be a true Christian while loving sin."[45] Thus, the pastor's counsel to the doubting congregant emphasized the need to crucify the old self with its vices and passions and to live a new life in and for Jesus Christ; without this, there is only deceit and hypocrisy. Throughout the rest of the work, the hypothetical pastor counsels his disciple to live each day *coram Deo*, even providing seventy-one different maxims for doing so.[46] In summary, the eight extensive conversations between counselor and counselee demonstrate Pictet's pastoral theology as he patiently persisted in walking an immature believer through deep-seated spiritual struggles and doubts.

COLLECTION OF PRAYERS

Pictet's *Prayers for Every Day of the Week* (1712) is a third work that provides a window into his pastoral theology.[47] Just over 150 pages in the earlier versions, this shorter volume contains a wide array of prayers suitable for a variety of circumstances and roles his Genevan congregants would have encountered.[48] While the table of contents lists eighty-five instances of prayer, one—"Short Prayers for the Sick and Dying"—is composed of forty-three brief prayers, thus bringing the total collection to 127 prayers. Pictet's aim was to provide models of prayer that could be used in all occasions of life. Whether they were prayed by a pregnant mother experiencing labor pains, an artisan about to begin his work for the day, a believer readying herself for communion, an orphaned child

---

45. Pictet, *Entretiens Pieux*, 268.

46. Pictet notes that the seventy-one maxims he lists are an abridged version received from "a pastor of the Reformed Church" and recorded in French by a "celebrated Jesuit." Cf. Pictet, *Entretiens Pieux*, 322–37.

47. Pictet, *Prières pour tous les jours de la semaine, et sur divers sujets*. All quotations will reference this edition.

48. The work is expanded in the 1853 edition to just under three hundred pages and includes ninety-one instances of prayer, to which are also added several liturgies, historic prayers, and songs. See Pictet, *Prières pour tous les jours de la semaine, et sur divers sujets* (1853).

grieving a lost parent, or a regular saint on a regular Tuesday morning, Pictet's desire was to encourage within his congregants frequent and habitual patterns of praying to God. De Budé notes that Pictet worked on several manuals of prayers throughout his lifetime, often writing these prayers during periods of his own sickness or poor health.[49]

Although the work is relatively short, the prayers, as already noted, reflect a wide range of circumstances or trials that an early-modern believer might have encountered. That Pictet was cognizant of these diverse situations illustrates his pastoral sensitivity and awareness. Some prayers were more general in nature, intentionally broad so as to accommodate a wider range of applicability. And yet, even in these more generic prayers, pastoral warmth and tenderness shine through. Consider, for example, this longer excerpt from prayer 52, which was to be prayed by a person enduring great affliction:

> Father of grace and God of consolation, have pity on me! There is no sorrow like mine; one abyss calls to another abyss; all your waves and all your billows have passed over me. You have given me the bread of tears to eat, and you have made me drink from a cup of weeping. What afflicts me most is that I fear all these afflictions are signs of your anger and effects of your just vengeance. In these sorrowful thoughts, I throw myself at your feet, and I come to seek my consolation in your embrace. It is true, my God, that I recognize your chastisements are sweet when I consider what I have too much deserved; but your mercy is infinite, and my flesh is utter weakness. The cup you make me drink is extremely bitter, and my pain is more than I can carry. My God, will you not have compassion on me? You are near to the brokenhearted; you console those who call to you from the depths; you heal broken bones. O my heavenly Father, will you not reach out your hand to me? It is through your Son that I call upon you. It is by his blood, by his merit—not for the love of me, but for the love of that Son—that I ask you to sustain me, strengthen me, and deliver me from my afflictions.[50]

---

49. De Budé suggests that *Prières pour tous les jours de la semaine* was first published in 1712, although he gives it this title: *Prières sur chaque jour de la semaine et sur divers sujets*. See De Budé, *Vie de Bénédict Pictet*, 95. De Budé lists five other manuals on prayer or prayer-related works that Pictet authored. De Budé writes, "Pictet was persuaded that the collections of prayers were of great use for action in families, especially in countries where the assembly of saints was forbidden, and so he composed a great number of this genre" (94).

50. Pictet, *Prières pour tous les jours de la semaine*, 110.

It is immediately evident that Pictet's prayers for the afflicted reflect undertones of biblical lament; reminiscent of David's psalms of lament or Jesus's prayer in the garden of Gethsemane, Pictet, through his prayers, taught those who are afflicted to pour out their hearts to God. His prayers also demonstrate that he was sensitive to the deep hurt that comes with the trials of life. And yet, despite this, Pictet modeled how weakness, pain, tears, and despondency all submit to the fatherly compassion and grace of God shown in and through Jesus Christ.

This same pastoral care is demonstrated in Pictet's forty-three prayers for the sick and dying. Noticeably shorter than the rest—often only two or three sentences long—these prayers illustrate how to offer quick, impromptu prayers to God, especially in the face of sickness or impending death. Passion and urgency are unmistakably present in these prayers, two characteristics that are understandable in the face of death. Consider this shortest prayer of the collection: "O my Savior, remember me. You are in your kingdom; let me hear the same words [*la même voix*] that you once spoke to the good thief: 'Today you will be with me in Paradise.' Amen."[51] While Pictet showed how urgent and passionate prayers can be made to God, at the same time, he taught those facing illness and death to succumb to God's will, encouraging his congregants to fully trust in God's gracious provisions (even if they are not immediately perceived that way). Thus, prayer 15 of this section reads: "O God, who brings down to the grave and who raises up, if you deem it fitting for my salvation, deliver me from the evil that presses on me. At the very least, Lord, let this affliction produce in me patience, and let this patience produce endurance, and endurance hope, and let this hope not confound me. Amen." Through forty-three such prayers, Pictet urged his flock to put their steadfast hope and trust in God, even in the face of the foremost difficulty of human existence: sickness and impending death.

Pictet's pastoral concern was not, however, limited to the sick and dying. In the opening prayer designed to be offered on the first day of the year—which also happens to be the longest prayer in the collection, totaling eight and a half pages—Pictet explicitly asked for God's blessing and favor on *all* those who made up the Genevan church.[52] Pictet prays:

---

51. Pictet, *Prières pour tous les jours de la semaine*, 74. This is prayer 24 of this section, and is only thirty-three words in the original French. The second shortest is prayer 31 (thirty-nine words long). See Pictet, *Prières pour tous les jours de la semaine*, 76.

52. This opening prayer is uniquely followed by a paraphrase of Ps 90, as well as several Scripture citations with brief prompts for meditation or reflection.

> Bless all the families who make up this church, of every age, sex, and condition; old men, grown men, young people and children, citizens and bourgeois, *habitans*, foreigners, and those whom the misfortunes of time have compelled them to seek here an asylum, to serve you according to the light of their conscience, all in particular, each according to the vocation with which you have honored him, and according to the state in which he finds himself.[53]

As earlier noted, Pictet had a particular concern for those who were displaced from France following the revocation of the Edict of Nantes.[54] Such concern is reflected briefly in this opening prayer, but Pictet also wrote separate prayers for believers who were imprisoned for professing their faith, for believers who were exiled from their country due to religious reasons, for believers who were condemned to death because of a true profession, for believers who were forced to worship in private because they were deprived of public worship, and for children who lost or were separated from their parents.[55] Pictet's prayers also reflected other real-life concerns of seventeenth-century Genevans: prayers offered by a servant; a widow; a scholar beginning his studies; a person who recently lost his sight; a believer struggling with assurance; a criminal who has been imprisoned (both justly and unjustly); a man who lost his wealth (for either just or unjust reasons); someone setting out on a journey; a husband for his wife, and vice versa; prayers for times of famine, war, and the plague; prayers for one's magistrates; prayers for one's pastor; prayers for family worship; and, as the title of the work makes clear, prayers to begin and end each day of the week. Each prayer reflected Pictet's desire to pastorally care for the Genevan people entrusted to him.

---

53. Pictet, *Prières pour tous les jours de la semaine*, 9. "Béni toutes les familles qui composent cette Eglise, de tout âge, de tout sexe et de toute condition; vieillards, hommes faits, jeunes gens et enfans, citoyens et bourgeois, habitans, étrangers, et ceux que les malheurs du tems ont contraint de chercher ici un asile, pour te servir selon les lumières de leur conscience, tous en particulier, chacun selon la vocation dont tu l'as honoré, et selon l'état où il se trouve."

54. Consider also Pictet, *Marrow of Christian Ethics*, 309. Here Pictet considers the moral question of what someone should do who is driven out of their fatherland because of religion. His answer is to submit to this affliction, comforting themselves with the knowledge that they are being persecuted for righteousness' sake, that they are imitating Abraham, that God remains their protector and leader, that heaven (the "true fatherland") awaits, and that the "days of their sojourning will be brief."

55. See, respectively, prayers 57, 53, 59, 83, and 70.

CONCLUSION

Upon consideration of these three relatively unknown works of Bénédict Pictet—his *Fivefold Catechism, Pious Conversations of a Believer and His Pastor,* and *Prayers for Each Day of the Week*—this essay has argued that pastoral sensitivity and awareness formed the core of the Genevan professor's identity and work. Pictet's aim in life, whether in theological education, private one-on-one counseling, or prayer, was to shepherd and lead God's people in such a way that they would live their lives more fully dependent on him and for his glory. Cognizant of his own dependence and weakness in this work, I close this chapter echoing Pictet's prayer that the Great Shepherd would enable him for a task that went far beyond him:

> O Sovereign Shepherd of souls, who has honored me with your holy ministry, grant that I may fulfill it with all the care I am capable of. Teach me everything that I must teach others and lead me by your Spirit of truth. Give me strength of body and spirit to carry out all my functions. Give me true humility and an ardent zeal for your glory, and make me to be an example of virtue to the flock you have given me, so that I may have a part in the crown of righteousness you promise to your faithful servants. Amen.[56]

BIBLIOGRAPHY

Beza, Theodore. *Confession de la Foy Chrestienne* [. . .]. [Geneva]: Imprimé par Conrad Badius, 1559.

Boisson, Didier. "The Revocation of the Edict of Nantes and the *Désert*." In *A Companion to the Huguenots*, edited by Raymond A. Mentzer and Bertrand Van Ruymbeke, 221–45. Brill's Companions to the Christian Tradition 68. Leiden: Brill, 2016.

de Budé, Eugène. *Vie de Bénédict Pictet, Théologien Genevois (1655-1724)*. Lausanne: Georges Bridel, 1874.

DeYoung, Kevin. *The Religious Formation of John Witherspoon: Calvinism, Evangelicalism, and the Scottish Enlightenment*. Routledge Studies in Evangelicalism. New York: Routledge, 2020.

Duley-Haour, Pauline. "La Correspondance d'Antoine Court, une Correspondance Pastorale?" *Bulletin de La Société de l'Histoire Du Protestantisme Français (1903-2015)* 159 (Jan./Feb./Mar. 2013) 143–58.

Gaberel, Jean. *Histoire de L'Église de Genève depuis le Commencement de la Réformation jusqu'à nos jours*. 3 vols. Geneva: Joël Cherbuliez, 1858-62.

---

56. Pictet, *Prières pour tous les jours de la semaine*, 134–35.

Klauber, Martin I. "Family Loyalty and Theological Transition in Post-Reformation Geneva: The Case of Benedict Pictet (1655–1724)." *Fides et Historia* 24 (Winter/Spring 1992) 54–67.

———. "Reformed Orthodoxy in Transition: Bénédict Pictet (1655–1724) and Enlightened Orthodoxy in Post-Reformation Geneva." In *Later Calvinism: International Perspectives*, edited by W. Fred Graham, 93–113. Sixteenth Century Essays and Studies 22. Kirksville, MO: Sixteenth Century Journal, 1994.

Manetsch, Scott M. *Calvin's Company of Pastors: Pastoral Care and the Emerging Reformed Church, 1536–1609*. Oxford Studies in Historical Theology. New York: Oxford University Press, 2013.

Miller, Matthew S. "Geneva's First New Church After Calvin and Bénédict Pictet's Dedication Sermon (1715)." In *Generation to Generation: Writings in Honor of Douglas F. Kelly*, edited by Matthew S. Miller and D. Blair Smith, 215–36. Fearn, UK: Mentor, 2023.

Muller, Richard A. "Calvin and the 'Calvinists': Assessing Continuities and Discontinuities Between the Reformation and Orthodoxy, Parts 1 and 2." In *After Calvin: Studies in the Development of a Theological Tradition*, 63–102. Oxford Studies in Historical Theology. New York: Oxford University Press, 2003.

Olsen, Jeannine. "The Edict of Nantes and Its Revocation: A Balanced Assessment?" In *The Theology of the Huguenot Refuge: From the Revocation of the Edict of Nantes to the Edict of Versailles*, edited by Martin I. Klauber, 9–34. Reformed Historical-Theological Studies. Grand Rapids: Reformation Heritage, 2020.

Pictet, Bénédict. *Cinq Catechimes [sic] pour Instruire les jeunes gens dans la Réligion Reformèe*. Amsterdam: Chez la Veuve Schippers, 1707.

———. *Cinq Catechismes*. Lausanne: Chez Jean Zimmerli, 1729.

———. *Cinq Catechismes pour Instruire les jeunes gens dans la Religion Reformée*. Geneva: Pour Jean Antoine Querel, 1715.

———. *Entretiens Pieux, d'un Fidele avec son Pasteur. Dans lesquels on trouve divers Conseils pour s'avancer dans la Sainteté, la Résolution de plusieurs Cas de Conscience, l'Explication d'un grand nombre de Passages, & l'Histoire de plusieurs Saints Hommes, comme des Martyrs, &c*. Geneva: Chez Fabri & Barrillot Libraries, 1710.

———. *The Marrow of Christian Ethics*. Translated by Michael Hunter. Kernersville, NC: Michael Hunter, 2024.

———. *Prières pour tous les jours de la semaine, et sur divers sujets*. Lausanne: Chez Emanuel Vincent fils, 1827.

———. *Prières pour tous les jours de la semaine, et sur divers sujets*. Toulouse: Société des Livres Religieux, 1853.

———. *Sermon fait le Jour de la Dedicace du Nouveau Temple, le XV. de Décembre de l'an MDCCXV*. Geneva: Chez Jean Antoine Querel, 1716.

———. *La Théologie Chretiene, et la Science du Salut*. 3 vols. Geneva: Chez Cramer, Perachon & Cramer Fils, 1721.

Rouwendal, Pieter L. "Late Orthodoxy—Benedict Pictet." In *Predestination and Preaching in Genevan Theology from Calvin to Pictet*, 245–299. Studies in the History of Church and Theology 1. Kampen: Summum Academic, 2017.

Selles, Otto. "A Case of Hidden Identity: Antoine Court, Bénédict Pictet, and Geneva's Aid to France's Desert Churches (1715–1724)." In *The Identity of Geneva: The*

Christian Commonwealth, 1564–1864, edited by John B. Roney and Martin I. Klauber, 93–109. Westport, CT: Greenwood, 1998.

van Asselt, Willem J. "Scholasticism in the Time of Late Orthodoxy (ca. 1700–1790)." In *Introduction to Reformed Scholasticism*, edited by Willem J. van Asselt, 167–93. Reformed Historical-Theological Studies. Grand Rapids: Reformation Heritage, 2011.

van Asselt, Willem J., and Pieter L. Rouwendal. "The State of Scholarship: From Discontinuity to Continuity." In *Introduction to Reformed Scholasticism*, edited by Willem J. van Asselt, 10–25. Reformed Historical-Theological Studies. Grand Rapids: Reformation Heritage, 2011.

Wolfe, Stephen. "Bénédict Pictet: Small Steps Toward Rationalism?" *Journal of Reformed Theology* 11 (Jan. 2017) 203–22.

Yardeni, Myriam. *Le réfuge protestant*. Paris: Presses Universitaires de France, 1985.

PART 2

Pastoral Care in Reformation
Readings of Scripture

6

Religion, Revelation, and the People of God in Matthew Henry's Commentary on the Psalms

RICHARD A. MULLER

HENRY THE COMMENTATOR: CONTEXT, INTENTION, AND METHOD

MATTHEW HENRY (1662–1714) is surely one of the most prominent and most published yet least studied of the major later Puritan or Nonconformist theologians and commentators. His *Exposition of the Old and New Testaments* has graced the studies of innumerable pastors, whether in the famous six-volume editions begun in the early eighteenth century and continued into the present or in various other formats, including single-volume abridgements and, most recently, a multivolume set in modernized English.¹ Nonetheless, Henry's theology and exegesis have seldom been the subject of scholarly study.²

Henry was born in the year of the Act of Uniformity, shortly after the ejection of his father, Philip Henry, from the parish of Worthenbury. After early studies under a Latin and Greek tutor at Broad Oak, the young Matthew Henry was sent, in 1680, to study at the academy of Thomas Doolittle, a Nonconformist minister of Islington, only to have his studies cut short by the move of the academy to Battersea, probably in late 1682. Henry continued studies with his father.³ Having completed this initial stage of his education, Henry took up residence as a law student at Gray's Inn in Holborn Court, London, in April 1685. During this time he attended the Anglican services of Edward Stillingfleet and John Tillotson.⁴ He studied for approximately a year, returned to Broad Oak, accepted several invitations to preach, and decided not to pursue the law but rather to enter the ministry. His intention and calling were sketched out in a series of questions and observations he composed at the time, entitled *Serious Self-Examination Before Ordination*.⁵ Henry was ordained on May 9, 1687, under the terms of James II's declaration of liberty of conscience.⁶

Henry's ordination was Presbyterian, and his theology consistently Reformed. The confession of faith delivered by Henry on the occasion of his ordination and in his *Scripture Catechism, in the Method of the Assemblies* (1703) both testify to his belief in the sovereignty of God, the inability of the human race in its fallenness and the necessity of salvation by grace alone, the two-covenant schema (covenant of works, covenant of

---

1. See Henry, *Exposition*. I have cited Henry from the third edition of 1725. Perhaps the best known of the many editions is the "new edition, carefully revised and corrected," undated, printed by Fleming H. Revell. This latter edition, unfortunately, alters spelling and punctuation and disturbs the pattern of the original by redistributing the contents of the volumes devoted to the Old Testament and obscuring Henry's reliance on the traditional design of Pentateuch, historical books, Writings, and Prophets.

2. On his life and writings, see Tong, *Account*; Williams, *Memoirs*; also note Roberts, *Matthew Henry*. On Henry's thought, note Murray, "Matthew Henry"; Murray, "More Than a Commentator"; Joo, "Communion with God"; Campbell, "Matthew Henry"; Harman, *Matthew Henry*; Harman, "Legacy of Matthew Henry"; and the essays in Collins and Middleton, *Matthew Henry*, which notes the scarcity of scholarly assessment (p. 1).

3. Cf. Tong, *Account*, 28–30, who notes that the problem of illness contributed to the closing of the academy; and Williams, *Memoirs*, 13, 15, 17; with Burden, *Biographical Dictionary*, 140–52.

4. Williams, *Memoirs*, 33.

5. Williams, *Memoirs*, 45–58.

6. Williams, *Memoirs*, 2–3, 9, 18, 31–35, 47–48.

grace), a fundamentally infralapsarian doctrine of predestination, and a doctrine of justification by graciously given faith—all typical of the Westminster Standards and of the Reformed orthodoxy of the era.[7] Within those theological boundaries, Henry leaned toward a form of hypothetical universalism and the universal offer of the gospel.[8]

He began his work on the *Exposition of the Old and New Testaments* in November 1704 and continued steadily to work through the text until the final months of his life. The last book for which he finalized the text of his commentary was the Acts of the Apostles, leaving Romans nearly complete, but the remainder of the Epistles and the Revelation in a fragmentary state.[9] Had he lived long enough to complete his plan for the work, Henry would not only have completed the exposition through Revelation, but he would also have added a seventh "critical" volume dealing with the "difficult places of scripture" and an eighth volume containing "a body of divinity in sermons."[10] The remainder of the exposition of the New Testament was completed by Henry's colleagues in ministry from notes taken in shorthand during both private talks and public sermons.[11] The proposed seventh and eighth volumes never materialized—but the doctrinal content as well as the structure and flow of the individual theological topics of the projected *Body of Divinity* may be gathered directly

---

7. Cf. Henry's confession in Williams, *Memoirs*, 64–69; with Henry, *Scripture Catechism*; also in *Miscellaneous Works*, 2:864–928.

8. Cf. Henry, *Exposition*, Isa 53:6, in loc. (4:158); with Henry, *Scripture Catechism*, 65–66; and note Burden, *Biographical Dictionary*, 148, where Henry's tutor, Thomas Doolittle, is described as "decidedly Baxterian."

9. See Evans, "Advertisement," appended to Henry's preface; and cf. Weeks, "Matthew Henry's Commentary," 85–86; and Alexander, "Matthew Henry," 250–52, including Evans's comments from the 1715 printing of the *Exposition*, vol. 5.

10. Williams, *Memoirs*, 315. An outline of the projected *Body of Divinity*, including detailed subtopics, can be found in Tong, *Account*, 178–97. Henry's sermons and short tracts are found in the *Miscellaneous Works*, also in *Works*; and *Select Works*. These sermons are largely occasional, and, although they offer a clear sense of Henry's method in organizing his sermons, only a few of them offer indications of how he would have fully elaborated the doctrinal topics. A clearer indication comes from his *Unpublished Sermons*, which, unlike the occasional sermons found in Henry's *Works*, presents a series of sermons that elaborate on a portion of a particular doctrinal topic. The original series on covenant consisted of three parts: (1) "God in the Covenant," seven sermons; (2) "Christ in the Covenant," nine sermons; (3) "The Holy Spirit in the Covenant," fourteen sermons, followed by a concluding sermon that summarized the basic doctrine: see Tong, *Account*, 166–70; also in Williams, *Memoirs*, note F (ad fin., v–vi). The *Unpublished Sermons* only contains the recovered final ten sermons, along with the concluding "Repetition."

11. Henry, *Exposition*, preface to the Epistles (6:iii).

from the outline found in Tong's *Account*, and its method further confirmed from the patterns of argument and topical elaboration found in Henry's extended catechism.[12]

Henry's work as a commentator, albeit pastoral and homiletical in focus, reflected both the major doctrinal issues of his age and the text-critical work of the seventeenth-century orthodox tradition of biblical interpretation. This grasp of theological issues and knowledge of the exegetical developments is particularly evident in his prefaces to various biblical books. Henry described his own efforts as a "Methodizing and Practical Exposition of the Inspired Writings."[13] He also indicated, reflecting on the content of his commentary, that he endeavored to "make these Writings serviceable to the Faith, Holiness, and Comfort of good Christians,"[14] an effort that, if faith is related to teaching, holiness to conduct, and comfort to Christian hope, echoes the concerns of the *quadriga*, adjusted to a more direct reading of the text as having a single meaning at once literal and spiritual.[15]

Henry introduced his entire project and identified its intention with the statement that "Religion is the one thing needful" to all of humanity: it provides the knowledge and fear of God that is the support of human nature and the foundation of human society. True religion, moreover, rests on divine revelation, and that revelation "is not now to be found or expected any where but in the Scriptures of the Old and New Testament."[16] In view of the fundamental purpose of religion and the nature of Scripture as divine revelation, Scripture exists not merely

---

12. Tong, *Account*, 85–91. Henry's exposition of the Westminster Shorter Catechism, the *Scripture Catechism*, provides some indication of how he might have handled the topics of a body of divinity. Henry's catechism divides each question into a series of sub-question paragraphs, each of which is further divided into a series of questions and answers. Taken together, the paragraphs exhibit an argumentative structure that begins with basic problems concerning the topic and concludes with a paragraph that returns, with a pastoral resolution, to the main catechetical question. This structuring of the main questions in the *Scripture Catechism* has affinities with the structure of Henry's sermons and with the outlines of the *loci* in his projected *Body of Divinity*. Given the length and detail of the sermons on covenant, the full homiletical theology would have been massive. We also have Henry's *Confession of Faith* from the time of his ordination in 1687.

13. Henry, *Exposition*, Joshua to Esther, preface (2:A2r).

14. Henry, *Exposition*, Gospels and Acts, preface (5:A2r).

15. Cf. Childs, "*Sensus Literalis*," 87.

16. Henry, *Exposition*, preface (1:A2r).

for the sake of "learning" but as "the settled standing Rule of our Faith and Practise, by which we must be governed now, and judged shortly."[17]

Henry went on to clarify his intention by contrasting his work with that of other commentators, beginning with those "Learned in the Languages." The date of his preface, 1706, adds significance to his comment that "The *Philology* of the *Critics* hath been of much more Advantage to Religion, and lent more Light to Sacred Truth, than the *Philosophy* of the *School-Divines*,"[18] inasmuch as he was aware of late seventeenth-century developments in critical exegesis, notably the work of Richard Simon, but still offered a broad and unqualified recommendation of the technical study of Scripture. Henry praised Simon Patrick's commentaries and Matthew Poole's English *Annotations* and Latin *Synopsis*,[19] and in numerous places he explicitly followed or adapted Henry Hammond's interpretations.[20] He knew Calvin's commentary on the Psalms and cited it at least three times.[21] Other English commentaries that he might have examined include Henry Ainsworth's *Annotations*,[22] William Ames's *Lectiones*,[23] the so-called *English Annotations*,[24] the *Dutch Annotations* as

17. Henry, *Exposition*, preface (1:A2r).
18. Henry, *Exposition*, preface (1:A2r).
19. Henry, *Exposition*, preface (1:A3v, A4r); e.g., Patrick, *Commentary upon the First Book of Moses*; Patrick, *Commentary upon the Fifth Book of Moses*; Patrick, *Commentary upon the Books of Joshua, Judges and Ruth*; Patrick, *Book of Psalms*; also Patrick, *Commentary upon the Historical Books of the Old Testament*; and Poole, *Annotations*. I have seen no explicit citation of Poole's *Annotations* on the Psalms. Patrick's *Book of Psalms* is cited only once, at Ps 116.
20. E.g., Henry, *Exposition*, Psalms, preface; Pss 5, 8, 11, 29, 34, 35, 37, 49, 50, 55, 58, 68, 72, 73, 77, 83, 85, 89, 94, 97, 98, 99, 103, 104, 106, 109, 111, 112, 119, 121, 126, 130, 131, 134, 137, 138, 141, 146, 148, 150, citing or mentioning Hammond (3:138, 149, 154, 162, 196, 207, 208, 217, 242, 243, 245, 255, 260, 279, 281, 291, 293, 302, 320, 324, 335, 344, 345, 350, 351, 353, 360, 361, 362, 369, 378, 382, 382, 410, 413, 419, 423, 427, 428, 431, 436, 437, 442, 450, 453, 456), referencing Hammond, *Paraphrase and Annotations*. Note the discussion of contemporary commentaries by Weeks, "Matthew Henry's Commentary," 88–93. Weeks makes no mention of Hammond.
21. Henry, *Exposition*, Pss 48; 109; 115 (3:240, 378, 389).
22. Ainsworth, *Annotations*. Henry cites Ainsworth's commentary on the Song of Songs in Henry, *Exposition*, Song 3:4 (3:623).
23. Ames, *Lectiones*.
24. *Annotations upon All the Books of the Old and New Testament*. The multi-authored work is typically identified as the *English Annotations*, in contrast to the *Dutch Annotations* commissioned by the Synod of Dort: see my essay, "'Entire Commentary,'" 11–29. Note that the *English Annotations* are unpaginated and that citations refer to chapters and verses, "in loc."

translated by Theodore Haak,[25] Jean Diodati's *Annotations*,[26] John Mayer's commentary on the Old Testament,[27] David Dickson's commentary on the Psalter,[28] and John Trapp's *Annotations*,[29] none of which are explicitly referenced in Henry's exposition of the Psalms, although there are some parallels in interpretation. The most influential predecessor to Henry's interpretation of the Psalter was clearly Henry Hammond.[30]

Matthew Henry's expositions of those portions of the Old Testament that were not commented on by Hammond evidence some reliance on, or at least relationship to, Matthew Poole's *Annotations*, and arguably less so to Simon Patrick's commentaries, despite the occasional reference. Like other commentators of his time, Henry recognized that Moses could not have written the final chapter of Deuteronomy, and like Calvin and Mayer, he suggested either Joshua or Eleazar as potential authors, noting also Patrick's hypothesis of Samuel.[31] In accord with Poole but at odds with Patrick, Henry offered a lengthy note on the unknown authorship and composite character of Joshua through 2 Kings—noting sources like the Chronicles of the Kings of Israel and the books of Jasher, Gad, Nathan, and Iddo and assigning the final "form" of the canonical books to an unknown compiler "long afterward."[32] Henry hypothesized later editorial work perhaps by Jeremiah, or even a postexilic effort by Ezra, granting that phrases like "the Kings of Judah" (1 Sam 27:6) could only arise "after Solomon" and that the statement "he that is now called a Prophet, was

25. *Dutch Annotations*.
26. Diodati, *Annotations*.
27. Mayer, *Commentary*.
28. Dickson, *Brief Explication*.
29. Trapp, *Commentary*.
30. Cf. Kuivenhoven, "Songs of the Son," 27.
31. Henry, *Exposition*, Deut 34, argument (1:510), citing Patrick, *Commentary upon the Fifth Book of Moses*, Deut 34:1 (678); Mayer, *Commentary*, 1:337, notes the tradition that Joshua wrote the final chapter and adds that Calvin also suggested Eleazar; Diodati, *Annotations* (1664) refers to the author as "some prophet"; and cf. Gataker et al., *Annotations*, vol. 1, Deut 34, in loc.; Poole, *Annotations*, Deut 34:1, in loc.
32. Henry, *Exposition*, Joshua, preface (2:1); cf. Poole, *Annotations*, Joshua, argument, noting the "insertions" like those previously observed "in the five Books of Moses"; Judges, argument, "the Author of this Book is certainly not known; whether it was Samuel, Ezra, or some other Prophet: nor is it material to know"; Ruth, argument, "This little Book, by whomsoever Written, which it is not material to know"; 1 Samuel, argument, "It is certainly not known who was the Pen-man of this Book, or whether it was Written by one or more Hands, not is it of any great Importance"; and note Patrick, *Commentary upon the Books of Joshua, Judges and Ruth*, 1, 311, arguing for Joshua's authorship of the book of Joshua, as well as Samuel's authorship of Judges.

then called a Seer" (1 Sam 9:9) implies later compilation or insertion.[33] So, too, various identifications and explanations of place names, "Rights and Possessions," and "Customs and Usages" clearly "have been since added to the History by the Inspired Collectors, for the Confirmation and Illustration of it to those of their own Age."[34]

Henry, then, was neither ignorant of nor averse to the critical and textual work of his time—but he did indicate a contrast between his work and that of the more critical-textual exegetes and of the various annotators, particularly Poole, whose *Annotations* Henry declared to be "of Admirable Use, especially for the explaining of Scripture-Phrases, opening the Sense, referring to parallel Scriptures, and the clearing of Difficulties."[35] Henry's own exposition, however, would follow a different method, for a different purpose:

> The Exposition which (like this here) is put into a continued Discourse, digested under proper Heads, is much more easy and ready, to be *read through* for one's own or other's Instruction. And, I think, the observing of the connexion of each Chapter, (if there be Occasion) with that which goes before, and the general Scope of it, with the Thread of the History or Discourse, and the collection of the several Parts of it to be seen at one View, will contribute very much to the Understanding of it, and will give the Mind abundant satisfaction in the general Intention, tho' there may be here and there a difficult Word or Expression which the best Criticks cannot easily account for. This, therefore I have here endeavoured.[36]

He continued, even more to the point:

> But we are concerned not only to *understand* what we read, but to *improve* it to some good Purpose, and in Order thereunto to be affected with it, and to receive the Impressions of it.... We must therefore in searching the Scriptures enquire, not only *What is this?* but *What is this to us?* What Use may we make of it? How may we accommodate it to some of the Purposes of the Divine and Heavenly Life, which by the Grace of God we are resolved to live? Enquiries of this Kind I have here aimed to answer.[37]

---

33. Henry, *Exposition*, Joshua, preface (2:1); noted by Poole, *Annotations*, 1 Sam 9:9 and 27:6, in loc.; but not by Patrick, *Commentary upon the Historical Books*, 2:212, 265.
34. Henry, *Exposition*, Joshua, preface (2:1).
35. Henry, *Exposition*, preface (1:A3v).
36. Henry, *Exposition*, preface (1:A3v).
37. Henry, *Exposition*, preface (1:A3v).

The *Exposition*, then, chose a distinct path. Henry was hardly oblivious to critical issues—he noted them, but he chose not to devote his work to them. Nor did he find the method of annotation conducive to a sense of the scope and flow of the text or to an understanding of its religious purpose. It is worth noting that "improve," in the language of the day, did not indicate an intention to increase the value of something. Rather, it meant to use something to a good purpose. Accordingly, Henry's chosen model was directed to the practical use of Scripture to the good purpose of preaching and worship, whether corporate or personal. It consisted in an extended initial comment or argument concerning an entire book of Scripture followed by discourses on each chapter, section by section. The sections are of varied length, consisting in several verses, typically identified as units suitable to a discourse on the meaning of the verses within it, followed by a series of "observations" directed toward faith and life. Henry's final applicatory comments draw on the theme of the discourse and consistently recognize that Psalms are both hymns and prayers intended for worship. He begins each brief counsel, "In singing this, and praying it over ... ," as in, for example, his closing of Ps 6: "In singing this, and praying it over, we must give Glory to God, as a God ready to hear our Prayer; and must own his Goodness to us in hearing our Prayers, and must encourage ourselves to wait upon him, and to trust in him in the greatest Straits and Difficulties."[38]

THE AUTHORSHIP, SCOPE, AND CONTENT OF THE PSALTER

From the very beginning of his *Exposition*, Henry affirmed that the direction of the Spirit in the writing of Scripture extended to the "Language and Expression" of the human authors, assisting "their understandings and Memories, in recording those Things which they themselves had the Knowledge of," in addition to revealing truths of God beyond the capability of human knowledge.[39] This understanding of inspiration allowed him to account for differences in style, vocabulary, and expression among the human authors of biblical books as well as to acknowledge diversity of authorship, sources drawn on by the writers of the biblical books, and, in some cases, unknown authors. When dealing with the

---

38. Henry, *Exposition*, Ps 6, ad fin. (3:152).
39. Henry, *Exposition*, preface (1:A2v).

authorship of the Psalter, he first indicated that the entire Psalter "deriv'd originally from the *Blessed Spirit*," but he added that the Psalms also had various "pen-men," that the whole "Collection" had been "compos'd at several times, and upon several Occasions," and that it had been "here put together without any reference to, or dependance upon one another."[40] This apparent lack of interdependence of the Psalms led Henry to dismiss the theological significance of various hypothetical divisions of the text, including what he recognized as the ancient division into five books.[41]

Henry, then, assumed that the Psalter was a compilation of texts written over a long period of time by multiple authors. David, he notes, was called "the Sweet Psalmist of Israel" (2 Sam 23:1) inasmuch as he was the "penman of most of them," as assumed by the inscriptions set prior to the text of various psalms. Further, some psalms that are not directly assigned to David in the Psalter itself are "expressly ascribed to him elsewhere," as Ps 2 is attributed to David in Acts 4:25, and Pss 96 and 105 attributed to David in 1 Chr 16.[42] Other psalms, however, were clearly not written by David: Psalm 90 is identified as a "Prayer of Moses," and the authorship of other psalms by Asaph is indicated in the ascriptions found in the text of the Psalter and "intimated" in 2 Chr 29:30. Psalms are also ascribed to the sons of Korah and others.[43] Echoing Hammond, Patrick, and Poole, Henry notes that "some of the Psalms seem to have been pen'd long after, as Psal. cxxxvii, at the time of the Captivity in Babylon."[44]

Henry's ascriptions of authorship were not merely pro forma—they played a role in his interpretations. By way of example, he noted that it must remain uncertain how Ps 90 was "preserv'd from *Moses's* Time

---

40. Henry, *Exposition*, Psalms, preface (3:137; cf. Henry, *Exposition*, Ps 137 [3:434]); Diodati, *Annotations*, "Argument of David's Psalms," in loc.; and Patrick, *Book of Psalms*, 1:A4r-v, A4[5]v-A7v, who followed Jewish tradition in assuming a compilation by Ezra in connection with the gathering of the Hebrew canon of the Old Testament.

41. Henry, *Exposition*, Psalms, preface, in 3:133, noting that each of the proposed "books" concludes with "Amen, Amen," or "Hallelujah," and that the divisions were Pss 1–41, 42–72, 73–89, 90–106, and 107–50. Far more support for the division, together with reflection on its interpretive significance, is found in Hammond, *Paraphrase and Annotations*, Bv; and Patrick, *Book of Psalms*, 1:A4[5]v-A6r; and 1:1, 285–86; 2:1–2, 164–65, 305–6. Unlike Patrick and Hammond, who explicitly divide their expositions into five books, Henry does not mark the traditional divisions of the Psalter.

42. Henry, *Exposition*, Psalms, preface (3:137).

43. Note Patrick, *Book of Psalms*, 1:A4[5]v, noting that the authors of each "book" of the Psalter are noted at the beginnings of the books.

44. Henry, *Exposition*, Psalms, preface (3:137); cf. Hammond, *Paraphrase and Annotations*, 2; Patrick, *Book of Psalms*, 1:A4r-v; Poole, *Annotations*, Psalms, argument.

till the Collection of *Psalms* begun to be made."[45] Various predecessors of Henry had elaborated on the question of Mosaic authorship: Poole located the psalm in relation to Num 14 and the "righteous sentence" of God against "that sinful Generation in the Wilderness."[46] By contrast, Calvin expressed doubts, indicating that one of the prophets may have turned a "formula of prayer written by Moses" into a song for religious use.[47] Hammond indicated that the psalm was either written by Moses "or else, as in his person, by some other, with reflexion on those times wherein Moses lived."[48] As for Henry, although he draws on the doctrine of the providential preservation of the text of Scripture as part of his explanation of the presence of a prayer of Moses in the Psalter, he also hypothesizes that the psalm was preserved in one or another of the known sources of the biblical histories, namely the Book of Jasher or the Book of the Wars of the Lord. More importantly for Henry, the ascription identifies Moses as the "Man of God" because he was "the Father of the Prophets, and an eminent Type of the great Prophet," who taught the people of Israel to pray to God.[49]

It should not be entirely surprising that Henry's introductory comments on the Psalter, notably concerning its scope and purpose, reflect an ongoing exegetical tradition. By the time Henry began his *Exposition* in 1704, the Protestant, and specifically Reformed, interpretation of Scripture had established itself in a well-defined but also variegated tradition. Various comments found throughout the text of his Psalter exposition reflect the text-critical results of the era, while the primary direction of his interpretation has affinity with lines of Reformed exegesis that, as distinct from the more Calvinian interpretation, held to a Christological reading grounded in typology that extended beyond the Christological reading of specifically messianic psalms.[50]

Protestant exegetes of the seventeenth century, for all of the emphasis given to the literal and grammatical meaning of the text by Reformation-era exegesis and by the increasingly text-critical approach to Scripture characteristic of the late sixteenth and seventeenth centuries,

---

45. Henry, *Exposition*, Ps 90 (3:335); cf. Patrick, *Book of Psalms*, 2:164; Hammond, *Paraphrase and Annotations*, 257.

46. Poole, *Annotations*, Ps 90, in loc.

47. Calvin, *Commentary*, Ps 90 (3:460).

48. Hammond, *Paraphrase and Annotations*, 257.

49. Henry, *Exposition*, Ps 90 (3:335).

50. See Kuivenhoven, "Songs of the Son," 21, 41, 43.

retained strong ties with the older tradition of exegesis and its Christological interpretation of large portions of the Old Testament—most notably, the messianic sections of the prophetic writings and of the Psalter. In addition, the seventeenth-century exegete still assumed the relevance and rectitude of the interpretation of Scripture by the comparison or collation of text with text on the principle of the *analogia scripturae*: the one divine purpose underlying the inspired text demanded that the whole give meaning to the parts and that the course and goal of the sacred history be recognized as contributing to the meaning of individual passages. In this view, the literal sense of a text could easily look beyond the limited horizon of its human author's historical situation toward the ultimate horizon of its divine author's infinite wisdom.[51] "The sense of the Scripture," wrote Edward Leigh, "is that which God, the Author of the Scripture in and by the Scriptures gives men to know and understand."[52]

Close attention to the "scope" of a passage, of a book of the Bible, and (at an entirely different hermeneutical and theological level) of the entire Scripture was characteristic of sixteenth- and seventeenth-century Reformed exegesis.[53] Particularly in the case of the Psalter, the older exegesis assumed a broad scope, encompassing the range of Christian prayer, praise, and spiritual expression and, therefore, also reflecting the range of God's revelation, both natural and supernatural, both "general" as given by God to the faithful in the world around them and "special" as given by God in his revelation of the promise of salvation and in the fulfillment of salvation in Christ. At the beginning of his introduction to the Psalter, Henry commented:

> We have now before us one of the choicest and most excellent Parts of all the Old Testament: Nay, so much is there in it of CHRIST and his Gospel, as well as of GOD and his Law, that it had been call'd the Abstract, or Summary, of both Testaments.... This Book brings us into the Sanctuary, draws us off from Converse with Men, with the Politicians, Philosophers, or *Disputers of this World*, and directs us into Communion with GOD, by solacing and reposing our Souls in him, lifting up and letting out our Hearts towards him. Thus may we be in the

---

51. Cf. Childs, "*Sensus Literalis*," 86–87, 94–95; with Muller, "Hermeneutic of Promise and Fulfillment"; and Steinmetz, "Superiority of Pre-Critical Exegesis," 31–35.

52. Leigh, *Treatise of Divinity*, I.ix (171).

53. Cf. the discussion in Sheppard, "Between Reformation and Modern Commentary"; with Muller, "William Perkins," 79; and Muller, *PRRD*, 2:206–23.

Mount with GOD; and we understand not our selves, if we say not, *It is good to be here.*[54]

This understanding of the Psalter was characteristic of the older exegetical tradition—its presence is a sign of the clear continuity between the exegesis of the reformers and that of their successors in the era of orthodoxy, and its passing is one of the historical markers of the shift from so-called "pre-critical" to "historical-critical" exegesis. Luther began his "Preface to the Psalter" with the comment that "many of the holy fathers prized and praised the Psalter above all the other books of the Scripture" and that Christians in his own time ought similarly to give "praise and thanks."[55] He then meditates on the neglect of the Psalter for the sake of other devotional writings—notably, lives of the saints and books of Christian example. This, he continues, is just a bit ironic, inasmuch as the Psalter is the finest book of examples and saints' lives ever collected:

> For here we find not only what one or two saints have done, but what he has done who is the very head of all saints. We also find what all the saints still do, such as the attitude they take toward God, toward friends and enemies, the way they conduct themselves amid all dangers and sufferings. Beyond that, there are contained here all sorts of divine and wholesome teachings and commandments.[56]

Luther's point assumes the identification of the Psalter as the mirror of the Christian soul, the prayers, songs, praises, and laments of the daily life of the people of God.

Similarly, in the preface to his commentary on the Psalms, Calvin identified the book as a whole as "an anatomy of all the parts of the soul" in which "all the griefs, sorrows, fears, doubts, hopes, cares, [and] perplexities" are portrayed. The Psalter, then, is unlike other books of Scripture that declare God's commandments—here the "prophets themselves ... are exhibited to us as speaking to God, and laying open all their inmost thoughts and affections."[57] Nowhere else in Scripture is the care of God for his church so fully revealed, and, accordingly, nowhere else is the "right manner of praising God" set forth; nowhere else is God's word so "replete with all the precepts which serve to frame our life to every part of

---

54. Henry, *Exposition*, Psalms, preface, 3:137.
55. Luther, "Preface to the Psalter" (1545), in *LW*, 35:253.
56. Luther, "Preface to the Psalter" (1545), in *LW*, 35:254.
57. Calvin, *Commentary*, author's preface, 1:xxxvii; and see De Jong, "Anatomy."

holiness, piety, and righteousness," so clear in teaching believers to bear their cross and submit themselves "entirely to God."[58] A decade after the publication of Calvin's commentary, his characterization was echoed in Matthew Parker's publication of the metrical Psalter: "All holye Scripture is certenly the teacher of all vertue and of the true faith: but the booke of the Psalmes doth expresse afer a certaine manner the verye state and condition of the soule," reflecting "all of [the] affections and passions, whereto [the] soule is inclined," and designed to instruct the believer how to "amend himselfe & how to geve God due thanks."[59]

Later Reformed exegetes maintained this sense of personal piety and folded it more fully into an objective, theological understanding of the scope of the Psalter. Jean Diodati referred to the Psalter as "an epitome of all Scripture, reduced into practise."[60] David Dickson also speaks broadly of the Psalter: "the scope of this book," he writes, is "not only to teach us the grounds of divinity for our information, but also to direct us how to apply saving doctrines practically to ourselves."[61] Similarly, in Henry Hammond's view, a proper reading of the Psalter should bring "home of every Mans Understanding . . . and intire Body of necessary *Theology*, in directions of Life, Fundamentals of Faith, and Incentives and Helps of Devotion, and copious and various Matter of divine Meditation."[62]

Henry, much like Diodati, understood the "scope" of the entire Psalter as an "abstract, or summary, of both Testaments."[63] As such, elaborating the point, the "scope" of the Psalter is

> (1.) To assist the *Exercises of Natural Religion*, and to kindle in the Souls of Men those devout Affections which we owe to GOD as our Creator, Owner, Ruler, and Benefactor. . . . Other parts of Scripture shew that God is infinitely above Man, and his Sovereign LORD; but this shews us, that notwithstanding that, He may be convers'd with by us sinful Worms of the Earth; and there are Ways, in which . . . we may keep up Communion with Him in all the various Conditions of Human Life. (2.) To advance the *Excellencies of Reveal'd Religion*, and in the most

---

58. Calvin, *Commentary*, author's preface, 1:xxxviii. Note Selderhuis, *Calvin's Theology of the Psalms*, which demonstrates that a full theology directly related to piety and the Christian life can be elicited from Calvin's commentary.

59. *Whole Psalter*, C.ii verso.

60. Diodati, *Annotations*, Psalms, argument, in loc.

61. Dickson, *Brief Explication*, 1:1.

62. Hammond, *Paraphrase and Annotations*, preface, §18, (a)r.

63. Cf. Henry, *Exposition*, Psalms, preface (3:139–40).

pleasing powerful manner to recommend it to the World. . . . The Word and Law of GOD, those parts of it which are moral and of perpetual Obligation, are here all along *magnify'd* and *made honourable*; nowhere more: And CHRIST, the Crown and Centre of *Revealed Religion* . . . is here clearly spoken of in Type and Prophecy, his *Sufferings* and the *Glory that should follow*, and the Kingdom that he should set up in the World, in which GOD's Covenant with *David*, concerning his Kingdom, was to have its accomplishment.[64]

Given this scope, the entire Psalter can be called "a Mirror or Looking-Glass of Pious and Devout Affection."[65]

THE CHRISTOLOGICAL INTERPRETATION OF THE PSALTER

There was much debate among early-modern Protestants concerning the extent of the Trinitarian and Christological content of the Psalter, given Calvin's relative hesitance to extend beyond a literal reading of the text and the Lutheran accusation of a "Judaizing" tendency in his interpretations.[66] Although Calvin's interpretations were defended at length in the early orthodox era by David Pareus,[67] they did not serve as a significant indicator of Reformed confessional development, if only because they did not provide the norm for Reformed exegesis of the Psalter.[68] By the time of Henry's exposition, the Reformed exegetical tradition had moved past the stage of defense against Lutheran complaints, not only because of the temporal distance from the original controversy but also because of a fairly settled understanding of the book's scope and, in some contrast to Calvin, a more consistent Christological reading of the messianic psalms and of the promises of future redemption found in the Psalter. There remained, however, differences among Reformed writers concerning the patterns of Christological interpretation of particular psalms, with some, like Hammond, stressing a literal-prophetic, David–Christ

---

64. Henry, *Exposition*, Psalms, preface, 3:137–38.
65. Henry, *Exposition*, Ps 42, preface, 3:227.
66. See Pak, *Judaizing Calvin*; also see Kuivenhoven, "Songs of the Son."
67. Pareus, *Libri duo*; cf. Pak, *Judaizing Calvin*, 104–24; with Merkle, *Defending the Trinity*, 118–48.
68. Contra Pak, *Judaizing Calvin*, 125–27; see Kuivenhoven, "Songs of the Son," on Musculus, Ainsworth, Rivetus, and others.

pattern with both David and Christ as subjects.[69] Ames had argued similarly that the Jews understood the psalms as merely referencing David, whereas the church fathers read them as merely referencing Christ, while the most "learned of our theologians" interpret them as partly referencing David but properly and principally referencing Christ.[70] Others, like Ainsworth, held to a more distinctly Christological reading based on the David–Christ parallel, with Christ, prophetically, as the primary subject—sometimes understood as David prophesying concerning Christ, other times understood as Christ speaking through David.[71] Still others, like Dickson, adopted a more directly Christological reading of the text's assumed literal sense, with Christ as subject of the text.[72]

Henry was heir to this broader understanding of the scope of the Psalter and to the several patterns of Christological interpretation. The basic David–Christ model can also, as frequently is the case in Henry's work, take the form of a David–believer–Christ typology that rests on the literal sense but echoes the full *quadriga*. A few examples will suffice. The kingdom of Christ is a major theme that Henry sees as uniting the entire Psalter. The Christological reference in Ps 1 is confined to the final pronouncement of blessing on the righteous and doom on the ungodly in Christ's second coming. The theme is more explicit in the second psalm. According to Henry, the primary referent of Ps 2 is Christ, "under the Type of David's Kingdom,"[73] with the result that the type fades into the background, and, at the very beginning of the psalm, the rage of the heathen and the counsel of rulers against the Lord are references to the "very great struggle about the Kingdom of CHRIST" between heaven and hell for rulership of the earth.[74] So also, at verse 7, "Thou art my son, this day have I begotten thee," Henry comments that the kingdom of the Messiah "was not a sudden resolve . . . but the Result of the Counsels of divine Wisdom" determined before all worlds: the "Precept or Statute"

69. E.g., Hammond, *Paraphrase and Annotations*, Pss 2, 22 (5–12, 69–74).
70. Ames, *Lectiones*, 16.
71. Ainsworth, *Annotations*, Pss 8, 16, in loc.
72. Dickson, *Brief Explication*, Ps 2:7–8 (1:10); *Dutch Annotations*, Ps 2:7, in loc.; Poole, *Annotations*, Ps 2:7, in loc.; and Trapp, *Commentary*, Ps 2:7 (567), refer the verse to Christ's eternal generation.
73. Cf. *English Annotations*, Ps 2:1, identifying the David–Christ typology but maintaining both David and Christ as subjects of the psalm, David the more immediate fulfillment, Christ the more remote.
74. Ainsworth, *Annotations*, Ps 2 (A4r–B2r); cf. Henry, *Exposition*, Ps 2, argument and vv. 1–6 (3:140–41).

mentioned in the text is the eternal covenant between the Father and the Son, here "represented by the Covenant of Royalty made with *David* and his Seed."[75] Henry here echoes the reading of the psalm by Dickson and, in effect, sets aside both Ainsworth's more Calvinian interpretation, according to which David prophesies of Christ, and Hammond's reading, in which David and Christ are both subjects of the psalm.[76] At the conclusion of the Psalter, Henry reiterates, is the kingdom typology in eschatological vision, where the victory and vindication of Israel ultimately refer "to CHRIST's Victories, by the Power of his Gospel and Grace over Spiritual Enemies, in which all Believers are more than Conquerors."[77]

A David–believer–Christ typology, where David both represents the believer in the midst of earthly struggles and ultimately points the believer to Christ, is arguably Henry's preferred approach in the exposition of individual psalms. This is clearly seen in Pss 18 and 20. Here the spiritual life of the type, David, receives the emphasis of interpretation. Psalm 18, for Henry, is a Davidic account of distress and deliverance. Even verses 4–7, where the speaker is encompassed by the "sorrows" of death and hell and prays to God for deliverance, after which the deliverance begins with an earthquake of anger against the enemies of God, are identified solely with reference to David in the main exposition. Only at the very end of his exposition of the passage does Henry engage the typological reading and declare that "our Salvation" and "great Deliverance" are accomplished by "the son of David." At that point, by way of conclusion, Henry returns to the images of verses 4–7: "In singing this, we must *triumph* in GOD, and *trust* in him: And we may apply it to CHRIST the Son of *David*; the *Sorrows of Death* surrounded him, in his Distress he pray'd, Heb. v:7. GOD made the Earth to shake and tremble, and the Rocks to rend, and brought him out in his Resurrection *into a large place*; because he *delighted* in him, and in his Undertaking."[78] Similarly, Ps 20 is identified as a prayer of David, and the first portion of Henry's exposition of the text references only David as the speaker. Then, in the second portion of the exposition, the prayer of David is described as the prayer

---

75. Henry, *Exposition*, Ps 2:7–9 (3:142).

76. Cf. Dickson, *Brief Explication*, Ps 2:7–8 (1:10); with Hammond, *Paraphrase and Annotations*, Ps 2:7 (6). *English Annotations*, Ps 2:7, in loc.; *Dutch Annotations*, Ps 2:7, in loc.; Poole, *Annotations*, Ps 2:7, in loc.; and Trapp, *Commentary*, Ps 2:7 (567), refer the verse to Christ's eternal generation.

77. Henry, *Exposition*, Ps 149 (3:455); cf. Ps 1 (3:130).

78. Henry, *Exposition*, Ps 18:1–19 (3:172).

or hymn of present-day believers, and finally, as in the exposition of Ps 18, Henry concludes with an application by way of the gathered believers singing the psalm: "But we may look farther; these Prayers for *David* are Prophesies concerning CHRIST."[79]

VARIED GENRES: HENRY'S EXEGESIS OF PENITENTIAL, DOCTRINAL, AND IMPRECATORY PSALMS

Matthew Henry was also a product of an exegetical tradition that, long before Gunkel, recognized the varied genres or forms of the prayers and hymns in the Psalter—which led to specific applications to the lives of believers, not all of which have a direct Christological interpretation. Thus, the English translation of Beza's paraphrase of the Psalter divided the Psalms into categories of doctrine, prophecy, prayer, consolation, thanksgiving, and victory, as well as the mixed categories of "thanksgiving and prophesie" or "doctrine and thanksgiving."[80] The *English Annotations* note that "the Argument of many Psalms, is mixt and various, so that the same Psalm may be reduced to several titles, according to its several parts, as *Petitory, Deprecatory, Imprecatory, Eucharistical, &* the like."[81] The English editor-translator of Diodati's *Annotations* distinguished the Psalms into psalms of instruction and psalms of devotion, in the former category identifying doctrinal, prophetical, historical, consolatory, and exhortatory psalms; in the latter category identifying psalms of invocation and psalms of praise, each grouping being distinguished into a series of subcategories.[82]

This understanding relates directly to Henry's sense of the scope of the Psalter, stated at the outset of the commentary: "This Book brings us into the Sanctuary ... and directs us into Communion with GOD." The Psalter addresses foundational issues of the knowledge of God and self

---

79. Henry, *Exposition*, Ps 20:1–5 (3:177).

80. Beza, *Psalmes of David*, note sig. a7r, where the chart is given and only Beza's name is mentioned as providing the "direction." The table does not appear in Beza's *Psalmorum Davidis*.

81. *English Annotations*, Psalms, preface.

82. Diodati, *Annotations*, analysis, prefaced to the exposition. The Diodati classification is as elaborate as Gunkel's hymns of praise and of thanksgiving, individual and corporate prayers of lament, psalms of trust, and royal psalms, with various subdivisions and mixed forms. Note Gunkel, *Psalms*; and cf. Bellinger, "Psalms and the Question of Genre," 313–15.

and does so, not after the manner of technical theology or disputation, but by direct address to the soul with a series of counsels and directives concerning the whole of religious life as doctrine, praise, petition, exhortation, consolation, thanksgiving, and other expressions of faith and obedience.[83]

Psalm 38 is one of the seven traditional "penitential psalms" and is identified as such in Diodati's commentary (as a subcategory of invocation) and in the *English Annotations*. Beza's *Psalms Paraphrased* does not acknowledge the penitential category and places Ps 38 in a group designated simply as prayers. Henry specifically notes that "this is one of the *Penitential Psalms*."[84] Its purpose, as indicated in the superscription, is "Remembrance," specifically the remembrance of times of affliction in order to awaken the conscience, to "set our Sins in order before us for our Humiliation," and through that to lead to hope for divine deliverance, peace, and salvation.[85] Henry does not interpret the psalm as one that is primarily Christological. Rather, he follows a David–believer–Christ typology, with David as the primary subject of the psalm: "Herein *David* in his Sufferings was a Type of CHRIST, who being in his Agony, cryed out, *My Soul is exceeding Sorrowful*."[86] The typology is what brings comfort to believers in their sufferings: given that David's sufferings are to be understood in the light of Christ's, Christians "have not Reason to complain, as long as he preserves to us the Use of our Reason, and the Peace of our Consciences."[87] Henry concludes that, if like David, any Christian is "afflicted, let him pray, let him thus plead, let him thus hope in singing this *Psalm*."[88]

The categorizations of psalms found in Beza's and Diodati's expositions both identify Ps 90 as a doctrinal psalm. In the former, it is described as a psalm concerned with "doctrine onelie," in the latter as an "invocatory or precatory" psalm concerned with "the vanity and shortness of this life" and, therefore, as one of a subset of "supplicatory or petitory" psalms. The *English Annotations* identify the psalm as one of an

---

83. Cf. Joo, "Communion with God," 97–109.

84. Henry, *Exposition*, Ps 38, preface (3:217).

85. Henry, *Exposition*, Ps 38 (3:218).

86. Henry, *Exposition*, Ps 38:8, similarly, vv. 11, 13–14, 19 (3:218–19); cf. Poole, *Annotations*, Ps 38:13, in loc.; Dickson, *Brief Explication*, Ps 38 (254–61), surprisingly, does not draw a Christological conclusion.

87. Henry, *Exposition*, Ps 38:8 (3:218).

88. Henry, *Exposition*, Ps 38, ad fin. (3:220).

extended list of penitential psalms.[89] Henry's reading of Ps 90, in accord with its superscription as a prayer of Moses, places it in the "invocatory or precatory" category and offers a significant example of the intersection of his more technical sense of authorship and historical context with his view of the scope of the Psalter and its homiletical, pastoral implications. Moses, Henry notes, had also written a song of praise following the deliverance of Israel at the Red Sea (Exod 15) and a valedictory song of instruction prior to the Israelite entrance into Canaan (Deut 32). By contrast, Ps 90 is a prayer for a repentant Israel that reflects her wandering in the wilderness.[90]

Of interest to Henry was the juxtaposition of Ps 89 with Ps 90, inasmuch as the former "was suppos'd to be penn'd as late as the Captivity in Babylon" and the latter "was penn'd as early as the Deliverance out of Egypt."[91] This juxtaposition, together with the assumption that Ps 90 reflects the situation recounted in Num 14, leads Henry to the focus of his interpretation and his pastoral point: as the first verses of the psalm teach, the Lord has been the "dwelling-place" of Israel "in all generations," but he is also the God who both "turnest man to destruction" and calls on his people to "return." At the time of Moses's psalm, Israel had been in bondage in Egypt, was murmuring against God, and was threatened with forty years of wandering in the wilderness before they might return to the land of the patriarchs. In the midst of these troubles, the psalm reminds Israel that it is God who is their true refuge and habitation. Even so, there is a lesson to Christians: "True Believers are *at home* in God, and that's their Comfort, in reference to all the Toils and Tosses they meet with in this World. In him we may repose and shelter ourselves, as in our Dwelling-Place."[92]

Henry's readings also occupy a particular place in the rather varied early-modern Reformed trajectory of the interpretation and use of imprecatory psalms, a place defined by his general use of a prophetic, type–antitype structure of interpretation, which is particularly evident in his

---

89. The *English Annotations*, Psalms, preface, indicates the seven traditional penitentials and then comments, "To these, may be added, for remission of sins, increase of Grace, and deliverance from sicknesse, and other prevailing calamities," Pss 25, 39, 88, and 90.

90. Henry, *Exposition*, Ps 90 (3:335); similarly, Poole, *Annotations*, Ps 90, in loc.

91. Henry, *Exposition*, Ps 90 (3:335). Henry was aware of the possible dating of Ps 89 to the time of Solomon and the alternative dating to the captivity: see *Exposition*, Ps 89 (3:330); cf. Poole, *Annotations*, Ps 89, in loc.

92. Henry, *Exposition*, Ps 90 (3:335).

interpretation of Ps 35. Calvin had warned that the imprecatory psalms should not be understood as advocating "revenge for private injuries" and that their use rested on both the integrity of the divine righteousness and the innocence of the one praying for vindication.[93] He held that Ps 35 was primarily about David in his struggles with Saul but that it extended more broadly by David himself to spiritual enemies of the faithful.[94] Diodati's editor commented that these psalms are prayers "against *Gods*, and the *Churches*, and our *souls* incorrigible and irreconcileable enemies, which are rather predictory of their ruine by the spirit of *prophesie*, then personal execrations from the private spirit of *bitterness* and *revenge*."[95] Even more than Diodati, Dickson maintained that the psalm primarily concerns Christ as "set forth under the shadow of *Davids* context with his irreconcileable enemies."[96] The *English Annotations* offer an extended comment at verse 4, "Let them be confounded and put to shame that seek after my soul," noting that the verse introduces a section of the psalm containing "divers Imprecations." The annotator, Meric Casaubon, argued that David, given his status, was a special case and that he had reason to go beyond the norm of conduct and pray for revenge against his personal enemies—whereas "good and godly men" in general ought to follow a "mystical, or anagogical sense" and understand the imprecations as directed against "the grand and Original enemy to mankind," namely, the devil.[97] Hammond, who often provided Henry with a model of interpretation, reads the imprecations as "no more than so many *testimonies*" to the promises of God for the deliverance of his people.[98]

Henry's initial argument, or summary, of Ps 35 indicates that "David in this Psalm appeals to the Righteous Judge of Heaven and Earth, against his Enemies that hated, and persecuted him."[99] Unlike Diodati and Dickson, Henry assumes that the psalm is primarily a prayer of David and,

93. Calvin, *Commentary*, Ps 28:4 (1:469); cf. Calvin, *Commentary*, Ps 35:4 (1:579); Ps 59:1 (2:381); Ps 69:22 (3:67); similarly, Poole *Annotations*, Ps 34:4, in loc.

94. Calvin, *Commentary*, Ps 34, argument and vv. 1, 4 (1:574-75, 578-79); similarly, Ames, *Lectiones*, Ps 35 (180-84).

95. Diodati, *Annotations*, Psalms, analysis (Rr3v).

96. Dickson, *Brief Explication*, Ps 34, argument (227).

97. *English Annotations*, Ps 35:4, in loc.; and Ps 143:3, in loc.; and see *English Annotations*, Psalms, preface, "As for Imprecatory Psalms, which are many, and how to be read, and applyed, see upon Psal. 35:4," which in turn refers the reader to Ps 143:3. For identification of the various annotators, see Muller, "'Entire Commentary,'" 20-26.

98. Hammond, *Paraphrase and Annotations*, Ps 35:4 (107).

99. Henry, *Exposition*, Ps 35 (3:207).

echoing Calvin, indicates that the enemies against whom David prays are chiefly "Saul and his Party." The psalm begins with a complaint concerning injuries done to David—his enemies fought against him, persecuted him, falsely accused him, and abused him. David then "plead his own Innocency" and prays for divine comfort and deliverance. The psalm also contains prophecy of the destruction of David's enemies. Here, like most of his predecessors in the interpretation of imprecatory psalms, Henry argues that David's prayer for the destruction of his enemies did not arise out of "Malice or Revenge" but from the just cause of God against enemies of salvation—specifically that the enemies of true religion might either be made to repent or, failing that, be defeated. The imprecations, moreover, given the David-Christ typology, are predictive of "the doom of the Enemies of CHRIST and his Kingdom."[100]

Henry, however, presses the point of application to believers further than his various predecessors. Rather than postpone his application to the end of the psalm, Henry inserts it at the end of his initial argument, prior to interpreting the first verses of the psalm. Like his predecessors, Henry rules out personal vengeance as a motive for imprecatory prayer, but he invokes the teaching of Christ more directly than they do, without initially invoking the typology: "In singing this *Psalm*, and praying over it, we must take heed of applying it to any little peevish Quarrels and Enmities of our own, and of expressing by it any uncharitable revengeful Resentments of Injuries done to us, for CHRIST has taught us to forgive our Enemies, and not to pray against them, but to pray for them, as he did."[101] Christ's teaching directs the believer toward assurance. On the condition that his conscience inwardly testifies to his innocence, the psalm promises "that GOD will, in his own way and time, right us, and, in the mean time support us."[102] Henry's second application of the psalm's teaching on the David-believer-Christ typology explains how the psalm, which Henry maintained was primarily about David's struggles, relates directly to the church and its members:

> We ought to apply it to the publick Enemies of CHRIST and his Kingdom, typified by David and his Kingdom, to resent the Indignities done to CHRIST's Honour, to pray to GOD to plead the just and injur'd Cause of Christianity, and serious Godliness, and to believe that GOD will, in due time, glorify his own Name

100. Henry, *Exposition*, Ps 35 (3:208).
101. Henry, *Exposition*, Ps 35 (3:207).
102. Henry, *Exposition*, Ps 35 (3:207).

in the Ruin of all the irreconcilable Enemies of his church; that will not repent to give him Glory.[103]

CONCLUSIONS

Matthew Henry's *Exposition of the Old and New Testaments* remains the preeminent early-modern commentary from the pen of an English Protestant. Other major expositions like John Mayer's commentaries, the *English Annotations*, and John Trapp's *Commentary* have faded from memory, whereas Henry's work remains available in various forms. This continued interest in Henry's commentary is grounded in the characteristics that rendered it a significant work in its own time. It seamlessly combines exegetical, doctrinal, and pastoral elements by situating itself in the tradition of Reformed and Puritan commentaries, recognizing issues of authorship, identifying some of the text-critical issues addressed in the more technical commentaries of the seventeenth century, offering a theologically unified understanding of the scope of Scripture and a balanced approach to the issue of faith and reason, and providing a theological understanding of the text both in whole and in part oriented toward homiletical instruction, corporate use, and personal meditation.

Henry's exposition of the Psalter is eminently illustrative of these characteristics. Following the long tradition of commentators on the Psalms, he understood the Psalter as a whole as a summation of the message of both Testaments, instructing in law and gospel, in natural and supernatural theology, and addressing all the needs of piety, both personal and corporate. The Psalter's address to the needs of piety is identified from a more technical perspective in Henry's reception of extant understandings of the various genres of psalm, as illustrated here in his treatment of penitential, doctrinal, and imprecatory psalms.

Henry's interpretation of the Psalms, moreover, stands in the line of Reformation and post-Reformation Reformed discourse concerning the question of Christological interpretation and the way in which that interpretation serves to represent the Psalter as an "Abstract, or Summary, of both Testaments." Henry distanced himself both from a minimalistic Christological reading like Calvin's and from a highly Christologized interpretation like Dickson's. Henry's Christological interpretations are often concentrated in his comments at the end of pericopes or at the

---

103. Henry, *Exposition*, Ps 35 (3:207–8).

conclusion of a psalm, leaving the body of the text as the prayer or meditation of David or of one of the other writers. He employed the David–Christ or David–believer–Christ typologies not so much to Christologize the Psalter as to identify it as a summation of the whole of Scripture and to reveal the text in its several genres as embracing the spiritual and doctrinal concerns of all members of Christ's kingdom through the presentation of the concerns of David and his kingdom. Henry's repeated conclusion—which comprised variants of the admonition, "In singing this and praying it over, we should have our hearts filled..."—built on his typological reading and directed the piety and instruction of the Psalter toward the whole people of God.

BIBLIOGRAPHY

Ainsworth, Henry. *Annotations upon the Book of Psalms. Wherein the Hebrew Words and Sentences Are Compared with, and Explained by the Ancient Greek and Chaldee Versions; but Chiefly by Conference with the Holy Scriptures*. 2nd ed. N.p.: n.p., 1617.

Alexander, Philip S. "Matthew Henry: An Annotated Bibliography." In *Matthew Henry: The Bible, Prayer, and Piety; A Tercentenary Celebration*, edited by Matthew A. Collins and Paul Middleton, 245–75. London: T&T Clark, 2019.

Ames, William. *Lectiones in omnes Psalmos Davidis: in quibus per analysim, &c, ubi opus est, per quaestiones sensus dilucide ac succincte enodatur, nec non documenta ubivis eliciuntur, & ad usus suos dextre applicantur*. London: J. D. for Andreas Kembe & Johannes Hardesty, 1647.

Annotations upon All the Books of the Old and New Testament This Third, Above the First and Second, Edition So Enlarged, as They Make an Entire Commentary on the Sacred Scripture: the Like Never Before Published in English. Wherein the Text Is Explained, Doubts Resolved, Scriptures Parallel'd, and Various Readings Observed; by the Labour of Certain Learned Divines Thereunto Appointed, and Therein Employed, as Is Expressed in the Preface. 2 vols. London: Evan Tyler, 1657.

Bellinger, William H., Jr. "Psalms and the Question of Genre." In *The Oxford Handbook of the Psalms*, edited by William P. Brown, 313–25. Oxford: Oxford University Press, 2014.

Beza, Theodore. *The Psalmes of David, Truly Opened and Explained by Paraphrasis... to the Which Is Added a Briefe Table, Shewing Whereunto Every Psalme Is Particularly to Be Applied, according to the Direction of M. Beza and Tremellius*. London: Henrie Denham, 1581.

———. *Psalmorum Davidis et aliorum Prophetarum libri quinque. Argumentis et latina paraphrasi illustrati, ac etiam vario carminum genere latine expressi Theodoro Beza Vezelio auctore*. Geneva: n.p., 1579.

Burden, Mark. *A Biographical Dictionary of Tutors at the Dissenters' Private Academies, 1660–1729*. London: Dr. Williams's Centre for Dissenting Studies, 2013.

Calvin, John. *Commentary on the Book of Psalms*. Translated by James Anderson. 4 vols. Edinburgh: Calvin Translation Society, 1845–49.

Campbell, Iain D. "Matthew Henry on the Aim of Exposition." *Banner of Truth* 383 (Aug./Sep. 1995) 23–27.

Childs, Brevard S. "The *Sensus Literalis* of Scripture: An Ancient and Modern Problem." In *Beiträge zur alttestamentlichen Theologie: Festschrift für Walther Zimmerli zum 70. Geburtstag*, edited by Herbert Donner, Robert Hanhart, and Rudolf Smend, 80–93. Göttingen: Vandenhoeck & Ruprecht, 1977.

Collins, Matthew A., and Paul Middleton, eds. *Matthew Henry: The Bible, Prayer, and Piety; A Tercentenary Celebration*. London: T&T Clark, 2019.

De Jong, James A. "An Anatomy of All Parts of the Soul: Insights into Calvin's Spirituality from His Psalms Commentary." In *Calvinus Sacrae Scripturae Professor: Calvin as Confessor of Holy Scripture*, edited by Wilhelm H. Neuser, 1–14. Grand Rapids: Eerdmans, 1994.

Dickson, David. *A Brief Explication of the . . . Psalms*. 3 vols. London: T. M. for Ralph Smith and Thomas Johnson, 1653–55.

Diodati, Jean. *Pious and Learned Annotations upon the Holy Bible, Plainly Expounding the Most Difficult Places Thereof*. 4th ed. London: T. Rycroft for Nicholas Fussell, 1664.

The Dutch Annotations upon the Whole Bible: Or, All the Holy Canonical Scriptures of the Old and New Testament . . . as . . . Appointed by the Synod of Dort, 1618, and Published by Authority, 1637. Translated by Theodore Haak. 2 vols. London: Henry Hills, 1657.

Evans, John. "Advertisement." In *Exposition of All the Books of the Old and New Testament*, by Matthew Henry, 5:viii. 3rd ed. London: for J. Clark et al., 1725.

Gataker, Thomas, et al. *Annotations upon All the Books of the Old and New Testament: Wherein the Text Is Explained, Doubts Resolved, Scriptures Parallelled, and Various Readings Observed*. Edited by John Downame. 2 vols. London: J. Legatt and J. Raworth, 1645.

Gunkel, Hermann. *The Psalms: A Form-Critical Introduction*. Translated by Thomas M. Horner. Facet Books Biblical Series 19. Philadelphia: Fortress, 1967.

Hammond, Henry. *A Paraphrase and Annotations upon the Psalms: Briefly Explaining the Difficulties Thereof. Also a Paraphrase and Annotations upon the Ten First Chapters of the Proverbs*. 2nd ed. London: T. Newcomb and M. Flesher, 1683.

Harman, Allan. "The Legacy of Matthew Henry." *Reformed Theological Review* 73 (2014) 181–97.

———. *Matthew Henry: His Life and Influence*. Fearn, Scot.: Christian Focus, 2012.

Henry, Matthew. *Exposition of All the Books of the Old and New Testament*. 6 vols. 3rd ed. London: for J. Clark et al., 1725.

———. *Matthew Henry's Unpublished Sermons on the Covenant of Grace*. Edited by Allan Harman. Fearn, Scot.: Christian Heritage, 2002.

———. *Miscellaneous Works of the Rev. Matthew Henry, V.D.M. Containing in Addition to Those Heretofore Published Numerous Sermons, Now Printed from the Original Mss. An Appendix, on What Christ Is Made to Believers in Forty Real Benefits*. 2 vols. London: Joseph Ogle Robinson, 1833.

———. *A Scripture Catechism, in the Method of the Assemblies*. London: R. J. for T. Parkhurst, 1703.

———. *Select Works of the Late Rev'd. Mr. Matthew Henry, Being a Collection of All His Practical Pieces*. Edinburgh: John Wood, 1776.

———. *The Works of the Late Reverend Mr. Matthew Henry; Being a Complete Collection of All the Discourses, Sermons and Other Tracts, That Were Published by Himself. Together with an Account of His Life, and a Sermon, Preach'd on the Occasion of His Death*. London: for Emanuel Matthews et al., 1726.

Joo, Jong Hun. "Communion with God: Liturgical Resources in the Theology and Practice of Matthew Henry's English Presbyterian Worship." PhD diss., Fuller Theological Seminary, 2010.

Kuivenhoven, Maarten. "Songs of the Son: Exegetical Method, Christology, and Piety in Reformation and Post-Reformation Interpretations of Select Messianic Psalms." PhD diss., Calvin Theological Seminary, 2022.

Leigh, Edward. *A Treatise of Divinity Consisting of Three Bookes: The First of Which Handling the Scripture or Word of God, Treateth of Its Divine Authority, the Canonicall Bookes, the Authenticall Edition, and Severall Versions, the End, Properties, and Interpretation of Scripture: The Second Handling God Sheweth That There Is a God, and What He Is, in His Essence and Several Attributes, and Likewise the Distinction of Persons in the Divine Essence: The Third Handleth the Three Principall Works of God, Decree, Creation and Providence*. London: E. Griffin for William Lee, 1646.

Mayer, John. *A Commentary upon the Whole Old Testament; Consisting of Four Parts, I The Pentateuch, of Five Books of Moses. II The Historicall Part, from Joshua to Esther. III Job, Psalms, Proverbs, Ecclesiastes, and Solomons Song. IV All the Prophets, both Great and Small*. 4 vols. London: R. L. and R. I., 1654.

Merkle, Benjamin R. *Defending the Trinity in the Reformed Palatinate: The Elohistae*. Oxford Theology and Religion Monographs. New York: Oxford University Press, 2015.

Muller, Richard A. "'An Entire Commentary . . . the Like Never Before Published in English': Annotating the Scriptures in the Era of the Westminster Assembly." In *Scripture and Worship: Biblical Interpretation and the Directory for Public Worship*, edited by Richard A. Muller and Rowland S. Ward, 11–29. Phillipsburg, NJ: P&R, 2007.

———. "The Hermeneutic of Promise and Fulfillment in Calvin's Exegesis of the Old Testament Prophecies of the Kingdom." In *The Bible in the Sixteenth Century*, edited by David C. Steinmetz, 68–82. Duke Monographs in Medieval and Renaissance Studies. Durham, NC: Duke University Press, 1990.

———. "William Perkins and the Protestant Exegetical Tradition: Interpretation, Style and Method in the Commentary on Hebrews 11." In *A Cloud of Faithful Witnesses: Commentary on Hebrews 11*, by William Perkins, 71–94. Edited by Gerald T. Sheppard. Pilgrim Classic Commentaries 3. New York: Pilgrim, 1991.

Murray, David P. "Matthew Henry (1662–1714): The Reasonableness and Pleasantness of Christianity." PhD diss., Free University Amsterdam, 2019.

———. "More Than a Commentator: Matthew Henry the Apologist." *Puritan Reformed Journal* 12 (July 2020) 167–74.

Pak, G. Sujin. *The Judaizing Calvin: Sixteenth-Century Debates over the Messianic Psalms*. Oxford Studies in Historical Theology. New York: Oxford University Press, 2010.

Pareus, David. *Libri duo: I. Calvinus orthodoxus de sacrosancta Trinitate & aeterna Christi divinitate. II. Solida expositio XXXIIX difficilimorum scripturae locorum & oraculorum: & de recta ratione applicandi oracula prophetica ad Christum.*

Oppositi Pseudocalvino iudiazanti nuper a quodam emisso. Neustadt, Germany: Matthaeus Harnisch, 1595.

Patrick, Simon. *The Book of Psalms Paraphras'd; with Arguments to Each Psalm.* 2 vols. London: M. Flesher, 1680.

———. *A Commentary upon the Books of Joshua, Judges and Ruth.* London: for Ri. Chiswell, 1702.

———. *A Commentary upon the Fifth Book of Moses, Called Deuteronomy.* London: for Ri. Chiswell, 1700.

———. *A Commentary upon the First Book of Moses, Called Genesis.* London: for Ri. Chiswell, 1695.

———. *A Commentary upon the Historical Books of the Old Testament, viz. Genesis. Exodus. Leviticus. Numbers. Deuteronomy. Joshua. Judges. Ruth. I. Samuel. II. Samuel. I. Kings. II. Kings. I. Chronicles. II. Chronicles. Ezra. Nehemiah. Esther.* 2 vols. 3rd ed. London: for John Darby, et al., 1727.

Poole, Matthew. *Annotations upon the Holy Bible. Wherein the Sacred Text Is Inserted and Various Readings Annex'd, Together with the Parallel Scriptures. The More Difficult Terms in Each Verse Are Explained. Seeming Contradictions Reconciled. Questions and Doubts Resolved, and the Whole Text Opened.* 2 vols. 3rd ed. London: for Thomas Parkhurst et al., 1686.

Roberts, H. D. *Matthew Henry and His Chapel, 1662–1900.* Liverpool: Liverpool, 1901.

Selderhuis, Herman J. *Calvin's Theology of the Psalms.* Texts and Studies in Reformation and Post-Reformation Thought. Grand Rapids: Baker Academic, 2007.

Sheppard, Gerald T. "Between Reformation and Modern Commentary: The Perception of the Scope of Biblical Books." In *A Commentary on Galatians*, by William Perkins, 42–71. Edited by Gerald T. Sheppard. Pilgrim Classic Commentaries 2. New York: Pilgrim, 1989.

Steinmetz, David C. "The Superiority of Pre-Critical Exegesis." *Theology Today* 37 (Apr. 1980) 27–38.

Trapp, John. *A Commentary or Exposition upon the Books of Ezra, Nehemiah, Esther, Job and Psalms, Wherein the Text Is Explained, Some Controversies Are Discussed, Sundry Cases of Conscience Are Closed, and Many Remarkable Matters Hinted.* London: T. R. and E. M. for Thomas Newberry, 1657.

Tong, William. *An Account of the Life and Death of the Late Reverend Mr. Matthew Henry, Minister of the Gospel at Hackney, Who Died June 22d, 1714, in the 52d Year of His Age. Chiefly Collected Out of His Own Papers.* London: for M. Lawrence, 1716.

Weeks, Stuart. "Matthew Henry's Commentary in Context: Reading Ecclesiastes." In *Matthew Henry: The Bible, Prayer, and Piety; A Tercentenary Celebration*, edited by Matthew A. Collins and Paul Middleton, 83–96. London: T&T Clark, 2019.

The Whole Psalter Translated into English Metre, Which Contayneth an Hundreth and Fifty Psalmes. The First Quinquagene. London: Iohn Daye, 1567.

Williams, John Bickerton. *Memoirs of the Life, Character, and Writings of the Rev. Matthew Henry.* 3rd ed. London: Joseph Ogle Robinson, 1829.

7

Pastoral Care in Reformed Interpretations of Isaiah

Comforting God's People in the Reformation from Isaiah 40–66

JEFFREY A. FISHER

INTRODUCTION

PASTORAL CARE AT THE time of the Reformation took on a shape that substantially differed from that of previous generations. As the reformers challenged and overturned many of the long-standing practices and expectations regarding the sacraments, liturgical elements, and popular spirituality, the means of offering pastoral care also shifted.[1] In particular, those collectively referred to as Reformed (in distinction from the Lutherans, Anabaptists, or Roman Catholics) insisted on the preaching and teaching of Scripture as foundational and instrumental in offering care, consolation, and comfort. Although the actual practices of pastoral care varied among different Reformed groups regarding household visitations, the moral authority of church leaders in carrying out discipline,

---

1. See earlier chapters in this volume, Amy Nelson Burnett, "Pastoral Care in the Swiss Reformation," and Todd R. Hains, "By the Word Alone: Martin Luther's Pastoral Care in His Sermons on the Temptation of Jesus."

caring for the sick and dying, and the function of the Lord's Supper, yet the application of God's word to the individual lives of men and women, boys and girls, for spiritual consolation remained a consistent feature among all the Reformed communities.

This chapter aims to bring together two major themes in Scott Manetsch's scholarly and ministry career: pastoral care and biblical interpretation. In his book *Calvin's Company of Pastors*, Manetsch summarizes that in sixteenth-century Geneva, "the ministry of the Word involved more than the public exposition of Scripture; it also entailed the application of the divine message to the people in every stage of life, from cradle to grave." These reformers produced a variety of "writings that equipped preachers for their pulpit ministries and provided instruction and spiritual comfort for their parishioners."[2] This study explores what several significant leaders in the Reformed tradition preached and taught regarding where a person finds comfort in difficult times. Ultimately, they emphasized that comfort comes from God alone but through particular means. This theme of comfort undoubtedly served a major pastoral purpose, as indicated by the opening question of one of the most enduring Reformed catechisms from the sixteenth century. The Heidelberg Catechism begins with the first and overarching question, "What is your only comfort in life and in death?"[3] Another relatively prominent place from which Reformed pastors expounded on the theme of comfort was the second part of Isaiah, which starts with the refrain, "Comfort, comfort my people, says your God" (40:1).

Throughout the rest of Isaiah, this theme arises again at various points, reminding the people how much God cares for them, especially using two notable analogies: God as a shepherd and God as a mother. The Lord's comfort as analogous to a mother's love appears most prominently in Isa 49:13–15 and 66:12–13. In this second part of Isaiah, from chapter 40 to the very end of chapter 66, the prophet repeatedly communicates the Lord's comfort to his people. These passages provided preachers and teachers with the opportunity to tell their people how to receive that comfort.

---

2. Manetsch, *Calvin's Company of Pastors*, 305–6. No one has shaped my vocational calling as a teacher for the church and a scholar of the history of biblical interpretation more than my doctoral advisor, Scott Manetsch.

3. Cochrane, *Reformed Confessions of the Sixteenth Century*, 305. See also Bierma, *Theology of the Heidelberg Catechism*, 13–21, on the theme of comfort in many Reformation-era documents.

While other documents (treatises, handbooks, catechisms, manuals) provide us with great insight on some of the contemporary practices related to pastoral care, the commentaries reveal the theology behind those practices and the instruction people repeatedly heard from the pulpits. Commentaries on the book of Isaiah in particular serve as a useful source from which to uncover what people in Reformed churches heard regarding how God comforts his people. These specific passages allowed preachers and teachers to express essential elements, applications, and dimensions of that comfort. Several of these Isaiah commentaries are compilations of sermons, sometimes preached over the course of years. Others were published from teachings intended for individuals who would preach on these passages in their own churches. These commentaries capture both the messages heard directly from some preachers and the material used by later preachers who learned it in the classroom or from the published versions.

ISAIAH COMMENTARIES

Several Reformed theologians produced Isaiah commentaries that show how they proclaimed God's comfort for his people.[4] Johannes Oecolampadius (1482–1531), the reformer of Basel, was the first Protestant to produce a Reformation commentary on Isaiah, publishing the work in 1525 based on his lectures from 1523.[5] Not long after Oecolampadius's Isaiah commentary appeared, Ulrich Zwingli (1484–1531) published his annotations on Isaiah in 1529 and a compilation of sermons on Isaiah he preached before his death in 1531.[6] Then, three key leaders in Zurich after Zwingli's death produced commentaries on Isaiah. Konrad Pellikan (1478–1556) published a relatively short commentary on Isaiah in 1534 that often draws from Oecolampadius's longer commentary.[7] Heinrich Bullinger (1504–75) preached a series of 190 sermons on Isaiah that was published as a commentary in 1567.[8] Similarly, Rudolf Gwalther (1519–86) had his 327 weekday homilies on Isaiah published as a commentary

---

4. For an overview of the numerous commentaries published on Isaiah during the Reformation, see Fisher, *Isaiah 1–39*, xlii–xlvii.

5. Oecolampadius, *Iesaiam*.

6. Zwingli, *Jesaja-Erklärungen*, in Z 14:1–412; Zwingli, *Homilien zum Propheten Jesaja*, in Z 15:1–245.

7. Pellikan, *Commentaria Bibliorum*.

8. Bullinger, *Isaias*.

in 1583.[9] In addition to these lengthy preaching commentaries on Isaiah, two additional commentaries in the 1550s provide significant engagement with the biblical text. The Isaiah commentary by John Calvin (1509–64) was published in 1551 based on his lectures in 1549.[10] And the teaching of Wolfgang Musculus (1497–1563) in Bern was published as an Isaiah commentary in 1557.[11] We will now look at the care these reformers expected people to receive when they engaged with such biblical texts on comfort.

COMFORT FOR ALL GOD'S PEOPLE

The opening words of Isa 40, "Comfort, comfort my people, says your God," signaled to Reformed interpreters that much of this portion of Isaiah's book applied not only to the people in Isaiah's time but to the faithful in any time period. When Bullinger began his 111th sermon on Isaiah, which picked up with this passage, he asserted, "I do not believe there exists in the Scriptures any consolatory saying as lengthy and magnificent as this one. Therefore, it will be suitable for all ages, for all persons, and for those in any afflictions, that we may seek from it both instruction and comfort."[12] Like other commentators considered here, he spent time explaining how these words pertained to the people in Isaiah's time, "but not solely, since they are written not only for them; they also pertain to our benefit and are written for us; therefore, they must also be applied to our use, for comfort, I say, and for the admonition of institutions."[13] Similarly, Wolfgang Musculus argued, "Therefore, it seemed good to the Holy Spirit to prepare this kind of comfort for future use, so that soon at the beginning of their coming tribulations, the godly would be encouraged and strengthened against despair by the hope of liberation."[14] Calvin

---

9. Gwalther, *Isaias*.

10. Calvin, *Commentarii in Isaiam Prophetam*, in CO 36–37. An English translation is available as John Calvin, *Commentary on the Book of Isaiah*, in CTS 13–16. An asterisk (*) with a citation of CTS indicates that I have updated or amended that translation to read more smoothly or accurately in contemporary English.

11. Musculus, *Esaiam*.

12. Bullinger, *Isaias*, 189r. In the following sermon, Bullinger also contended, "These words . . . comfort today all who are laboring under various difficulties" (191r).

13. Bullinger, *Isaias*, 189r. Gwalther similarly maintained that the prophet Isaiah and Christ addressed their own time and "at the same time instructed us with the most beneficial precepts and full promises of comfort" (*Isaias*, 242v).

14. Musculus, *Esaiam*, 549. See also Oecolampadius, *Iesaiam*, 210v.

referred to the message of comfort from Isa 40 as "a perpetual doctrine, which must not be restricted to a time period," and a prophecy "of greater importance to us, because it speaks to us directly."[15] Like Zwingli had categorized this passage earlier, Calvin interpreted it anagogically—that is, it both addressed the Jews in their time and especially applied to Christians in his own time.[16]

These reformers identified other passages in Isaiah where the prophet communicates God's comfort for his people in such a way that it is universally applicable across time. In Gwalther's 251st homily on Isaiah, where he preaches on Isa 49, he affirmed that "Isaiah foresaw in the Spirit" the calamities that would come about in Isaiah's day, and "at the same time he begins to present the fruit that was going to flow from him to the Church and individual believers."[17] On that same passage, Bullinger preached that Isaiah's words "greatly and sweetly comfort not merely the afflicted church of God, but each individual Christian in all their temptations and afflictions."[18] Another way the reformers maintained the direct application of these words was to contend that whenever the prophet spoke of Jerusalem or Zion, it was a figure of speech that denotes, or at least encompasses, the church, with some even specifying that it included "each member of the church."[19]

In his exposition of the final chapter of Isaiah, Oecolampadius rejected the view of those who interpreted it as "only pertaining to future glory" and instead asserted that it refers to the time of "the present kingdom of Christ, in which he reigns here over the godly through faith."[20] Calvin further noted that because Isaiah "can neither express the greatness and warmth of the love which God bears toward us, nor satisfy himself with speaking about it, for that reason he mentions and

15. CO 37:3; CTS 15:197. Calvin later called it a "doctrine that is common both to the Jews and to us" (CO 37:3).

16. CO 37:3; CTS 15:197–98. See Z 14:327.

17. Gwalther, *Isaias*, 310v. See also his comments on Isa 52:7–9 (330v).

18. Bullinger, *Isaias*, 246v.

19. Bullinger, *Isaias*, 246r. See also CO 37:5; CTS 15:201; Gwalther, *Isaias*, 422r. Musculus differs from the other interpreters in that he understood Jerusalem to be the physical, geographical Jerusalem where the exiles "would be brought back to dwell . . . happily and securely." He interpreted the phrase "You will be comforted in Jerusalem" to express that "however desolate and forsaken it may become, I will make it so that you will be comforted there" (*Esaiam*, 849).

20. Oecolampadius, *Iesaiam*, 308r. Oecolampadius quoted from Rom 5:1, 8:18, 8:38–39, and 1 Cor 1:4–9.

repeats it frequently."²¹ He even asserts that Isaiah proclaimed these promises of comfort as a "general rule" such that "those statements must not be limited exclusively to a single period."²² Bullinger followed their views, expressing that whenever Isaiah warns "the church that they will be trained through various afflictions, he then attaches the consolation, exhibiting the most abundant promises of God and the benefits that are greatest in every way, by which God established to always support and comfort the church and each of its members."²³ In one of his final homilies, the 324th, Gwalther summarized the reason for the repetition of Isaiah's message: "Since in this world there are infinite troubles and dangers, much comfort is needed for the godly."²⁴ In each of these passages where Isaiah communicates God's comfort for his people, these Reformed interpreters held that the teaching was relevant and directly applicable to their day—and indeed, to all times.

As these preachers and teachers used God's word from Isaiah to convey pastoral care to the people, they frequently referred to the way external circumstances precipitated the need and longing for God's comfort. Especially in the sermons, but also in some of the published lectures, the recurring themes they identified included disruption, division, persecution (both from those who claimed to be part of the church and from those in broader society), fierce wars, heresies, hypocrites in the church, prolonged illnesses, the pursuit of private gain, and, of course, general weariness and despair.²⁵ In his 203rd homily, Gwalther asserted that "we must consider not only what pertained to the Jews at that time, but also that these things serve for our comfort and instruction. For today there are also tyrannical persecutors, and their fates always press upon the Church, which in the meantime Christ protects, preserves, and liberates."²⁶ Bullinger reproached those who seek comfort in "their own flesh, their leisure, and pleasures . . . and live entirely for this world."²⁷

---

21. *CO* 37:446; CTS 16:426.

22. *CO* 37:445; CTS 16:424–25. Gwalther also refers to "a general doctrine that must still be observed today" in his comments on Isa 66:12–13 (*Isaias*, 422r).

23. Bullinger, *Isaias*, 345v.

24. Gwalther, *Isaias*, 422r. In the margin is written, "What he promises the church is applied to every believer."

25. Bullinger, *Isaias*, 246r-v, 343v; *CO* 37:446; CTS 16:426; Gwalther, *Isaias*, 422r; Oecolampadius, *Iesaiam*, 259r; Musculus, *Esaiam*, 549.

26. Gwalther, *Isaias*, 242v.

27. Bullinger, *Isaias*, 246v.

Perhaps because of the themes in the surrounding verses of the Isaiah passages, but also likely due to the realities of their own day, one of the most common ways these reformers applied the message of comfort from Isaiah was in dissuading people from withdrawing from the church. Commenting on 51:22—52:2—which he identified as where Isaiah "now applies the comfort"—Oecolampadius described "the insolence of tyrants, who think they can do anything to the saints, afflicting them for their own pleasure, and trampling over them with their feet, marching like people crossing the streets, without any mercy."[28] This kind of persecution seems to have pressured many to consider leaving, or actually to leave, the church. Calvin, for his part, included multiple references to the apparent smallness of the church. In his introductory remarks on chapter 40, Calvin noted that the prophet encourages "the godly who would live afterwards, or will yet live, even when they will appear to be reduced very low and to be utterly ruined."[29] This sentiment is echoed in his comments on the final chapter of Isaiah, where he exhorted that when we "see the sad and melancholy condition of the Church, let us remember that these promises relate to us no less than to that people."[30]

These preachers and teachers insisted that despite all hardships, one must believe and know that God will provide true and ultimate comfort. To varying degrees and depths, they drew from these passages in Isaiah as well as their own circumstances to illustrate how God conveys comfort to his people. The major themes that emerge from these Reformed theologians' teaching can be collated in this way: God comforts his people through pastors who preach the promises of provision that bring peace and protection. Next, we will consider each of these components of divine comfort in turn.

PASTORS

In many of these commentaries, the first way God provides comfort that the writers identify is through pastors. While the opening words of Isa 40, "Comfort, comfort," are attributed to God, they are addressed to those

---

28. Oecolampadius, *Iesaiam*, 259r. On that same passage, Oecolampadius added that God's people were "exposed to persecutions, despised and trampled by all . . . attacked by the uncircumcised nations and those completely ignorant in the faith, and by those who are polluted, that is, false brothers, heretics," and others (259r).

29. *CO* 37:3; CTS 15:197.

30. *CO* 37:446; CTS 16:426*.

who should communicate this message to his people. These interpreters reasoned that God communicates his comfort through pastors who proclaim and apply the gospel. For example, Musculus observed that the prophet "introduces God himself, crying out to his prophets, commanding them to bring the gospel of comfort to his people."[31] Gwalther asserted that in this passage, "the prophets and ministers are reminded of their duty, which is to comfort the afflicted people of God."[32] He specifically labeled this section of Isa 40 "God gives ministers of the Word," and he paralleled it with Eph 4:11, where Christ gives to the church those who are apostles, prophets, evangelists, pastors, and teachers.[33] He repeated that it is "the ministers of the Word of God, who comfort and admonish us," and that while ministers also bring instruction and correction, "the end of the entire ministry is that people be brought to God and reconciled with him whom they have offended, who is the source of all consolation. Therefore, all corrections must lead to consolation."[34] For these Reformed theologians, God provides comfort to his people through pastors, sometimes calling them ministers, or prophets, or shepherds.

Pastoral language features prominently in their expositions of Isa 40:9–11, where the prophet states that the Sovereign Lord himself "tends his flock like a shepherd." Because the very word "pastor" is derived from the Latin word for shepherd, several commentators made the connection that pastors in the church are to shepherd the people in a way that emulates how God himself shepherds. Musculus even summarized Isa 40:9–11 this way: "All this grace is compared to *pastoral care*. And it encompasses this in two parts: namely, feeding and guiding.... This comparison is both familiar and beautiful, and is greatly suitable for the purpose; it requires not so much laborious explanation as diligent consideration."[35] Not only does this passage show how God "will faithfully fulfill the duty of a good shepherd," but in it we "also have an example to which those who take the title of pastor in the church of Christ should conform."[36] Likewise, Bullinger insisted, "The pastors of the churches are commanded to imitate that supreme shepherd in feeding the sheep and

---

31. Musculus, *Esaiam*, 549.
32. Gwalther, *Isaias*, 242v.
33. Gwalther, *Isaias*, 242v. See also Calvin, CO 37:4; CTS 15:199 on "raising up" men to communicate the message that God cares for his people.
34. Gwalther, *Isaias*, 242v.
35. Musculus, *Esaiam*, 560. Emphasis mine.
36. Musculus, *Esaiam*, 561.

in caring for the weak."³⁷ Gwalther also reiterated that Christ "established the ministry of the gospel and instituted the apostles and their successors for this purpose," namely, that "those whom he deems worthy of such honor should imitate the example of that chief shepherd and tend the flock entrusted to them."³⁸ He particularly applied this text to his own day, calling his people to "leave far behind the fake shepherds who domineer over the flock and lead those who are miserable down paths and alleys for their own advantage."³⁹ Calvin even refers to those whom God sends to his people as "ministers of comfort."⁴⁰ He noted that this passage in Isa 40 not only exhibits "an excellent commendation of the prophetic office that sustains the godly in adversity" but also "warns that the vengeance of God has great severity when faithful teachers are lacking, from whose mouths in the church of God comfort resounds, which raises the down-trodden and restores the exhausted."⁴¹

Several of the commentators drew attention to how Isa 40:9–11 insists that a good shepherd, or pastor, will "not only feed the flock he has, but also take particular care of the weak, like lambs and sheep giving birth."⁴² They observed that in the church, as in any flock of actual sheep, there will be some who are healthy and some who are weak and in need of additional care or feeding.⁴³ They insisted that God's comfort of his people should be exemplified in the ministry of those who are called to be pastors.

PREACHING

These reformers specifically connected the pastor's duty to provide comfort with that of preaching the gospel appropriately. Nearly all of them

37. Bullinger, *Isaias*, 192r. Homily CXII (#112). Bullinger also noted that "this passage is explained more fully by Ezekiel in chapter 34, and John 10, and Luke" (191r).

38. Gwalther, *Isaias*, 248r. Homily #206. Gwalther refers to Jeremiah, Ezekiel, Luke, and John for other passages where God "humbles himself to take on the role and duty of a shepherd" (246v–47r).

39. Gwalther, *Isaias*, 248r.

40. *CO* 37:7; CTS 15:203.

41. *CO* 37:5; CTS 15:200. Calvin reiterated that God's comfort is given and received through ministers sent by God in his comments on Isa 52:7–9 and 59:15 (*CO* 37:247–48, 346–47; CTS 16:100–101, 263).

42. Musculus, *Esaiam*, 561.

43. Musculus, *Esaiam*, 560; *CO* 37:14–15; CTS 15:216; Bullinger, *Isaias*, 191r–v; Gwalther, *Isaias*, 246v.

explained the phrase "speak tenderly," or "to the heart," in Isa 40:2 as essential in caring for the flock. Musculus explained, "We are admonished here about gospel comfort, by which the minds of sinners are to be lifted against despair through the preaching of the gospel, which should be frequent, diligent, and earnest, presented with appropriate words and directed to their hearts."[44] Oecolampadius conveyed that those entrusted with this calling should "teach them gently, not imperiously, not coldly, but fervently, so that the words penetrate to the innermost heart."[45] He reasoned that Isaiah "speaks first to the prophets and priests, that they may fulfill the apostolic duty, and no longer preach the harsh law, but proclaim the comforting gospel. . . . No one comforts unless they preach faith."[46] Bullinger similarly concluded, "Therefore, let all ministers of the churches know that God requires this of them alone: to comfort the captives or the afflicted"; they are expected "to speak kindly, familiarly, and to comfort, so that we may capture a person's soul with our speech and persuasion."[47] Gwalther maintained that in this passage, "God prescribes the manner they ought to employ in comforting the people," specifying from Isaiah's words that ministers should speak "to soothe someone with gentle and friendly words to persuade them . . . and clearly and distinctly in such a way that the message penetrates the hearts."[48] Calvin insisted that "the power of comforting is especially present in the gospel."[49] Preaching the gospel in a compelling way was imperative in offering comfort to God's people.

PROMISES

Central to their preaching of comfort was knowing and trusting the promises of God. Zwingli briefly summarized Isaiah's word to pastors, writing that God "commands those whose duty it is to comfort the weak, to soak and refresh withering consciences with the dew of divine

---

44. Musculus, *Esaiam*, 550.
45. Oecolampadius, *Iesaiam*, 210v.
46. Oecolampadius, *Iesaiam*, 210v.
47. Bullinger, *Isaias*, 189r–v.
48. Gwalther, *Isaias*, 243r. Gwalther noted that this passage taught "how the Word of God, or the Gospel, should be preached." Calvin uses similar language of "soothing" and "friendly" speaking to God's people (*CO* 37:3; CTS 15:197–98).
49. *CO* 37:4–5; CTS 15:199.

promise."⁵⁰ Calvin addressed the need for the godly to "rest firmly on the promises of God," especially in times of affliction, trouble, or doubt.⁵¹ He observed that people "either remain in suspense, or tremble, or utterly fall and even faint. So long as they are oppressed by fear, anxiety, or grief, they scarcely accept any comfort; and therefore they need to be reassured in various ways."⁵² For Calvin, "our unbelief uncovers and exposes itself when we do not rest in the promises of God."⁵³ Gwalther began his 252nd sermon, which includes Isa 49:13–15, with a similar emphasis:

> Although God generously promises his help to the Church and to every believer, yet there remains, even in the elect, a weakness of faith, which is the reason that they tremble at any dangers and somewhat doubt having faith in God, if he does not immediately extend his hand as if from heaven.⁵⁴

Gwalther specifically asserted that Isaiah included his message of "comfort for those who might be disturbed by unexpected adversities or dangers, by which he strengthens the godly against such temptations."⁵⁵

Oecolampadius highlighted two aspects of Isa 66:12–13 where God's comfort is found in his promises. He held that, with the metaphor of children being nurtured and cherished by their mother, Isaiah "gives a double comfort: one from God the Holy Spirit, who is the παράκλητος [paraklētos] comforter and makes us cry out with great confidence, 'Abba Father'; the other is from Jerusalem, the mother of the living, where God comforts us daily with many promises."⁵⁶ Then, he briefly explained how "feeling the sweet breath of the Holy Spirit" and "drinking in the sweetness of the Spirit" provided comfort like a mother holding her child close and nursing her infant. Likewise, he compared the comfort found in the church to how "the cries of children are stopped" when a mother bounces her child on her knees and how mothers "wipe our tears, lighten our labors, and make the yoke sweet with both love itself and the most certain promises."⁵⁷

50. Z 14:327.
51. CO 37:203; CTS 16:28.
52. CO 37:203; CTS 16:28–29.
53. CO 37:204; CTS 16:30*. Calvin also emphasized the necessity of finding comfort in the forward-looking promises of Isa 59:15–19 (CO 37:346–47; CTS 16:262).
54. Gwalther, *Isaias*, 311r.
55. Gwalther, *Isaias*, 311r.
56. Oecolampadius, *Iesaiam*, 308r.
57. Oecolampadius, *Iesaiam*, 308r.

According to Bullinger, the unique addition to the imagery of a mother comforting her child in Isa 66:12 was found in the phrase "in Jerusalem, you will receive comfort."[58] Like many others, he connected Jerusalem with the church and understood the motherly imagery as an indication of the comfort one receives from the church, especially from the "divine word and the Holy Spirit."[59] Bullinger acknowledged that in promising this comfort, "it could also be that the prophet considered when the Lord ... gave the Spirit, the Paraclete, to the disciples" or when Jesus commanded his earliest followers to wait in Jerusalem for the promised Holy Spirit.[60] Gwalther also took this perspective on the nursing infant in 66:12, explaining, "The sense is, 'You will enjoy your mother church, and you will be partakers of all the good things which the Lord has promised her.'"[61] He explained that the comfort crying infants find in their mother's lap and bosom refers to the certain and effective comfort one receives "if they return to the Scriptures of both testaments and apply for themselves the promises by which God has built the church."[62] From each of these passages, Reformed interpreters emphasized that God's comfort requires knowing and trusting in God's promises, especially those related to the church, the word, and the Holy Spirit.

PROVISION

As already indicated in the quotations above, these promises of comfort focus on what God provides for his people. Most commonly, among these Reformed writings, such provision was in the form of salvation and forgiveness. In his 264th homily, Gwalther expressed that the way "the Lord has comforted his people" was through the redemption provided in Christ:

---

58. Bullinger, *Isaias*, 346r. Homily #188. Bullinger observed that 66:12 repeated phrases found in chapter 40 and continued the allegory from chapter 49 (346r).

59. Bullinger, *Isaias*, 345v. Bullinger cited 2 Cor 1.

60. Bullinger, *Isaias*, 346r. Earlier in this sermon, Bullinger asserted that comfort for the church requires the Holy Spirit, whom the Lord calls another comforter (345v).

61. Gwalther, *Isaias*, 422r. This section is labeled "comforts for the church." In his earlier sermon on 40:11, Gwalther had pointed out that God "feeds his Church, not only with the Word of eternal life, but also with his flesh and blood, which he gave for the life of the world, so that he might become for us the bread and drink of life" (246v–47r).

62. Gwalther, *Isaias*, 422r.

God sent His Son, who redeemed us according to the promises given to the fathers; and not only redeemed us, but also revealed himself to the whole world through the preaching of the gospel, so that all the ends of the earth have seen this salvation, of which God is the author.[63]

Oecolampadius identified Isa 49:13–15 as "another comfort . . . proclaimed to the congregation of the church."[64] In contrast to the feeling that God has forgotten them, he paraphrased God as saying, "For no mother loves her offspring with such affection as I love you."[65] He makes the comparison that "whatever a mother does for her children, Christ does for us. A mother fasts so that her child may eat; she stays awake so that he may sleep; she endures poverty so that he may be enriched; she allows herself to be despised so that he may be glorious."[66] Like a mother who will do anything to provide for her child, God will provide even more, especially in Christ's saving work on our behalf. Further, Calvin broadened the application of this metaphor, writing that "all believers, whatever may be their age, are made like children to remind them of their weakness and be assured of the Lord's strength."[67]

Musculus especially emphasized the necessity of God's providence for embracing the comfort God provides. He commented on Isa 40, "We are admonished that all our matters are subject to certain times by the disposition of divine providence. Neither our sad nor joyful affairs are under our control, but they begin and end at their own times, as they are arranged according to the will of God."[68] He later added that "Scripture often uses the metaphor of a shepherd" to depict God's care for the faithful as "displayed in divine providence."[69] Moreover, according to Musculus, the passages that portray God's comfort like "the maternal tenderness toward the child of her womb" develop an analogy that is "the most beautiful and most enlightening example of divine providence."[70] When explaining the

---

63. Gwalther, *Isaias*, 330v. Gwalther quoted from Ps 98 to reinforce the point that this comfort is the Lord's salvation revealed to all the nations.

64. Oecolampadius, *Iesaiam*, 250v.

65. Oecolampadius, *Iesaiam*, 250v.

66. Oecolampadius, *Iesaiam*, 250v.

67. *CO* 37:445; *CTS* 16:425*.

68. Musculus, *Esaiam*, 550.

69. Musculus, *Esaiam*, 560. Multiple times Musculus refers to Jesus as the Good Shepherd (John 10).

70. Musculus, *Esaiam*, 687. See also Bullinger, *Isaias*, 246r.

use of the motherly imagery in the last chapter of Isaiah, he summarized it as "the kind of nourishment that is sweetest and most beneficial to infants," reminding us of the "most indulgent and faithful care" of God.[71] These Reformed pastors communicated that one could find comfort in the knowledge that God provides what his people need.

PEACE

A related and recurring theme among these Reformed writings concerned the comfort that comes from peace of mind, or peace in one's conscience. Musculus highlighted this theme in his comments on Isa 40:1–2, where he expressed that as long as one's sense of God's wrath for sin "endures, there can be no place for comfort."[72] He was particularly concerned with this lack of peace because of false teachings that "obscured and perverted" the assurance a believer could have. He bemoaned that too many people had either trusted in the papacy, with its "horrible distraction and fluctuation of consciences," or relied on "the false security of trusting in works, merits, and contrived satisfactions."[73] He went so far as to claim that we cannot embrace any of God's other promises "unless we are first firmly convinced about the remission of our sins."[74]

This theme more commonly appears in comments on Isa 66:12–13. In one of Bullinger's last sermons on Isaiah, he articulated that the Lord provides "especially the peace of consciences and a tranquil mind in God. . . . But he also grants temporal peace after disturbances and perpetual persecutions."[75] In Zwingli's sermon on this chapter, the mother's comfort for her child reminds us that "if the conscience suffers from many tribulations and pains, the grace of God will heal and comfort it."[76] Gwalther repeated this notion in his sermon on Isa 66:13:

71. Musculus, *Esaiam*, 849. Musculus connected the parable in 66:12–13 with earlier passages in Isa 49 and 60.

72. Musculus, *Esaiam*, 450. See also Oecolampadius, *Iesaiam*, 210v; CO 37:6; CTS 15:201–2.

73. Musculus, *Esaiam*, 451. He specifically identified Masses, indulgences, and other documents as "sordid" ways in which people sought this kind of peace and comfort. Bullinger similarly contrasted Isaiah's positive example of mothers with monks and nuns who "have no testimony in scripture that their voluntary or monastic works please God" (246v).

74. Musculus, *Esaiam*, 451.

75. Bullinger, *Isaias*, 345v. Homily #188.

76. Z 15:226. He stated, "Just as a mother comforts the child at her breasts, so does

> This passage should be diligently observed, as it provides remedy for the most serious temptations that commonly befall us, when our own consciences snarl at us that the promises of Scripture, which have been given to the elect and the Church, do not apply to us, who are unworthy to be called children of the Church. Against these thoughts, this passage can be a shield for us, where the Holy Spirit testifies that the breasts of the Church are also presented to us, so that we may enjoy the comfort with which the Lord has blessed her—even all the way to being satisfied.[77]

These Reformed theologians recognized that God's people need the peace of mind that God provides when we are assured of his grace. The imagery of the mother's comfort in Isaiah conveys that needed reassurance.

PROTECTION

Finally, God comforts his people by protecting them. The two analogies of God guiding like a shepherd and loving like a mother gave these Reformed interpreters the material to explore this theme. Calvin summarized the message of comfort in Isa 40:9–11 with the statement that "God has determined to protect and guard his Church."[78] In Gwalther's 206th sermon, which includes Isa 40:11, he described how God, as a shepherd, "cares for the individual ones, gathering the scattered, carrying the lambs in his bosom, and gently leading the pregnant and those about to give birth, so that they may suffer no harm from haste or violent disturbance."[79] In comparing himself to a shepherd, God comforts his people by reminding them that he will feed his flock, handle them gently, lead them with patience, and watch over them with care.

In a similar way, the analogy of God comforting like a mother includes this sense of protection. Calvin summarized the metaphor as it appears in chapter 49 this way: "The prophet here describes to us the immense care of God by which he ceaselessly watches over our salvation so that we may be certainly persuaded that he is never going to abandon us, even if we are afflicted by great and numerous calamities."[80] Preaching

---

the grace of God comfort the conscience of godly children." On Zwingli's brief comments about God comforting his children like a mother, see also Z 14:408 and Z 15:180.

77. Gwalther, *Isaias*, 422v.
78. *CO* 37:14–15; CTS 15:216.
79. Gwalther, *Isaias*, 246v.
80. *CO* 37:205; CTS 16:31*.

on Isa 66:11–14, Gwalther observed from this analogy how a mother comforts her children in many ways—when nursing or holding them close, or when bouncing them on her knees in delight. He remarked that the prophet Isaiah "persists in the parable and also promises protection, so that we do not succumb to any dangers."[81] Similarly, a mother who comforts her children "soothes them in her lap or on her knees with all kinds of caresses, carefully and diligently ensuring that nothing harmful or bad happens to them."[82] Gwalther then applied this metaphor to the church, "which does not allow her children to wander carelessly, so that they become prey to enemies or wolves, but will gather them to herself and will cherish them, embraced with maternal love."[83] He acknowledged that the comforter is Christ himself but that "the church receives from him whatever it communicates to its children," and because all comfort and help is found in Jesus, "therefore it is necessary for those who wish to benefit from the avenger and Savior to remain in this fellowship."[84] The church is a place of comfort, particularly as she protects her children by preventing them from wandering away and withdrawing from the help that Christ provides.

CONCLUSION

The analogy of a mother comforting her infant contained all the key themes that these Reformed theologians emphasized in their preaching of pastoral care from Isaiah. Many of them commented on the prophet's choice of a mother's love as the analogy rather than a father's love. Calvin noted that while Scripture often refers to God as father, here in Isaiah, "in order to express his [God's] most ardent affection, he preferred to compare himself to a mother."[85] He maintained that a mother's "love for her offspring is so concerned and careful that it surpasses a father's love by a great distance" and referred to motherly affection as "warmer" and "incredible." Representative of a common view, Musculus held that there

---

81. Gwalther, *Isaias*, 422v. Oecolampadius noted that the security and peace the Lord provides do not take the form of earthly riches; rather, "we are enriched with the greatest heavenly abundance—not only safe from our enemies, but also rich with all the spiritual gifts" (Oecolampadius, *Iesaiam*, 308r).

82. Gwalther, *Isaias*, 422v.

83. Gwalther, *Isaias*, 422v.

84. Gwalther, *Isaias*, 422v.

85. *CO* 37:204; CTS 16:30–31*.

exists "a nature divinely bestowed upon us that mothers love their children more tenderly than fathers."[86] Similarly, in his comments on the Isa 49 passage, Gwalther referred to "the nature of things" to explain why God would use this comparison:

> For this affection is innate in mothers by nature, and is birthed itself in childbirth, so that although they may be tormented by the most acute pains, as soon as they feel themselves relieved by childbirth, they no longer remember those because of the greater joy that follows when they see a person brought forth into the light from them. The same affection ensures that mothers are not fatigued by any labor, sleeplessness, or cares, but rather derive pleasure from them, as long as they can take care of the health of their children.[87]

Some of these commentators observed that this kind of motherly care is seen not only among humans but also among "savage and cruel beasts."[88] Musculus further pondered why Isaiah's analogy is not that of a husband being loved or comforted by his wife. He asserted that although "you may find a man who is more intensely loved by his wife than by his mother, however, we frequently and commonly see such a comparison that the power of nature in a mother is stronger than the bond of marriage in a wife."[89] A more helpful insight from Musculus is that when God communicates that he "will take care of you—not in just any way—but as a mother comforts her child," this includes not only what they need in their infancy but also the security she provides as they grow up, as well as the concern she still has for them even when they become adults.[90] While these comments perhaps give us some insight on male perspectives regarding mothers and marriage in the sixteenth century, the point from these preachers and teachers is that God's love and care for his people extends from before birth, all throughout life, and beyond. So, these reformers declare that we should take comfort from this unique analogy of a mother's unceasing care for her child.

Yet they also acknowledged that some mothers may not show this kind of maternal affection, especially based on the phrase "though she

86. Musculus, *Esaiam*, 687. See also Bullinger, *Isaias*, 246r.

87. Gwalther, *Isaias*, 311r.

88. CO 37:204; Gwalther, *Isaias*, 312v.

89. Musculus, *Esaiam*, 849. Musculus asserted, "the maternal affection in a mother is stronger than the law of marriage in a wife."

90. Musculus, *Esaiam*, 849.

may forget" in Isa 49:15. While Oecolampadius merely commented on this implication, Bullinger and Gwalther develop the possibilities further.[91] Bullinger identified several reasons a mother may behave like this:

> It sometimes happens that mothers, driven by hunger or overcome by the fear of disgrace, neglect or even kill their own children.... Experience also testifies that sometimes girls, lacking modesty, either inflict harm on their unborn children or cruelly kill their newborns, without any punishment, no matter how dire.[92]

Noting this stark contrast with honorable mothers, Gwalther considered "the women of prostituted chastity, who through some poison of their own, seek to abort or expose or cruelly slay those born to them."[93] But no one should think this is how God operates. Bullinger reasoned:

> But God, who is incorruptible and most holy, not subject to any affections, yet also most loving toward the human race, can never think of or establish anything cruel against his faithful ones. Indeed, he gave his own Son over to death for his faithful so that they may live through him and not die eternally. Therefore, it is absolutely certain that God can never forget his own, can never forsake his own, but always has mercy on them, always comforts, protects, and governs them.[94]

In Calvin's comments on 66:12, he alluded back to 49:15 and contended that when "the Lord expresses his affection toward us, he compares it to a mother's love which exceeds every other by a great distance."[95] Earlier, when he had explained the comparisons to different kinds of mothers, he concluded that the Lord's "affection towards us far surpasses the love of all mothers in passion and zeal."[96] Musculus not only considered the contrast between the behavior of different mothers but also explored how anyone who fails to live up to their created purpose contrasts with God, who as "the supreme uncreated one, being the creator, cannot fail, as he is perfect."[97] He drew comfort from this thought, stating, "In this I find

---

91. Oecolampadius, *Iesaiam*, 250v.

92. Bullinger, *Isaias*, 246v. Bullinger cites 2 Kgs 6:28–29 and Josephus for examples of this behavior.

93. Gwalther, *Isaias*, 311r.

94. Bullinger, *Isaias*, 246v.

95. *CO* 37:446; *CTS* 16:425*.

96. *CO* 37:205; *CTS* 16:31*.

97. Musculus, *Esaiam*, 687.

solace, that for me in heaven is a Father, with a supreme motherly nature, and in whom no defect nor mutability can occur."[98] This maternal imagery from the second part of Isaiah served as a meaningful illustration for preaching comfort.

These insights from Reformed commentaries on Isaiah exhibit one significant way these preachers communicated God's care for his people. God comforts his people through pastors who must imitate the kind of shepherd God himself is. Pastors are tasked with preaching the gospel persuasively and compassionately, as it serves to remind believers of God's promises. God promises that he will provide all that his people need, especially by sending the Comforter, the Holy Spirit, and by bringing his people together in the church. Among many other things, the Spirit grants the peace that is necessary to alleviate our feelings of unworthiness or condemnation. Further, the Spirit and the church together provide the protection that we need both within ourselves and from the outside world. The words these pastors preached and taught based on Isaiah intended to convey God's comfort as they offered pastoral care to the people in Reformed communities.

BIBLIOGRAPHY

Bierma, Lyle D. *The Theology of the Heidelberg Catechism: A Reformation Synthesis.* Columbia Series in Reformed Theology. Louisville: Westminster John Knox, 2013.

Bullinger, Heinrich. *Isaias Excellentissimus Dei Propheta . . . Expositus Homiliis CXC.* Zürich: Christoph Froschauer, 1567.

Cochrane, Arthur C., ed. *Reformed Confessions of the Sixteenth Century.* Louisville: Westminster John Knox, 2003.

Fisher, Jeff, ed. *Isaiah 1–39.* Reformation Commentary on Scripture OT Xa. Downers Grove, IL: InterVarsity, 2024.

Gwalther, Rudolf. *Isaias: In Isaiam Prophetam Rodolphi Gualtheri Tigurini Homiliae CCCXXVII.* Zürich: Christoph Froschauer, 1583.

Manetsch, Scott M. *Calvin's Company of Pastors: Pastoral Care and the Emerging Reformed Church, 1536–1609.* Oxford Studies in Historical Theology. New York: Oxford University Press, 2013.

Musculus, Wolfgang. *In Esaiam Prophetam Commentarii.* Basel: Johannes Herwagen, 1557.

Oecolampadius, Johannes. *In Iesaiam Prophetam Hypomnematon, hoc est, Commentariorum.* Basel: Andreas Cratander, 1525.

Pellikan, Konrad. *Commentaria Bibliorum et Illa Brevia Quidem ac Catholica.* Vol. 1. Zürich: Christoph Froschauer, 1582 [1534].

---

98. Musculus, *Esaiam*, 687.

8

Prophets, Preachers, and Potentates
Nikolaus Selnecker and the Late Lutheran Reformation

J. JEFFERY TYLER

NEARLY FIFTY YEARS AFTER Martin Luther posted his *Ninety-Five Theses*, another enterprising pastor and scholar turned to theology and Scripture. In 1566, Nikolaus Selnecker (1530–92) published a commentary on the Old Testament prophet Jeremiah, providing an exposition that was homiletic in style and written in German for the instruction and consolation of all readers, including the laity. At thirty-six years old, Selnecker was a rising star among the preachers and theologians of the late German Reformation. Throughout his career he would hold prominent positions as a court preacher, university professor, published theologian, ecclesial reformer, and catalyst for church unity. Selnecker turned to Jeremiah at a moment of profound crisis in his life, faith, and vocation; here he found a biblical prophet suffused with penetrating insight, deep consolation, and hard-earned wisdom for uncertain times.

    Moreover, Selnecker's commentary offers an intriguing German parallel to John Calvin (1509–64) in his final years in Geneva and to his successor, Theodore Beza (1519–1605), both of whom figure prominently in the scholarship and teaching of Scott Manetsch. In fact, Selnecker's acute focus in his commentary on ministry and faith formation—in Jeremiah's biblical past and in sixteenth-century Germany—serve to parallel

Manetsch's tireless training of pastors, missionaries, and scholars, as well as his dazzling and dogged commitment to the study of Scripture in the Reformation era.[1] Indeed, Selnecker's study of Jeremiah explores the difficulties of preaching, the perils of ministry among the powerful, and the uncertain survival of the Lutheran Reformation as a whole. Vivid quotes from Selnecker's work further capture the urgency of his vision, the vitality of his voice, and his abiding concern for church and society.

SELNECKER'S EARLY CAREER AND OLD TESTAMENT COMMENTARIES

Nikolaus Selnecker was in his mid-thirties when he turned to the prophecies of Jeremiah. Significant experiences and events shaped Selnecker's approach to and interpretation of the prophet: his upbringing in Nürnberg, Germany; his theological education under Philip Melanchthon and other Lutheran luminaries at the University of Wittenberg (1550–58); his first pastoral call as a court chaplain and preacher in Dresden under Elector Augustus of Saxony (1526–86, r. 1553–86); and, in 1559, his marriage to Margaretha Greiser, the daughter of a church superintendent. Although Selnecker had already offered lectures as a Privatdozent on Aristotle and the New Testament in Wittenberg, his publishing career began in earnest in the 1560s in Dresden with works on philosophy, church history, doctrine, and practical theology.[2] In fact, this decade would be a golden age of Selnecker's exegetical and homiletic commentaries, especially on the Old Testament. His first major expository work explored the Psalms in three volumes. The subtitle of this series underscores the broad audience Selnecker intended to reach: a work "preached and printed here in orderly fashion for the welfare, consolation, and instruction of common people and godly, simple Christians in this miserable time."[3] The choice of the Psalms as his first major exegetical work is all the more understandable,

---

1. Manetsch, *Theodore Beza*; *Calvin's Company of Pastors*; and preeminently the many volumes of the Reformation Commentary on Scripture, for which Manetsch has served as associate general editor since its inception and as editor for the volumes on 1 and 2 Corinthians (2017 and 2022, respectively).

2. For details on Selnecker's biography cited in this chapter, see Bode, "Selnecker"; Koch, "Selnecker"; Franz Dibelius's article based on earlier work by Wagenmann, "Selnecker"; Jungkuntz, *Formulators*.

3. Selnecker, *Gantze Psalter des Kœniglichen Propheten Dauids*. On the dating of Selnecker's Psalms volumes and subsequent sixteenth-century editions, see Kolb, "Doctrine of Christ," 314n5.

given Selnecker's musical mastery of the organ at a young age, his long career composing hymns, and his subsequent work in helping develop the St. Thomas Church boys choir (*Thomanerchor*) in Leipzig.[4]

After his volumes on the Psalms, Selnecker turned to the prophets of the Old Testament with similar homiletic commentaries for German-speaking audiences, including volumes on Lamentations (1565), Jeremiah and Zephaniah (1566), Ezekiel (1567), Daniel and the New Testament book of Revelation (1567), Amos and Obadiah (1567), and Isaiah (1569).[5] Thereafter, he produced a scholarly commentary on Genesis in Latin (1569).[6] For the remainder of his career, Selnecker continued to make progress on his biblical commentary project—including volumes on the New Testament Gospels and Epistles. But ultimately, he devoted most of his time and energy to publishing theological and catechetical works. Selnecker sought to establish common ground with fellow Lutherans divided over Luther's legacy, thereby helping to draft, garner support for, and defend the Lutheran Formula of Concord (1577). Throughout his career, Selnecker countered the persistent influence of Calvinism in Lutheran lands, churches, and theology.[7]

CONTROVERSY IN DRESDEN (1564)

Selnecker's encounter with the prophet Jeremiah emerged in a period of controversy and conflict in Dresden. As he grappled with events in the city and their aftermath, Selnecker contemplated a commentary that addresses timeless themes for church and ministry: the future and legacy of the Reformation, the perils and promise of preaching, and the daunting challenge of ministry among the potentates at the electoral court.

---

4. The *Thomanerchor* was later made famous by Johann Sebastian Bach (1685–1750); this world-renowned choir is still performing and recording in the twenty-first century. On Selnecker's musical legacy in Lutheran worship, see Kolodziej, "Early Lutheran Hymnody," 44; and Polack, *Handbook*, 578–79.

5. Selnecker published his prophetic commentaries with the Leipzig printer Jakob Bärwald: *Threni* (1565), *Der gantze Prophet Jeremias* (1566; hereafter *Jeremias*), *Der herrliche Prophet Ezechiel* (1567), *Der Prophet Daniel, und die Offenbarung Johannis* (1567), *Der Prophet unnd ernster Busprediger Amos unnd Obadias* (1567), and *Der herrliche Prophet Esaias* (1569).

6. See Selnecker, *In Genesin*.

7. On debates among Lutheran theological parties and the resulting Formula of Concord (1577), see articles by Kolb, "Formula of Concord" and "Wittenberg Circle"; for a more detailed account of Selnecker's role, see Jungkuntz, *Formulators*, 98–102.

The decisive event that changed Selnecker's future and shaped his work on Jeremiah occurred in the mid-1560s as he recovered from a near-fatal illness that left him unable to preach. For a time Selnecker was replaced by Martin Hofmann, a preacher in Dresden's nearby Frauenkirche, who seized the opportunity afforded him to offer a homiletic critique of the local nobility and its costly hunting practices. In fact, the very wild game that the nobility prized for sport and protected from harm had recently consumed the grain harvest of Hofmann's impoverished mother. The noblemen in question did not take kindly to such open critique and saw to it that Hofmann was dismissed from his pastoral position. When Selnecker returned to his post, he might well have moved on from the reckless preaching of his ministerial colleague. Instead, Selnecker took up Hofmann's cause and warned that "these lords and their servants would go straight to the devil."[8] Even when confronted by his prince, Elector Augustus, Selnecker doubled down on his critique of the nobility and the elector himself. Simultaneous pressure from theological adversaries furthered destabilized Selnecker's standing in Dresden, and he was forced to resign his pastoral position at the elector's court. Unemployed and uncertain, Selnecker prepared to return to his hometown of Nürnberg. Fortunately, an academic position became available, and Selnecker headed to the University of Jena in March 1565.[9]

What was Selnecker's state of mind as he departed his very first pastoral call for a new professorial post in Jena? A surprising source reveals his physical condition and spiritual struggle. As he prepared to leave Dresden, Selnecker was putting the finishing touches on his commentary on the Old Testament book of Lamentations. At the end of his dedicatory letter to the volume, Selnecker concludes, "Dated at Dresden, on the day of my traveling forth, in the year 1565."[10] This commentary on Lamentations not only marks his departure but also sheds light on Selnecker's health in his last years and months in Dresden—a time of emotional and theological despair. As he reflects on Lam 3:19–21, Selnecker writes:

> For a few years now I have often been so deathly ill that I could only think that the final hours of my life were at hand, that after

---

8. The exact dating of Hoffman's and Selnecker's sermons is unclear; the evidence is cited from Schriften D. Nic. Seln. 7169, Dresdener Staatsarchiv; as noted in Dibelius, "Selnecker," 186.

9. Dibelius, "Selnecker," 186; Jungkuntz, *Formulators*, 95–96.

10. "Dated in Dres[d]en, die peregrinationis meae. Anno 1565." Selnecker, *Threni*, A4r.

so much struggle at last I should give up. In part, I have experienced what it is like for someone who sees death before him, and searches for his courage.... I had fallen into very difficult, dangerous, and despairing thoughts—more difficult than I can say or have time to say. I could neither rest nor sleep. I often broke out in anxious sweats and often fell into unconsciousness. I would argue with myself for long stretches and think, Oh God, are you not mine? Shall I pass on in this melancholy state while doubting, anxious, and desperate, feeling no consolation and dying without faith? How did I get here? See God knew that while in such torment, my heart was coming alive, fresh, and happy once more. For I thought, what are you doing in such sorrow that you are serving the devil? Grab onto God and his word and promise. He is truly your God and Father through Christ his son. Why do you worry so?[11]

This very illness likely explains Selnecker's absence from his pulpit in Dresden, the ill-fated substitution of Hofmann, and thereby Selnecker's clash with his noble parishioners and his elector. Indeed, having faced physical illness, spiritual distress, and his own mortality, Selnecker was less likely to submit to his magisterial superiors and mute his pastoral admonitions.[12] Even so, as he prepared to move on to his new home in Jena, Selnecker still expressed continued concerns for his health.[13]

Once he had settled into Jena, Selnecker turned to the prophecies and narratives of Jeremiah.[14] This prophet's oracles brimmed with doom,

---

11. Selnecker, *Threni*, S3v–S4r. Selnecker's vivid description of his own struggle suggests why he was likewise gifted in delivering funeral sermons that honored the dead and consoled the faithful. See Kolb, "Pastoral Practice."

12. Selnecker's physical and psychological health as well as his faithful recovery were likely more decisive in fueling his critique of his superiors than the thesis of Dibelius and Jungkuntz—namely, that Selnecker's surly father-in-law, Daniel Greiser, had radicalized Selnecker's disposition, which originally shared a more irenic spirit in harmony with his theological mentor Philip Melanchthon. See Dibelius, "Selnecker," 186; Jungkuntz, *Formulators*, 93–94.

13. Selnecker conveys that after Lamentations, he next planned to expound on the all the Old Testament prophets, if God would grant him the grace and health to do so; see *Threni*, A3v.

Selnecker's caution was warranted; his tenure in Jena was short-lived, and he was deposed three years later in 1568. In Dresden, Selnecker had been the target of Lutheran theologians who found his doctrinal positions out of step with their views that were sympathetic to Calvinism. Now in Jena, he was let go because of his associations with Philip Melanchthon and the so-called Philippists. In 1568 he was hired by the University of Leipzig and was appointed as pastor to the St. Thomas Church in Leipzig.

14. Surprisingly, Selnecker did not write his first commentary on Isaiah—the first

destruction, and judgment, and yet they likewise offered glimpses of shimmering hope and divine promise;[15] Jeremiah's proclamations echoed prophets major and minor, and yet his biographical narratives rival the stories of Elijah and Elisha in drama and detail. Here Selnecker would find a mirror in which to consider the future of the Reformation, the challenges of preaching, and the recent difficulties in his own pastoral and academic career.

THE UNCERTAINTY OF REFORMATION: PAST AND PRESENT

As Selnecker deciphered Jeremiah chapter by chapter, he in turn addressed his contemporaries—pastors and their parishioners facing resurgent Catholicism, division among Protestants, and military aggression from abroad. Would the reforms of Luther survive? Would Protestant fortunes echo the fate of King Josiah (r. 640–609 BC) and his descendants two millennia before, whose reforms were righteous, but short-lived, proving insufficient to overcome the lingering sins and legacy of King Manasseh (r. 687–643 BC)?[16] In fact, Selnecker chose to expound on Jeremiah precisely because he was the sort of prophet and preacher well-suited to address the miserable times in which sixteenth-century Christians lived and the conditions they faced in the church, government, and everyday life.[17] Marking the passing decades since Luther had posted his *Ninety-Five Theses*, Selnecker comments on Jer 7: "You should listen to us, as we are now in the fiftieth year that God's voice, word, and gospel have been heard loud and clear. And God be praised, it can still be heard with the reform of our lives. That we know, see, and experience daily."[18] Yet at the same time, Selnecker was not at all sanguine regarding current conditions and the future of Protestantism; he looked back

---

prophetic book in the order of the Bible and the most cited and revered of the major Old Testament prophets. Selnecker offers several reasons for his selection of Jeremiah: Veit Dietrich, reformer of Nürnberg and a preacher Selnecker had heard in his youth, had already published a commentary on Isaiah in German: *Der gantz Prophet Esaias*; and Selnecker's recent commentary on Lamentations—attributed to Jeremiah's authorship in the sixteenth century—made Jeremiah's prophecies the logical choice over Isaiah; *Jeremias*, B1r.

15. See, for example, Jer 23:5–6; 30:18–22; 31:1–40; 32:1–25; 35:1–2.
16. See 2 Kgs 23:26–27.
17. Selnecker, *Jeremias*, B1v.
18. Commenting on Jer 7:13–16; Selnecker, *Jeremias*, P1r.

with nostalgia, and he resonated with Jeremiah, who feared that God no longer heard his prayers for divine mercy: "While [Luther] lived, peace and unity would remain. But he has died, so now one should watch and hold on to prayer.... It is certain that Germany at this time has long lain in the ashes and has God's word no longer."[19]

In fact, throughout his commentary on Jeremiah, Selnecker raises his eyes again and again to the eastern horizon of Europe and the ever-looming threat of the Ottoman Turks, who seem poised to take up the role of the ancient Babylonians and lay waste to Germany as Judea had been ravaged long before: "When today or tomorrow the Turks come—or another enemy—and we Germans have not improved ourselves, nothing will help; even if all the kings, princes, and cities are mobilized and gather together and build a great fortress."[20] Indeed, Selnecker surmises that his readers are intimately familiar with the plight of refugees and the brutality of invasion. Explaining the implications of Jer 6 with an ear attuned to the sounds of terror and eyes fixated on panic turned to paralysis, Selnecker writes:

> We are able to find this passage useful because of the Turks. And we know what sort of lamentation this is: godly parents can understand it and take it to heart. Their children have often experienced this in Hungary, in many places in Austria, and elsewhere. The enemies . . . arrive here as quickly as an arrow and they roar like a turbulent sea. When we hear of them our fists fall to our sides. We are terrified and fall in on ourselves, lose all courage, and have no hope. We fear the roaring horn. None are sure of themselves with a sword. What we have, we must give over to the enemy. The children are cut in two or otherwise captured and led away. The women and young girls are defiled. We become a poor people and concern ourselves with death.[21]

As women are violated and children butchered, the faithful will find no support from feeble lords and failing teachers. Societal breakdown ensues, and sources of mercy and relief are rare.[22] Selnecker explores the threat of violence not only to underscore the potential for divine judgment in any

---

19. Commenting on Jer 7:13–16; Selnecker, *Jeremias*, P1v.
20. Commenting on Jer 4:5; Selnecker, *Jeremias*, H2r–v.
21. Commenting on Jer 6:11–13; Selnecker, *Jeremias*, L2r–v.
22. Commenting on Jer 8:10; 10:19–21; and 31:15; Selnecker, *Jeremias*, R3r, V3v–V4r, 2B1r–v; see also commentary on Jer 46 and 50; 2P1v–2P2r; 2R3r–v.

age—including in the sixteenth century—but also to remind the faithful of the consolations they now enjoy:

> God shows us his countenance when we hear the Word of God in church and school, and can be led and have the right use of the most-worthy sacrament. He shows us his back, when we are robbed of the Word and cannot hear it, like the poor captive Christians in Turkey or wherever God's Word cannot be heard in a church. There is none of that because of heathen idolatry, the Muhammadan Qur'an, and other horrible blasphemy and errors.[23]

In short, Selnecker's application of Jeremiah's prophetic judgments reveals just how uncertain sixteenth-century Lutherans might be about the survival or longevity of the Reformation, given the division among Christians and the spread of Islam on the horizon.

THE PERILS OF PREACHING

Even as his vision is ever tempered by the savagery of war, the possibility of persecution, and the threat of divine judgment, Selnecker likewise sees Jeremiah's text as a guide to form pastors and preachers, teachers, and parishioners for the work of the gospel, the requirements of Christian vocation, and the hard times demanded of the faithful, especially as reforming ardor cooled. Selnecker's commentary is decidedly homiletic in tone and oriented to pastors deciphering Jeremiah as they pondered sermons to preach and congregants to console.[24] He describes Jeremiah's oracles as "difficult preaching."[25] Selnecker further offers the life and suffering of the prophet as a vivid example of the fierce commitment preaching requires, the suffering the preacher must endure, and the divine assurance that undergirds all faithful proclamation:

> [Jeremiah] was truly a wretched and miserable man, full of sorrow and misery. He had fully intended and committed himself to preach to the people; for in God's name one must go forth and fear no danger, disgrace, or suffering for the truth. But one must

---

23. Commentary on Jer 18:14–17; Selnecker, *Jeremias*, F4v.

24. Selnecker may have in mind a contrast to the magisterial and scholarly commentary in Latin of Johannes Bugenhagen, *In Ieremiam Prophetam Commentarium*.

25. Commenting on Jer 5; Selnecker, *Jeremias*, J1r.

give full attention to God's command and see how God's word will triumph over those who despise evil.[26]

Lutheran pastors of the mid-sixteenth century must be reminded to lean into their homiletical vocation and look to predecessors who accepted the mantle of proclamation: "All godly preachers in our own time should follow Jeremiah's example and effort." Selnecker continues:

> True preachers should look straight at their office and their calling and know this: they indeed have the office of Jeremiah, Micah, John, Paul, Ambrose, and other upright prophets, apostles, and teachers of the Old and New Testament; and they lead with the same word as led those above; they serve the same God which others have served. Teachers today have the same people and listeners as the others once had.[27]

Yet, one can imagine that Selnecker's praise of this prophet as an exemplar may have raised a few eyebrows. While Jeremiah might be put forward as a preacher for apocalyptic times, was he perhaps a bit too extreme and shrill for Lutheran pastors of the late sixteenth century? Granted, the text of Jeremiah is full of preaching and prophecy; his vision of covenants—old and new—provide a framework of biblical testaments, old and new. However, Jeremiah's task and calling are harrowing and terminal; over fifty-two lengthy chapters he proclaims unremitting judgment and doom to the people of Judea. Jeremiah's few consoling passages envision divine blessings for future generations but offer meager hope for the present.[28]

Not surprisingly, Jeremiah's message was universally panned by his own people; he was ignored, despised, insulted, assaulted, arrested, and left for dead.[29] In fundamental ways, Jeremiah—though faithful to divine revelation—is the decidedly failed preacher who converts or convinces no one. In response, Selnecker underscores Jeremiah's realism—the way he gives searing profile to the deep frustrations and frequent failings of preachers and their sermons. After nearly eight years of full-time preaching in Dresden, Selnecker was now keenly aware of the emotional life of preachers, the urgency of divine consolation, and the toll that the

---

26. Commenting on Jer 38:6; Selnecker, *Jeremias*, 2L1v–2L2r.

27. Commenting on Jer 26:14–15; Selnecker, *Jeremias*, V4v–X1r.

28. Even the oft-quoted Jer 29:11–13 is a promise for future generations proclaimed in the context of judgment on the current generation.

29. See Jer 26; 27; 36–38.

proclamation of the word takes on all who step into the pulpit and spark the attention of adversarial parishioners.

> In these words Jeremiah gives stunning expression—as he does in further chapters to follow—to the heavy burden of the preaching office and how the true teacher has enough to do and must endure so much angst, exhaustion, and work, and thereby be little honored. Just as the world is ungrateful, so true teachers are even less appreciated. We see how God also allows his saints to experience many misfortunes in the world, and thereby they gain patience and through difficulty they are shaped. While they are gifted at times, they are also impatient, often complain and are unwilling—as with Jeremiah, Job, Habakkuk, and others. But as God again helps up Jeremiah, so also he will do for us; we will be overcome by some of the same thoughts and impatience but also trust God to comfort, strengthen, and help us to know that we are not yet alone in this life and that we should be thankful eternally.[30]

However, at times in his anguish and exhaustion Jeremiah descends into doubt, despair, and even defiance before the divine. Is *this* Jeremiah a proper model for pastors and preachers? Given his singular calling and dire circumstances, should he serve as a template for the faithful in all times and seasons? The fifteenth and twentieth chapters of Jeremiah are a particular challenge to sixteenth-century commentators, who must contend with Jeremiah's despair. Some are willing to grant Jeremiah latitude in his suffering, while others are appalled by his lack of restraint and reverence before God.[31] For Selnecker, suffering and anguish are marks of true preaching. Jeremiah helps pastors face up to this dimension of their work and to the divine consolation that accompanies faithful preaching.

> God does not reject Jeremiah or other weak saints, but he consoles them. God helps Jeremiah get back on his feet, strengthens and instructs him, and promises him his grace and mercy, that he wants to protect and preserve him, that he does not want his poor little house and church to perish among enemies. [God shows us] what consolation we should have and hold in our difficulties, and in our calling, so that we forge ahead truly and diligently, and order our matters and lives to God. He will

---

30. Commentary on Jer 20:7–10; Selnecker, *Jeremias*, H2v.

31. See the responses of a variety of sixteenth-century commentators and preachers on the prophet's laments in Jer 15 and 20, in Tyler, *Jeremiah, Lamentations*, 146–54, 191–201.

not leave us orphans. We learn too and see how it goes for true preachers and teachers in their office and what kind of misery, temptation, pain, anxiety, and difficulty they carry and suffer—more and greater than many hundreds of people. All honest and true-hearted preachers in their office fully experience and can attest to this difficulty and can be run down by it. The rest of the world sleeps, snores, and lives in all their pleasures, goes into the spring and enjoys good weather. But preachers quake with sadness and have much anxious sweat, few good days, and great care and work all the time.[32]

Despite the labor and exhaustion of the pulpit, preachers must stay the course. They lead the faithful to Scripture, chastise the sinful, reprimand the overconfident, and call them all to true repentance.[33] They must prepare for unresponsive congregants, answer false charges of heresy and blasphemy, endure those who openly question a pastor's calling, and tolerate those who prefer pastors who offer consolation alone and avoid controversial, confrontational, or disruptive preaching.[34] Ultimately, Selnecker consoles the faithful pastor and congregant alike, not with the power of human endurance but with the deeper wellsprings of divine perseverance:

> The God-fearing person, who trusts in God and is filled with the Holy Spirit, has grace and blessings; and in every situation this person already belongs to what honors God; nothing hinders this person—neither hail nor lightning, neither rain nor snow. He is free in every case—through severe storms—because he has vigor and sap in his roots. Therefore, when a cross or persecution comes, he poses no questions about it; for he has the sap and he always moves forward. No one is able to fight against him, nor dampen his abilities, nor press out his sap, because he lives. He is oriented toward what God wants.[35]

---

32. Commenting on Jer 15:10; Selnecker, *Jeremias*, B3r–v.

33. Commenting on Jer 2:12; 2:20; and 7:13; Selnecker, *Jeremias*, B2v–V3v; C2v–C4v, P1r–v.

34. Commenting on Jer 7:13–16; 18:18–23; 26:9; Selnecker, *Jeremias*, P1r–v, F4v–G1v, V2r–v, X1v.

35. Commentary on Jer 17:7–8 and citing Pss 1:3 and 92:12–15; Selnecker, *Jeremias*, D1r.

MINISTRY AMONG THE POWERFUL

Even as Selnecker is drawn to Jeremiah as a vivid and unrelenting guide to the challenges of preaching, he is likewise attuned to the prophet's encounters with the ruling class, the king and the courtiers, who resist and ridicule the prophet's message—and threaten his life.[36] Like Selnecker in Dresden, Jeremiah was not only a prophet but also a *Hofprediger*—a "court preacher"—called to ring forth in the halls of power.[37]

Thus, the running clash between Jeremiah on the one hand and the king, his courtiers, and his preferred prophets on the other parallels Selnecker's own fateful encounter with leaders of church and state. In fact, Selnecker's exposition of Jeremiah gives him the opportunity to critique magistrates and their supporters in his own time. In a Europe where state churches were the rule, clergy had to navigate the preferences of princes and faced reprimand, dismissal, or worse when they chose to challenge the ungodliness and greed of rulers. Selnecker's critique of Elector Augustus and the nobility in Dresden—or his ducal and theological adversaries in Jena—echoes in his commentaries on Jeremiah. While discussing Jer 5, Selnecker summarizes the prophet in language that is vividly contemporary to his own time: "Oh dear lords, princes, magistrates, officers, nobles, and others who are at court, who sit in our councilmen's houses, in offices, and other places. Do you really want to see that the salvation of your soul depends on this Word [of repentance and salvation]?"[38] Commenting on Jer 4, Selnecker is even more emphatic. Both the rulers of ancient Judea and the current guardians of the church receive withering criticism:

> [They are] enraged tyrants who devastate and destroy everything.... They should be guardians of the churches and schools, and should support the common good. But most of them are wolves and destroyers of churches, lands, and people. They inquire about nothing according to the word of God. They are

---

36. In fact, Selnecker first encountered the powerful and their possible claims on one's life as a boy and young man. As a musical prodigy and an organist in the Kaiserburg in Nürnberg, he caught the attention of both royal choristers and Ferdinand—brother and chief representative of Emperor Charles V (r. 1519–56) in the German lands until he himself became emperor in 1556—who might have drafted Selnecker into imperial service. His matriculation at the University of Wittenberg effectively defied the empire and a purely musical career; Polack, *Handbook*, 578, Dibelius, "Selnecker," 184.

37. Selnecker, *Jeremias*, A4v.

38. Commentary on Jer 5; Selnecker, *Jeremias*, J3v.

surely Epicurean paunches, who look after their own bellies; they feed and drink themselves to exhaustion and pursue mischief. So other guardians must come, who make a certain end of these supposed guardians . . . and wipe them out. There will again be a cry against them because of their ways, as the foreign peoples—the Turks, Muscovites, and the like—unleash the horrifying, growling dog."[39]

Meanwhile, as Selnecker reminds his readers, the faithful suffer the consequences, even from those whom they have learned to trust: "This chapter [Jer 20] shows how it goes for true preachers. They are hated, beaten, imprisoned, and ridiculed. Despite this abuse they should be able to wait in their office in silence. Of course, it has to be their own friends and acquaintances that hate and strike them, and engage them in an unfriendly manner."[40] In contrast, pious rulers ought to rule with a reverent fear of God, promote instruction in the law and gospel, support and honor true teachers, defend their subjects, and encourage them toward faithful prayer. Likewise, they must avoid false preachers who please and pacify godless rulers.[41] Near the end of his commentary, Selnecker reprimands magistrates and princes yet again; the rulers of Moab condemned in chapter 48 of Jeremiah—fierce adversaries of Judea—do not conjure the contemporary Muslim Turks for Selnecker. Rather, Moabite rulers bring to mind the Christian potentates and palaces of Germany, including the hunting practices that led to Selnecker's reprimand and downfall in Dresden:

> Thus, in our own time princes and lords have a little something, but they build greater residences and build in the cities with great splendor, and with the people they excessively hunt, play, and indulge all their passions. Then poor people must extend all of their sweat and blood, and look to their own influence, power, and daily well-being. But what will happen if such splendor and defiance of God remain unchecked? What will happen if shame and ridicule must stop, and so one says, How did these people become so reckless that they did not conserve anything? What then? How does their wealth help them? I think, has God enriched them, and then humbled them? Where is their splendor and where are their fortresses? Where are the reliable people, whom they exploit? Where are they, the poor and miserable

---

39. Commenting on Jer 4:15–18; Selnecker, *Jeremias*, H4r.
40. Commentary on Jer 20:1–6; Selnecker, *Jeremias*, G3r.
41. Commentary on Jer 21:3–14 and 27:9–11; Selnecker, *Jeremias*, H4v4, X4v.

people? And where is flawless Germany with its fortresses and cities? And what is Germany coming to, when now every person, all the lords and other people are proud, ostentatious, and arrogant? They see and hear with a real affinity for a kind of blindness that angers God greatly."[42]

CONCLUSION

Clearly, Selnecker found parallels between his own unstable position—first as a court preacher in Dresden, and then as a university professor in Jena—and Jeremiah's suffering among the king, courtiers, and false prophets in Jerusalem. At the very least, Jeremiah's example prepared Selnecker to accept that his homiletical, theological, and pastoral convictions might lead to dismissal, transfer, or reassignment as he navigated the political and confessional waters of his own time. Selnecker not only moved from Dresden to Jena in 1565 but was forced out from Jena after only three years at the university, after which he took another academic position in Leipzig. Even after two decades at the University of Leipzig, Selnecker faced dismissal yet again in 1589. As the new Prince-Elector Christian I (1560–91; r. 1586–91) outlawed the critique of Calvinist influence in his territory, Selnecker defied his sovereign and continued to challenge "crypto-Calvinism" in public and in print.[43] After his departure from Leipzig, he accepted a post as church superintendent in Hildesheim, Germany. In accord with the strength of his convictions—and his willingness to change locations and callings even late in life—Selnecker was called back to Leipzig yet again in 1591. Perhaps it is fitting that Selnecker died as he transitioned and before taking up his final academic post and pastoral calling.

Given Selnecker's poor health in the mid-1560s, his sudden and frequent dismissals and transfers, his association with the trials and travails of Jeremiah, and his vivid prose on the perils of preaching and the unfaithfulness of the powerful, we might have expected him to descend into a fiercely contrarian academic and pastoral career; he might have succumbed to an irascible, uncharitable, and uncooperative frame of

---

42. Commentary on Jer 48; Selnecker, *Jeremias*, 2Q1r-v.

43. See, for example, Selnecker's work: *Calvinus Redivivus Das ist*. Selnecker also published his own *Institutio Christianae Religionis* in three volumes, which includes a substantial section on the *communicatio idiomatum*, a contested issue between Lutherans and Calvinists; see 125–65. On the context of these debates, see Dingel, "Calvin," 172–73.

mind. Rather, Selnecker's experiences in the 1560s seem to have prepared him for the rough-and-tumble of negotiations and compromises in the decades that followed.[44] Despite his clashes with princely and religious authorities, Selnecker navigated the theological and ecclesial landscape with considerable success. In addition to his academic and pastoral positions, Selnecker was appointed to a variety of ecclesial posts to oversee and further reforms in Lutheran churches and territories.[45] Most of all, he played a pivotal role in the drafting of the Formula of Concord, in the negotiations among various Lutheran parties, and in the defense of the Formula after its adoption.[46] Like Jeremiah, Selnecker understood that preaching, teaching, and church leadership required theological conviction and personal resilience, dexterity and boldness in princely courts, and the willingness to move where needed and when necessary.[47] Unlike his half brother, Georg, who became a pastor in Schwabach—close to the native lands of the Selnecker family—Nikolaus took on the mantle of court preacher, public theologian, and university professor. Still, he may well have resonated with Jeremiah, who longed for a quiet and peaceful life, for Selnecker recalls the words of worldly-wise folk and their advice to take the easier way: "It is preferable that you are not a Jeremiah, nor a prophet; that you are not a John the Baptist or an apostle, that you are not a Luther."[48]

BIBLIOGRAPHY

Bode, Gerhard. "Selnecker, Nikolaus." In *Dictionary of Luther and the Lutheran Traditions*, edited by Timothy J. Wengert et al., 678. Grand Rapids: Baker Academic, 2017.

Bugenhagen, Johannes. *In Ieremiam Prophetam Commentarium*. Wittenberg: Seitz, 1546.

---

44. On Selnecker's shift from Philippist views to the more Gnesio-Lutheran theological positions that came to dominate Lutheranism after the late sixteenth century, see Jungkuntz, *Formulators*, 96–100.

45. Selnecker held superintendencies in Leipzig, Gandersheim, and Hildesheim. He also assisted with reformation of the church in Braunschweig-Wolfenbüttel and introduced a Lutheran church order in Oldenburg; see Jungkuntz, *Formulators*, 96–98; and Koch, "Selnecker," 106.

46. See Kolb, "Formula of Concord"; and "Wittenberg Circle."

47. On his evolving views as a Philippist and then as a supporter of the Formula of Concord, see Jungkuntz, *Formulators*, 99–109.

48. Commentary on Jer 26:14–16; Selnecker, *Jeremias*, V4v.

Dibelius, Franz. "Selnecker, Nikolaus." In *Realencyklopädie für protestantische Theologie und Kirche*, 18:184-91. 3rd ed. Leipzig: Hinrich'sche Buchhandlung, 1906.

Dietrich, Veit. *Der gantz Prophet Esaias*. Nürnberg: VomBerg, 1548.

Dingel, Irene. "Calvin in the Context of Lutheran Consolidation." *Reformation and Renaissance Review* 12 (2010) 155-87.

Jungkuntz, Theodore R. *Formulators of the Formula of Concord: Four Architects of Lutheran Unity*. Eugene, OR: Wipf & Stock, 2001.

Koch, Ernst. "Selnecker, Nikolaus (1530-92)." In *Theologische Realenzyklopädie*, edited by G. Müller, 31:105-8. Berlin: de Gruyter, 2000.

Kolb, Robert. "The Doctrine of Christ in Nikolaus Selnecker's Interpretation of Psalms 8, 22, and 110." In *Biblical Interpretation in the Era of the Reformation*, edited by Richard A. Muller and John L. Thompson, 313-32. Eugene, OR: Wipf & Stock, 1996.

———. "Formula of Concord." In *Dictionary of Luther and the Lutheran Traditions*, edited by Timothy J. Wengert et al., 260. Grand Rapids: Baker Academic, 2017.

———. "Pastoral Practice in the Funeral Sermons of Nikolaus Selnecker (1530-1592)." *Lutheran Quarterly* 28 (Spring 2014) 22-48.

———. "Wittenberg Circle." In *Dictionary of Luther and the Lutheran Traditions*, edited by Timothy J. Wengert et al., 787-93. Grand Rapids: Baker Academic, 2017.

Kolodziej, Benjamin. "Early Lutheran Hymnody (1550-1650)." In *From Catholic Europe to Protestant Europe*, edited by Mark A. Lamport, Benjamin K. Forrest, and Vernon M. Whaley, 31-48. Vol. 2 of *Hymns and Hymnody: Historical and Theological Introductions*. Cambridge: Lutterworth, 2019.

Manetsch, Scott M. *Calvin's Company of Pastors: Pastoral Care and the Emerging Reformed Church, 1536-1609*. Oxford Studies in Historical Theology. Oxford: Oxford University Press, 2013.

———. *Theodore Beza and the Quest for Peace in France, 1572-1598*. Studies in Medieval and Reformation Thought 79. Leiden: Brill, 2000.

Polack, W. G. *The Handbook to the Lutheran Hymnal*. St. Louis: Concordia, 1942.

Selnecker, Nikolaus. *Calvinus Redivivus Das ist: Zwinglii, Calvini, Beze etc. Eigentliche Meinung von etlichen fürnemen streitigen Religions Artickeln unnd Sprüchen der H. Schrifft: mit jhren eigenen Worten, ohn alle Verbitterung vnd Verfälschung dargethan*. Lübeck: Kröger, 1590.

———. *Der gantze Prophet Jeremias/Zu diesen schweren vnnd gefehrlichen zeiten/ frommen Christen zum vnterricht vnd Trost/Ausgelegt*. Leipzig: Jakob Bärwald, 1566.

———. *Der gantze Psalter des Kœniglichen Propheten Dauids/außgelegt/vnd in drey Buecher getheylt . . . ordenlich nach einander dem gemeinen Mann vnd frommen einfeltigen Christen zu gut vnd in diser elenden Zeit zu Trost vnd vnterricht geprediget vnd in Druck gegeben*. Nürnberg: Christoph Heußler, 1563-64.

———. *Der herrliche Prophet Esaias/in diesen schweren vnd kuemmerlichen zeiten . . . Christlich/kuertzlich/vnd einfeltig fuer den gemeinen Man/erkleret*. Leipzig: Jakob Bärwald, 1569.

———. *Der herrliche Prophet Ezechiel*. Leipzig: Jakob Bärwald, 1567.

———. *In Genesin, Primum Librum Moysi, Commentarius: Ita Scriptvs, Vt Docentibvs Et Discentibvs Coelestem Doctrinam Magno Vsvi Esse Possit. . . . Addita est Chronologia ab initio mundi usq[ue] ad exitum populi Israelitici ex Aegypto*. Leipzig: Rhambau, 1569.

———. *Institutio Christianae Religionis*. 3 vols. Frankfurt am Main: Tröster, 1573.
———. *Der Prophet Daniel, und die Offenbarung Johannis*. Leipzig: Jakob Bärwald, 1567.
———. *Der Prophet unnd ernster Busprediger Amos unnd Obadias*. Leipzig: Jakob Bärwald, 1567.
———. *Threni. Klaglieder des Propheten Jeremie . . . Jetziger zeit allen Christen nœtig/ nuetzlich vnd trœstlich zu lessen*. Leipzig: Jakob Bärwald, 1565.
Tyler, J. Jeffrey, ed. *Jeremiah, Lamentations*. Reformation Commentary on Scripture, Old Testament 11. Downers Grove, IL: IVP Academic, 2018.

9

Pastoral Insights from Reformation Readings on Romans

Reigning Sin, Concupiscence, and the Mortal/ Venial Distinction[1]

JEB RALSTON

ALL SIN ARISES FROM a common sinful source, yet not all sins are necessarily equal: this was the pastoral and theological tension that many magisterial reformers faced following Luther's reconceptualization of original sin. In critiquing the traditional Catholic distinction between mortal and venial sins, Calvin once famously wrote, "Every sin is mortal," and yet, "the faults of the saints are venial, not from their own nature, but on account of the mercy of God."[2] While it is true that almost all

---

1. This essay is dedicated to my *Doktorvater*, Scott M. Manetsch, whose mentorship and friendship has cultivated in me both a love of church history and an even greater love for the Church herself. I am thankful for the comments and suggestions on an earlier draft of this chapter from my colleagues in the Swiss National Science Foundation research project, "16th-Century Exegesis of Paul." Stefan Krauter and Benjamin Manig were especially helpful in pointing out earlier weaknesses of this essay. All remaining errors are my own.

2. Calvin, *Institutes* II.8.59 (CO 2:309): "Quod si delirare perseverant, illis valere iussis, habeant filii Dei, omne peccatum mortale esse; quia est adversus Dei voluntatem rebellio, quae eius iram necessario provocat; quia est legis praevaricatio, in quam edictum est sine exceptione Dei iudicium: sanctorum delicta venialia esse, non ex suapte natura, sed quia ex Dei misericordia veniam consequuntur."

sixteenth-century Protestants denied the traditional *Catholic* distinction between mortal and venial sins (as well as the distinction between sin and concupiscence), many nevertheless maintained the categories of "mortal" and "venial" sins redressed as "reigning" and "un-reigning" sins in light of their developing hamartiologies and engagement with Pauline theology.[3] In other words, the Catholic distinction was criticized *and* reconfigured as Protestants found new grounding for their doctrine in their reading of Paul's letter to the Romans.

I will argue that in the Latin Western exegetical tradition, Rom 4:7–8 was typically treated as a *locus classicus* for discussing the distinction between sins, yet among several significant magisterial reformers, this *locus classicus* found a new home in Rom 6:12 as the distinction between mortal and venial sins itself was reconfigured and renamed. Following this, I will demonstrate the ways in which Lutheran and some Reformed theologians nuanced their own distinct articulations of the mortal–venial distinction while reckoning with Philip Melanchthon's 1540 reading of Rom 6. Finally, I will elaborate on the pastoral concern at the heart of this theological debate and exegetical development in the sixteenth century.

THE FORMATION OF A *LOCUS CLASSICUS*: ROMANS 4:7–8 FROM AMBROSIASTER TO THE *MAGNA GLOSSATURA*

Gradations of Sin in the Patristic Period

The Western Latin theological tradition has a long history of engaging various gradations of sin as expressed within Holy Scripture. Matthew 12:31 ("All sin and blasphemy shall be remitted to men, but blasphemy against the Spirit shall not be remitted"), 1 John 5:16–17 ("There is a sin unto death: for that I say not that any man ask . . ."), and 1 John 1:8–10 ("If we say we have no sin, we lead ourselves astray . . .") have especially elicited

---

3. Catholic–Protestant polemics have tended to obfuscate the complex reality regarding this distinction among sixteenth-century Protestants. For example, see the foreword of Durkin, *Theological Distinction of Sins*, where he writes: "Since the Protestant innovators of the sixteenth century denied the doctrine of the theological distinction of sins, an appreciation of this doctrine's development is especially valuable" (i). Protestants have also been prone to simple caricatures of this distinction. See Schaff, *Ante-Nicene Fathers*, 3:425. For more balanced perspectives in modern dogmatics (from a Protestant and Roman Catholic perspective, respectively), see Berkouwer, *Sin*, beginning on 302; and Ott, *Fundamentals of Catholic Dogma*, 263.

a variety of theological reflections on forgivable and unforgivable sins.[4] For example, in *Against Jovinianus*, Jerome (ca. 347–420) writes immediately after quoting 1 John 5:16, "You observe that if we entreat for smaller offenses, we obtain pardon: if for greater ones, it is difficult to obtain our request: and that there is a great difference between sins."[5] For context, Jerome's opponent, Jovinian—whose ideas we retain as mediated through Jerome's criticisms—was condemned by Pope Siricius around 393.[6] Jovinian was accused of holding a Stoic view that all sins are equally heinous (a view that finds expression in Cicero's *Paradoxa Stoicorum*).[7] Augustine (354–430) himself weighed in on this controversy, writing to Jerome:

> On the doctrine of the equality of sins, only the Stoics dared to argue against the unanimous sentiment of humanity: a vain thought, which in writing against Jovinian (a Stoic in this opinion, but an Epicurean in following after and defending pleasure) you have most clearly refuted according to the Holy Scriptures.[8]

Augustine and Jerome were not the first to articulate a distinction between sins, and Augustine (though not the inventor of the mortal–venial distinction) employed a sort of proto-distinction; as a result, he appears

---

4. For example, see Tertullian on remissible versus irremissible sin as part of his discussion of 1 John 5:16 in *Liber de Pudicitia* 2 (*PL* 2:985). On Cyprian's remedying of "the daily sins" in connection with 1 John 1:8–10 and the Lord's Prayer, see Cyprian, *De Opere et Eleemosynis* 3 (*PL* 4:604), and Cyprian, *De Oratione Dominica* 22 (*PL* 4:534). On Ambrose's use of lighter and heavier sins committed by the righteous in connection with 1 John 5:16–17, see Ambrose, *De Poenitentia* 10.45 (*PL* 16:480): "eui satis est si pro levioribus delictis Deum precetur, graviorum veniam iustorum orationibus reservandam putet."

5. Jerome, *Adversus Jovinianum* 2.30 (*PL* 23:327): "Cernis quod si pro peccatis minoribus deprecemur, impetremus veniam. Si pro maioribus, difficilis impetratio sit: et inter peccata et peccata, magnam esse distantiam. Unde et de populo Israel, quia peccaverat peccatum ad mortem, dicitur ad Jeremiam: *Noli orare pro populo hoc, nec assumas pro eis deprecationem, et non obsistas mihi, quia non exaudiam te.*"

6. For more on the Jovinianist controversy, see Hunter, *Marriage, Celibacy, and Heresy*.

7. This was more of a secondary accusation in light of Jovinian's views on celibacy and ascetic practice. Hunter sees this accusation as Jerome's attempt of "conjur[ing] up a philosophical pedigree for Jovinian's position" (Hunter, *Marriage, Celibacy, and Heresy*, 233). On the conflation of sins in Stoic thought, see Paradox 3 of *Paradoxa Stoicorum* in Cicero, *On the Orator*, 270–71: "Aequalia esse peccata et recte facta."

8. Augustine, *Epistolae* 167.2.4 (*PL* 33:735): "Illoc autem de parilitate peccatorum, soli Stoici ausi sunt disputare, contra omnem sensum generis humani: quam eorum vanitatem in Joviniano illo qui in hac sententia Stoicus erat, in aucupandis autem et defensandis voluptatibus Epicureus, de Scripturis sanctis dilucidissime convicisti."

to be the most widely quoted authority on the matter in the later Western theological tradition.⁹

Yet, even before Jerome, Augustine, and Jovinian, earlier commentators on Scripture found another critical place from which to detail the manifold diversity of transgressions: Rom 4:7–8. In these verses the apostle Paul quotes Ps 32:1–2 (VG/LXX Ps 31:1–2): "Blessed are they whose iniquities are forgiven and whose sins are covered. Blessed is the man to whom the Lord has not reckoned sin." The late fourth-century Latin commentator known as "Ambrosiaster" remarked that:

> The words *to forgive* and *to cover* and *not to reckon* have a single explanation and a single meaning.... However, to some people it seems that these words have a threefold explanation, because the prophet used different words and because he proceeds from the plural to the singular. For since the prophet wishes to relay the words of God about the abundance of grace by using several terms for transgressions—since there are various names for *sins*—he has spoken rather expansively. Nevertheless, the words have a single meaning, because when God covers he forgives, and when he forgives he does not reckon.¹⁰

Before this, Ambrosiaster explains that Paul uses David "the prophet" to reinforce the point that the Gentile who believes apart from the works of the law is reckoned righteous on account of his faith in Christ. Ambrosiaster adds that the person whose sins are forgiven is "blessed" because they need no works of repentance for this forgiveness, only faith. However, he

---

9. See Durkin, *Theological Distinction of Sins*, 150: "[Augustine's] development of the theological distinction of sins—a distinction previously quite secondary to the distinction of sins according to the manner of remissibility—gave to the Christian world a new phraseology. Because of his expression of the distinction between mortal and venial sin this fundamental doctrine was afterwards more easily anchored in popular conscience and more readily explored by his theological heirs." It should be noted, however, that while Augustine does use the phrase "*peccatum veniale*," nowhere does he use the expression "*peccatum mortale*." Though he does not use this term, he still possesses and utilizes a category of heavier, deadlier, and more grave sin.

10. The Latin text that I am consulting is from *CSEL* vol. 81/1, edited by H. J. Vogels [hereafter: *Ambrosiaster in Romanos*]. This translation is from De Bruyn, *Commentary*, 77–78. *Ambrosiaster in Romanos* 133.4–11: "remittere et tegere et non inputare una ratio et unus est sensus. omnia enim uno modo obtinentur et donantur. videtur autem quibusdam tripertita ratio in his dictis, quia diversis profeta usus est verbis, et quia a plurali numero ad singularem descendit. cum enim verba dei in ubertate gratiae, quia peccati diversa sunt nomina, per delictorum vocabula enumerare vult, latius locutus est; unius tamen significationis sunt verba, quia et cum tegit remittit, et cum remittit non inputat."

tries to explain why different terms are being used to communicate the same things. He grants that "to forgive," "to cover," and "not to reckon" all have the same meaning but that others have argued for a "threefold" explanation. Further, the prophet gives not only different terms for forgiveness but also different terms for sin. Here is where Ambrosiaster describes the three levels of sinning, which are nevertheless all forgiven in baptism:

> He created three levels on account of the diversity of transgressions. The first of these levels is wickedness or ungodliness, when the creator is not recognized; the second level consists in committing more serious [*gravium*] sins; the third level consists in lighter [*levium*] sins. Nevertheless, he says that these are all wiped out in baptism. With these three levels he has designated the entire body of sin.[11]

Unlike the terms for forgiveness, these terms for sin convey a gradation of sinning. Ambrosiaster makes an important qualification: The forgiveness for all these sins is in the context of baptism, *not* penitence or martyrdom. He argues that Paul/David cannot be speaking of either "penitents" or "martyrs" but rather of those whose sins are wiped out through baptism.[12] Penitents' sins are forgiven by "toil and sighing," whereas martyrs reach glory through "suffering and anguish."[13] This forgiveness of sin(s) is spoken of in relation to those who receive baptism and not for those who have already received it. For those already baptized, Ambrosiaster explains that there are other means of obtaining forgiveness—on this point we will see a development in thought throughout later centuries.

Lombard and the Gloss Tradition

By the time of Peter Lombard (1100–1160), the use of a distinction between mortal and venial sins was common, though not entirely

---

11. This translation is from De Bruyn, *Commentary*, 78. Ambrosiaster in Romanos 133.14–19: "tres enim gradus fecis propter delictorum varietatem. quorum primus gradus iniquitas est vel inpietas, dum non agnoscitur creator, secundus gradus gravium in operibus peccatorum, tertius vero levium. hos tamen omnes in baptismate obliterari. tribus his gradibus totius peccati corpus significavit."

12. Theodore S. de Bruyn has noted the variety of late fourth- and early fifth-century commentators who use this verse to distinguish between "sins [that] are forgiven in baptism, covered through penitence, and not imputed through martyrdom," which includes Origen/Rufinus, Pelagius, and Budapest Anonymous. See De Bruyn, *Commentary*, 77n16.

13. De Bruyn, *Commentary*, 78; Ambrosiaster in Romanos 133.19–25.

standardized with respect to penance, and the distinction of sin appears to have grown increasingly complex, especially "taking into account consent, will, and act and delineating between venial and mortal."[14] Lombard himself committed nine distinctions in book IV of the *Sentences* to the topic of penance and the mortal–venial distinction.[15] Also immediately preceding this century, there was an ongoing resurgence in biblical commentaries among students in Bec, Rheims, and Laon. The works of Anselm of Laon and his students are notable especially for their "authoritative presentation of the exegetical tradition, the *Glossa Ordinaria*."[16] The *Gloss* was a full edition of the Bible with both excerpts and summaries from medieval and patristic biblical commentators that were in marginal and interlinear glosses, and Peter Lombard likely helped standardize the *Gloss* as it was promoted within Parisian schools.[17] Lombard even added on to the *Glossa Ordinaria* with his own gloss, the so-called *Magna Glossatura* (*MG*).[18] While this claim is contested among some, for our purposes here, it is apparent that the *MG* expands upon the *Gloss*'s comments on Rom 4:7–8.[19]

The *MG* develops the *Gloss* in a distinctive way. It follows Ambrosiaster's reading of the three levels of sin being the sins that are removed in baptism, yet it develops this idea through an extended discussion of the nature of concupiscence post-baptism and more explicitly identifies original sin with concupiscence, or *iniquitas*, by following Ps 51:5 (VG 50:7): "Ecce enim in iniquitatibus conceptus sum, et in peccatis concepit

---

14. See Hause, "Abelard," 252: "The distinction between these two types of sin was in Abelard's day already an old and well accepted one." Abelard and Lombard were, of course, contemporaries who both wrote on the topic of the mortal–venial sin distinction. On the growing complexity of sin and the expanding role of the priest in confession in the twelfth century, see Briola, "Case Study," 79.

15. See Lombard, *Sententiae*, IV.14–22.

16. Hughes, *Constructing Antichrist*, 179.

17. Hughes, *Constructing Antichrist*, 209.

18. This is the traditional argument on the matter stemming back to Beryl Smalley's work. See Smalley, "*Glossa Ordinaria*." For a more recent discussion of the debate and defense of the traditional argument, see O'Hagan, "Teaching the Tradition," 95–96; O'Hagan, "Glossing the Gloss," 83–116. However, while there has been widespread agreement on this matter, there has also been some pushback to it, arguing that instead of Lombard's *Magna Glossatura* being considered an addition to the *Glossa Ordinaria*, it should instead be viewed in reverse—i.e., the *Glossa Ordinaria* was an abridgement of the *Magna Glossatura*. See the introduction to Woodward, *Glossa Ordinaria*, ix–xi.

19. I have consulted the *Glossa Ordinaria* on Rom 4 in Froehlich, *Biblia Latina* [hereafter: *Gloss*]. Similarly, I have consulted the *Magna Glossatura* on Rom 4 in *PL* 191 [hereafter: *MG*].

me mater mea." Original sin, for both Augustine and Lombard, is tied directly to this basic disorientation of the human nature: we are directed away from God, inward, and toward lesser goods. Lombard argues, following Augustine, that this concupiscence is not removed in baptism: its guilt (*culpa*) is removed, yet its punishment (*poena*) remains.[20] However, this disordered desire "no longer dominates if man perseveres in the grace of baptism."[21] In other words, concupiscence remains in the believer, but it is not counted as sin for those who do not consent to it.[22] It is this man, then, who is counted blessed, whose iniquities (i.e., original sin) are forgiven and whose sins (i.e., actual, willful sins) are removed in baptism.[23] Moving to verse 8, the *MG* following the *Gloss* states:

> Because there is no one without original (*originali*) or venial (*veniali*) sin, he adds, "Blessed is the man to whom the Lord has not imputed" for punishment "sin"—original sin, that is from another, or venial sin.[24]

For Lombard, verse 7 details the forgiveness of the guilt of original sin and the removal of actual sins in baptism, while verse 8 considers the blessedness of not being imputed original sin nor being punished for venial sin.[25] While the *Gloss* only briefly quotes Ambrosiaster, Lombard follows Ambrosiaster's logic and applies it to the guilt and punishment of original and venial sins, even explicitly quoting him on the threefold offenses and the one collective meaning of them all:

---

20. *MG* (*PL* 191:1369): "et quomodo in baptismate remittatur, ut scilicet non remaneat post baptismum culpa, sed poena." For Augustine's ideas on the matter, see *De Nuptiis et Concupiscentia* 1.25.28 (*PL* 44:852): "ad haec respondetur dimitti concupiscentiam carnis in baptismo, non ut non sit, sed ut in peccatum non imputetur."

21. *MG* (*PL* 191:1369): "et illud quod remaneat non iam dominetur, si perseveret homo in gratia baptismi."

22. See Augustine, *De Nuptiis et Concupiscentia* 1.23.25 (*PL* 44:428): "Nam ipsa quidem concupiscentia iam non est peccatum in regeneratis, quando illi ad illicita opera non consentitur, atque ut ea perpetrent a regina mente membra non dantur."

23. *MG* (*PL* 191:1369): "Ideo caute ait: *Beati quorum remissae sunt*, etc, mitigate et quantum ad culpam deletae, sed non quantum ad poenam, et *Quorum peccata*, actualia, *tecta sunt* in baptismo."

24. *MG* (*PL* 191:1370): "Et quia nullus est sine peccato originali, vel veniali, subdit: *Beatus*, vir cui non imputavit Dominus ad poenam *peccatum*, originale quod aliunde est, vel veniale."

25. Though, of course, the punishments on account of Adam's original sin—namely, concupiscence, mortality, etc.—remain.

> He committed three degrees of wrongdoing. For it seems that there is a threefold reason in these sayings, because of the variety of offenses. The first step is iniquity, or impiety, namely when the Creator is not recognized. The second step is in the works of grave sins. The third, however, is light (*levium*) [sins]. However, to forgive and to reign [*sic*],[26] and not to impute, are words of one reason and sense, because when he covers [sin] he forgives [sin] and when he forgives [sin] he does not impute it.[27]

Here Lombard, quoting Ambrosiaster, discusses the three sorts of sins forgiven in baptism: original sin, grave sins, and venial sins. Though Lombard nowhere in this section uses the term "mortal sins," he almost certainly had them in mind, and even later commentators on this passage, such as St. Thomas Aquinas (1224/1226–74), had no problem using Rom 4:7–8 to distinguish between "original, actual mortal, and actual venial" sin, especially as the doctrine of private penance had undergone several significant developments over the intervening centuries.[28] Among these significant Latin commentators, we can see the roots of and, subsequently, the emergence of a traditional place to discuss the distinctions of sins within biblical commentaries on Romans in the Western exegetical tradition.

---

26. This second verb is listed as "*regere*" (to reign) but should likely instead be "*tegere*" (to cover), as it is in the following sentence and in the Ambrosiaster commentary. Thanks to Stefan Krauter for pointing this out. See n11: "remittere et tegere et non inputare . . ."

27. *MG* (*PL* 191:1370): "Vel aliter, tres gradus delictorum fecit. Videtur enim tripertita ratio in his dictis propter delictorum varietatem. Primus gradus iniquitas, vel impietas est, scilicet cum Creator non agnoscitur, id est infidelitas. Secundus gradus est in operibus gravium peccatorum. Tertius vero, levium. Remittere vero et regere [*sic*], et non imputare unius rationis et sensus sunt verba, quia et cum tegit remittit, et cum remittit non imputat." The Ambrosiaster quote here in the *MG* is out of order. See n11 above for the original quote from Ambrosiaster. On the *Gloss*'s marginal gloss of Ambrosiaster here, see *Gloss* 4.1061v (facsim., 282a): "Tres gradus fecit: iniquitas vel impietas cum creator non agnoscitur. Peccata in operibus. Quod non imputat leve." This does seem to suggest either that Lombard had access to the Ambrosiaster commentary, with which he could have filled out the *Gloss*'s paraphrase more fully, or that the *Gloss* is an abridgement of the *MG*.

28. Aquinas, *Commentary*, 113; *Super Epistolam B. Pauli ad Romanos Lectura*, C.4 L.1 (§335): "Est autem triplex peccatum, scilicet originale, actuale mortale et actuale veniale." Aquinas explicitly names the same three steps listed in Ambrosiaster's commentary and the *MG*, but he names the sins of the second step as *actuale mortale*. See Aquinas, *Commentary*, 114; *Super Epistolam B. Pauli ad Romanos Lectura*, C.4 L.1 (§336): "Secundo, quantum ad actuale mortale, dicit *et quorum tecta sunt peccata*." On the development of private penance between the ninth and thirteenth centuries, see Tentler, *Sin and Confession*, 16–27.

FROM *LOCUS CLASSICUS* TO *LOCUS APOSTOLICUS*: REIGNING SIN IN ROMANS 6:12

Luther on Romans 4:7–8

Romans 4 played a significant role in the development of Luther's Reformation breakthrough, yet few have considered the way in which Luther read Rom 4:7–8 through the lens of the exegetical history traced above. The passage figures prominently within Luther's 1515–16 Romans lectures. In his scholia on these two verses, three themes connected to Luther's developing hamartiology are apparent: (1) his *simul* theology;[29] (2) his definition of original sin as *peccatum radicale*;[30] and, subsequently, (3) his redefinition of the mortal–venial sin distinction. There is not enough space here to expand on the former two entirely, but they are intimately interwoven in Luther's comments presented below. Luther's engagement with verse 7 notes how

> sin remains and at the same time it does not remain.... At the same time He [God] both takes away their sin and does not take it away.[31]

Shortly after this, he writes regarding the Christian person:

> He is at the same time both a sinner and a righteous man; a sinner in fact, but a righteous man by the sure imputation and promise of God.[32]

For Luther, original sin is not wholly removed with baptism. Original sin runs too deep, and Luther even conceptualizes it as the root [*radicale*] sin.[33] Concupiscence remains, and this concupiscence is sin itself.[34]

29. For recent work on the topic, see Kolb, Johansson, and Johansson, *Simul*.

30. This notion has been explored thoroughly by one recent scholar, especially as it was conceived in Luther's teaching on Ps 51. See Batka, *Peccatum Radicale*; and Batka, "Luther's Teaching."

31. *LW* 25:258; *WA* 56:270.10–11, 13: "Simul manet peccatum et non manet.... Simul tollitur eorum peccatum et non tollitur."

32. *LW* 25:260; *WA* 56:272.17–18: "Non, Sed simul peccator et Iustus; peccator re vera, Sed Iustus ex reputatione et promissione Dei certa."

33. See Luther's discussion on how this verse is describing both actual sin (the "fruit of sin") and original sin (the "root sin") at *WA* 56:271 (*LW* 25:259) and *WA* 56:277 (*LW* 25:264). As Ľubomír Batka has helpfully shown, this term appeared in Luther's works as early as these very Romans lectures, yet they emerged out of the parable of the tree and its fruit in Matt 7:17 and Matt 12:33. See Batka, "Luther's Teaching," 241.

34. *LW* 25:259: "Sin itself is the passion, the tinder, and the concupiscence"; *WA*

Luther positively identified original sin as concupiscence, but he explicitly maintains that original sin is truly *sin* after baptism. He follows Lombard's identification of original sin as expressed directly in the *MG*: "Behold, from these verses it is evident concupiscence is original sin."[35] Luther is likely engaging the *MG* in his scholia on these verses, even slightly modifying a quote from Augustine that appears in it: "Sin, or concupiscence, is forgiven in baptism, not in the sense that it no longer exists, but in the sense that it is not imputed."[36] Luther's ideas on sin here emerge as a further development in the Augustinian-Lombardian sin tradition born out of his study of Paul's Letter (and the Psalms).[37]

Finally, following this idea that sin remains even in the baptized, Luther is able to articulate what he means by "venial sin." After discussing the various Hebrew terms for sin David uses in Ps 32, he writes that, despite the fact that this evil sin lingers within us, "it becomes a venial sin and is not imputed to us only when we lament it and ask God not to condemn us on account of it."[38] A little later, he adds:

56:271.6–8: "Ergo Actuale (sicut a theologis vocatur) verius est peccatum i.e. opus et fructus peccati, peccatum autem ipsa passio fomes et concupiscentia sive pronitas ad malum et difficultas ad bonum."

35. *MG* (PL 191:1369): "Ecce ex his liquet concupiscentiam esse originale peccatum." For a good summary of these developing sin traditions, see Pitkin, "Nothing but Concupiscence," 353–56: "Martin Luther's identification of original sin with concupiscence in the scholion to Romans 4:7 locates him within Biel's Lombardian-Augustinian camp, even as contemporary scholars disagree about Luther's fidelity to that tradition" (355). Pitkin is engaging Heiko A. Oberman's work on Gabriel Biel in Oberman, *Harvest of Medieval Theology*, 120–28.

36. *LW* 25:261; *WA* 56:273.9–74.1: "Sed b. Augustinus preclarissime dixit 'peccatum concupiscentiam in baptismate remitti, non ut non sit, sed ut non imputetur.'" Cf. *MG* (PL 191:1369): "Dimittitur ergo concupiscentia carnis, in baptismate, non ut non sit, sed ut non imputetur peccatum, hoc est enim non habere peccatum, non esse reum peccati." See n20.

37. For a more detailed consideration and comparison of both Luther's and Augustine's views on this point, see Anderas, *Renovatio*, 166–99; and Pereira, *Augustine of Hippo and Martin Luther*, 326–29. On the impact of Luther's earlier study of the Psalms (especially Ps 51) on his hamartiology, see n30 above.

38. *LW* 25:264–65; *WA* 56:277–78. He uses and cites Johannes Reuchlin's Hebrew translation of these Hebrew terms (but develops his own definitions). See Reuchlin, *Ioannis Revchlin*, d.iiv–d.iiir. The first sin Luther defines is *crimen*, or פשע, which he understands to be actual sin. The second sin is *peccatum*, or האטה, which he connects to the idea of *peccatum radicale*, or "root" sin. The final sin he mentions is *iniquitas*, or עון, which he defines as hypocrisy and lowering God below the creature.

LW 25:268; *WA* 56:281.11–13: "Hoc solo autem fit veniale et non imputatur, Quod pro ipso gemimus, et ne forte Deus propter ipsum nos damnet, ne nobis imputet."

> *From all of this it is obvious that there is no sin which is venial according to its substance and to its nature, but also no merit.* For even the good works which are done while the tinder of sin and sensuality are fighting against them are not of such intensity and purity as the law requires, since they are not done with all of our strength, but only with the spiritual powers which struggle against the powers of the flesh. Thus we sin even when we do good, unless God through Christ covers this imperfection and does not impute it to us. *Thus it becomes a venial sin through the mercy of God, who does not impute it for the sake of faith and plea in behalf of this imperfection for the sake of Christ.*[39]

What is apparent here is that Luther sees all sin as mortal sin, though he does not use the word "mortal." All sin is deadly by its very nature. However, what makes sin venial is the fact that God does not impute it to the believer, who by faith trusts in Christ to cover this imperfection and confesses herself to be a sinner. However, for the one whose fear of God diminishes, who grows apathetic or prideful in this fight against internal sin, Luther claims, "God's imputation of sin returns, for God has determined that He will impute sin to no one who mourns and fears his sins and anxiously seeks his mercy."[40] In other words, for Luther here, venial sin becomes deadly again when the sinner refuses to acknowledge herself to be a sinner before God and subsequently refuses to struggle against sin and concedes to sin by willful consent.[41]

In his later comment on Rom 7:17, Luther wrote about what he saw as the struggle of each believer: "In itself the concupiscence is guilty, to be

---

39. Emphases mine. *LW* 25:276; *WA* 56:289.14–21: "Ex quo patet, Quod nullum est peccatum Veniale ex substantia et natura sua, Sed nec meritum. Quia etiam bona opera, quia renitente fomite et sensualitate, non tanta fiunt intensione et puritate, quantam lex requirit, cum non ex totis viribus fiant, Sed tantum ex viribus spiritus repugnantibus viribus carnis. Idcirco enim bene operando peccamus, nisi Deus per Christum nobis hoc imperfectum tegeret et non imputaret; fit ergo Veniale per misericordiam Dei non imputantis, propter fidem et gemitum pro ista imperfection in Christo suscepta."

40. *LW* 25:268; *WA* 56:281.16–19: "Cessante enim isto timore et sollicitudine mox ponitur securitas, posita securitate mox redit Imputatio Dei in peccatum, eo quod statuerit Deus nulli velle non imputare nisi gementi et timenti ac assidue misericordiam suam imploranti."

41. See also Luther's remarks on Rom 7:17 in *LW* 25:339; *WA* 56:350: "For he who does not earnestly strive to drive out sin certainly still possesses it, even if he has not committed any further sin for which he might be condemned. For we are not called to ease, but to a struggle against our passions, which would not be without guilt (for they really are sins and truly damnable) if the mercy of God did not refrain from imputing them to us. But only to those who manfully struggle and fight against their faults, invoking the grace of God, does God not impute sin."

sure, but yet it does not render us guilty unless we yield to it and commit sin." He then adds, "God in his mercy does not impute the guilt of the weakness but only the guilt of the will which consents to the weakness."[42] This attention to the will with respect to the culpability of sin is not a new idea. Thomas N. Tentler, who wrote extensively on confession and sin in late medieval religion, even stated that the "consent of the will, then, is a basic test of culpability.... Willful consent not only distinguishes mortal from venial sins, but also affects the general estimation of the gravity of the sinfulness of an action."[43] What was truly new in Luther's configuration of sin was that the guiltiness of concupiscence persisted in the life of the baptized but remained unimputed unless the will consented to these disordered desires: the believer is simultaneously guilty and not guilty.

Luther's reading of Rom 4:7–8 is consistent with the preceding exegetical tradition insofar as he continues to identify it as a place to distinguish between different sorts of sins, yet he strongly diverges from this tradition on the nature of *what* is being distinguished and *how* those distinctions are made: ultimately, he fundamentally challenged the traditional distinction between mortal and venial sins by denying a distinction in the essence or nature of sins. Following Luther, there appears to have been much less impetus in the Protestant tradition for attempting to locate distinctions of sin in Rom 4. Instead of Rom 4, a new place for locating a newly redefined distinction emerged among the Protestant reformers, most notably within the work of Luther's companion and collaborator, Philip Melanchthon.

Melanchthon on Romans 6:12

Luther never returned to lecturing on Romans after this early effort from 1515–16. Instead, he handed the task over to Philip Melanchthon (1497–1560), who began lecturing on Romans in 1519 as a Greek lecturer at

---

42. *LW* 25:340; *WA* 56:351.10–13: "Ex ista pulchra authoritate patet, Quomodo Concupiscentia sit ipsa infirmitas nostra ad bonum, que in se quidem rea est, Sed tamen reos nos non facit nisi consentientes et operantes. Ex quo tamen mirabile sequitur, Quod rei sumus et non rei. Quia Infirmitas illa nos ipsi sumus, Ergo ipsa rea et nos rei sumus, donec cesset et sanetur. Sed non sumus rei, dum non operamur secundum eam, Dei misericordia non imputante reatum infirmitatis, Sed reatum consentientis infirmitati voluntatis."

43. Tentler, *Sin and Confession*, 150–51. This is not to say that desire was considered morally neutral, as he writes: "Everyone carefully instructs penitents that it is possible to sin by desire even if one does not act on it."

Wittenberg University. It has also been suggested that Melanchthon likely had access to and made use of Luther's lectures on Romans in the work of his own commentaries on the book.[44] However, there is no sign of Luther's comments on the distinctions of sin in Rom 4:7–8 in Melanchthon's own commentary on these verses. Melanchthon instead makes these comments in some of the first lines of his *Loci Communes* of 1521:

> Scripture does not distinguish between actual and original sin, since original sin is also clearly an actual corrupt desire. Rather, Scripture simply calls both original vice and actual vice sin, though sometimes it calls what we consider actual sins "the fruits of sin" as Paul likes to do in Romans. And what we call original sin, David sometimes names "crookedness" [*curvitatem*] and sometimes "iniquity" [*iniquitatem*]. But there is no reason to discuss here those stupid distinctions concerning sin. Sin is a corrupt inner disposition and a depraved agitation of the heart against the Law of God.[45]

Given the close relationship between Melanchthon's *Loci* and his Romans commentary, there are a few things worth recognizing here. First, Melanchthon follows Luther on the close connection between the "root" and "fruit" of sin as original and actual sin, respectively. He believes it is erroneous to distinguish them too starkly. Further, Melanchthon also references what he sees as David's account of the distinctions of sin in the psalm. However, he finds a place a little later in his *loci* for a discussion of the distinction between mortal and venial sins. Melanchthon writes closely following Luther's own ideas:

> All the works of the saints are venial sins because they are forgiven to believers by God's mercy. God sometimes takes his Spirit from the saints with the result that they fall back into manifest sins. The Scholastics call these manifest sins "mortal sins," and I do not object to this at all, so long as they understand

---

44. The first major attempt to make this connection is in Bizer, *Theologie der Verheissung*, 216–18. A current expert on Melanchthon's commentaries has also assumed this. See Wengert, "Philip Melanchthon," 125.

45. Melanchthon, *Loci Communes*, 37–38; *CR* 21:97: "Scriptura non vocat hoc originale, illud actuale peccatum. Est enim et originale peccatum plane actualis quaedam prava cupiditas. Sed tam actuale quam originale vitium, peccatum simpliciter vocat, quanquam nonnunquam ea quae nos actualia peccata, vocet fructus peccati, ut ad Romanos Paulus solet, et David, quod originale nos, alias curvitatem, alias iniquitatem adpellat. Nec est quod hic de illis stultis relationibus in peccato disputemus. Pravus adfectus, pravusque cordis motus est contra legem dei, peccatum."

that I call everything done by people who lack the Spirit of God "mortal sins."[46]

Here we can see how Melanchthon connects mortal sins not to certain types of *sin* but to certain types of *people*, that is, those who lack the Spirit of God. Again, sin does not go away, yet the root sin is not imputed as guilt to the saints. However, giving into "manifest sins" is a sign of the Spirit's absence, which, according to Melanchthon, God does sometimes permit even in the saints.

This same idea was also communicated in the portion of the Smalcald Articles (1537) devoted to the topic of repentance. Luther echoes Melanchthon's earlier comments, which instruct us that "holy men," while feeling the tug of original sin, can still fall into "manifest sins, as David [fell] into adultery, murder, and blasphemy," and that this is an indication that they have "cast out" both "faith and the Holy Ghost."[47] The idea that mortal sin cannot coexist with faith and the Holy Spirit also appears in the *Apology of the Augsburg Confession* (1530).[48] The Articles also add, alluding to Rom 6:12, that "the Holy Spirit does not permit for sin to reign [*dominari*] . . . but restrains and curbs it."[49] This idea will be further developed by Melanchthon in his reading of Rom 6.

---

46. Melanchthon, *Loci Communes*, 166; CR 21:207–8: "Contra venialia peccata sunt, omnia sanctorum opera, nempe, quod per misericordiam dei, credentibus condonentur. Nonnunquam sanctis eripit deus spiritum, ita ut in manifesta vitia prolabantur, quae vocent sane, me nihil refragante peccata mortalia, modo sciant me mortalia ad eum modum adpellare quid quid fit ab iis qui spiritu dei carent." Strangely, two translations of the work have offered two very different readings of this passage. Preus's translation, which I have cited above, offers a reading indicating that Melanchthon does allow for the possibility of saints falling into mortal sin. By contrast, Hill's earlier translation presents this reading: "God never takes the Spirit from the saints so that they fall into the manifest crimes rightly denominated moral sins" (Melanchthon, *Loci Communes of Philip Melanchthon*, 237). Hill's translation here is erroneous due to his mistranslation of *nonnunquam*.

47. Smalcald Articles, pars. III., art. IV, in *BSELK* 319:43: "Si igitur, tales in posterum etiam orirentur, sciendum et docendum est, quod si sancti, qui originale peccatum adhuc habere se sentient et quotidie de eo penitent et cum eo luctantur, insuper ruant in manifesta peccata, ut David in adulterium, homicidium et blasphemiam, eos excutere fidem et Spiritum Sanctum, et abesse tum ab ipsis fidem et Spiritum Sanctum."

48. See *Apologia Confessionis*, art. IV (II), in *BSELK* 98:64: "Quum autem de tali fide loquamur, quae non est otiosa cogitatio, sed quae a morte liberat, et novam vitam in cordibus parit, et est opus Spiritus Sancti: non stat cum peccato mortali, sed tantisper, dum adest, bonos fructus parit, ut postea dicemus."

49. *BSELK* 319:44: "Spiritus enim Sanctus non sinit peccatum dominari, invalescere et victoriam obtinere ac consummari, sed reprimit et coercet, ne facere possit, quae vult."

Melanchthon's commentary on Romans was first published in 1532, yet his 1540 commentary represents a more finalized and revised edition of the work.[50] For the present matter at hand, there is a lengthy insertion that is made in his comments on Rom 6:12 in this later edition pertaining to the distinction between mortal and venial sins. Romans 6:12 ("Therefore let not sin reign in your mortal body so that you obey its concupiscences") is situated directly between the two chapters of Paul's letter describing the entrance of sin into the world (Rom 5) and the believer's personal struggle with sin (Rom 7). It is here in this chapter that Melanchthon details the baptism of the sinful old man and the rebirth of the spiritual new man through the twofold process of mortification and vivification. Given that we have been "buried with Christ," Melanchthon writes:

> The Holy Spirit is given at the same time in order that he might put to death our old nature and begin the new. We are buried with Christ, because after our nature has begun to be mortified, sin has been buried in a twofold way: first by imputation, for although the remnants of sin remain, they are forgiven, and second, as far as the effect is concerned, because our sinful nature ceases to be active, or begins to be mortified.[51]

Melanchthon, reflecting on Paul's words, held that the old man relates to these remnants of sin, while the new man is associated with the presence of the Holy Spirit putting to death the elements of the old. This helps contextualize these new comments Melanchthon makes on mortal-venial sin among the saints.

In discussing verse 12, Melanchthon writes that Paul says "Let not sin reign" because it indicates that sin is still within us; it has not been totally extinguished. However, he writes that this is the place in which we can clearly see the distinction between mortal and venial sins. First, he describes how mortal sins become venial:

---

50. The 1532 version is available within *Philipp Melancthon*, volume 5. The 1540 version can be found in *CR* 15:493–796.

51. Melanchthon, *Commentary on Romans*, 146; *CR* 15:637: "Quia simul datur Spiritus sanctus, ut mortificet veterem naturam, et incoet novam. Sepelimur autem una eum Christo, quia postquam natura nostra mortificari coepit, peccatum sepultum est dupliciter. Primum imputatione, Quanquam enim reliquiae manent, tamen sunt condonatae. Secundo, quod ad effectum attinet, quia natura vitiosa desinit esse efficax, seu incipit mortificari."

> These and similar passages [Rom 8:13] show the difference between mortal and venial sin. There remains in the saints concupiscence and evil desires; but since they resist these, and in faith seek and declare that theses sins are forgiven, the sins become venial, because when such sins are present, the Holy Spirit and faith can exist at the same time in the godly.
> But they become mortal sins in those who have been sanctified when they obey the evil desires contrary to their conscience.[52]

Rather than making the traditional move of connecting these distinctions to Rom 4:7–8 (he does not comment on those verses in relation to this passage), Melanchthon continues with the idea that sin remains in the saints but is forgiven and becomes venial through faith and the indwelling Spirit. However, Melanchthon also adds that these venial sins can become mortal again. He cites Rom 8:13 and 12:11 to argue that by consenting to these vestiges of sin, we betray our consciences and refuse the Holy Spirit. This is the heart of Melanchthon's distinction of mortal and venial sin: the allegiance of one's obedience to the Spirit or to Sin. The Holy Spirit and Sin cannot reign alongside one another in a person, and for Melanchthon, the direction of one's will is an indication of whether Sin or the Spirit is truly reigning.

Though Melanchthon was more critical of the mortal–venial distinction in his earlier works, his earliest writings still maintained this reconfigured definition. However, it was not until his later commentaries on Romans that he found a precise exegetical location in Romans for this newly worked out distinction. This new location (in conjunction with the penitential psalms) provided Melanchthon a scriptural tether for the idea, fomented by Luther, that the difference between mortal and venial sin lies not in the quality of sin but rather in the person who resists (or commits) such sins. A new *locus classicus* was thus established for the doctrine of reigning (mortal) sin and unreigning (venial) sin. In other words, Luther prompted this reconfigured *doctrine*, while Melanchthon found a new exegetical *location* for it.

---

52. Melanchthon, *Commentary on Romans*, 148; *CR* 15:639: "Hi loci et similes ostendunt discrimen peccati mortalis et venialis. Manent in Sanctis concupiscentia et vitiosi affectus: sed cum his resistunt, et fide petunt ac statuunt sibi condonari haec peccata, fiunt veniala, quia etiam cum adsunt talia, possunt simul existere in piis Spiritus sanctus et fides. Sed mortalia sunt in his, qui fuerant santificati, cum contra conscientiam obtemperant pravis affectibus."

PROTESTANT RECEPTIONS OF MELANCHTHON'S READING OF ROMANS 6:12

Nearly a century after Melanchthon's first commentary on Romans, Lutheran professor of theology Friedrich Balduin (1575–1627) found it possible to write in his *Catechesis Apostolica* (a commentary on Romans) on the connection between mortal-venial sin and Rom 6:12:

> *The distinction between "venial" and "mortal" sin has its origins in this apostolic locus*, where he expressly distinguishes between concupiscence or desire of sin and a voluntary compliance presented unto it. No man or woman is able to prevent evil concupiscences, on account of original sin, which is never idle. But as long as the godly person struggles against them and does not provide assent [to these desires], it is decreed only venial [sin], so called not because it is pardonable on account of its own nature or in any way deserves pardon, but because it is not imputed to the faithful for Christ's sake. But compliance to sin makes it mortal sin, which injures the conscience and casts out both faith and the Holy Spirit.[53]

Melanchthon's commentary established for Balduin and a line of other Lutheran commentators on Scripture a location and explanation (following Luther) for their distinct notion of the mortal–venial distinction.[54] Balduin names it a "*locus Apostolicus*" for this doctrine. What distinguishes these Lutheran theologians' understandings from traditional Catholic teaching is the opinion that mortal and venial sin are not distinguished by nature or substance but by the person who commits that sin: whether it is a repentant person or an unrepentant person. In other words, the difference between a mortal sin and a venial sin in this tradition does not

---

53. Emphasis mine. Balduin, *Catechesis apostolica*, 427: "Discrimen inter peccatum Veniale et Mortale sedem suam habet in hoc loco Apostolico, ubi expresse distinguitur inter concupiscentias et desideria peccati, et inter obsequium eis praestitum. Concupiscentias malas nemo hominum praecavere potest, propter peccatum originis, quod nunquam otiosum est: sed quamdiu homo pius iis reluctatur neque praebet assensum, peccatum constituent veniale, ita dictum, non quod natura sua venia dignum sit, aut veniam mereatur, sed quia fidelibus propter Christum non imputatur. Obsequium peccati facit peccatum mortale, quod ladit conscientiam, excutit Spiritum Sanctum et fidem."

54. For some other Lutheran commentators who follow this reading, see Cruciger, *In epistolam Pauli ad Romanos scriptam commentarius*, 240; Major, *Primus Tomus Operum Reverendi Viri D. Georgii Maioris*, 119; and Wigand, *In epistolam S. Pauli ad Romano annotationes*, 63v.

lie in the sin itself but in a person's willingness or unwillingness to lend consent to concupiscence.

Admittedly, the later Protestant Reformed tradition did not see much of a need for maintaining such a distinction so explicitly. However, some notable Reformed commentators in the sixteenth century did maintain a place for it. For example, Melanchthon's 1540 reading of Rom 6:12 was utilized directly by Peter Martyr Vermigli (1499–1562) in his own commentary on Rom 6:12–13.[55] Commenting on the verse, Vermigli writes:

> Out of this place the distinction between mortal [*mortalia*] sins and venial [*veniala*] sins is elicited. For when we loudly protest and resist these carnal desires, those unruly motions, and incitements erupting from our innate depravity—these are indeed sins since they are opposed to the law of God—however, because they are displeasing to us, and we struggle against them, we leave some place in us for faith and the Spirit of God, therefore, they are forgiven of us. Neither are they imputed [to us] unto death. On the contrary, however, when we submit to them, we repel the influence of the Spirit of God, and act contrary to our conscience, or at very least when we act with a faulty conscience so that we call those things which are evil, good, or judge good things evil. *Only then do we sin mortally, for we make sin to reign in us.*[56]

Vermigli paraphrases Melanchthon's comments on this verse without naming him (though Vermigli names him in the dedication of the commentary). Vermigli explains that this passage in Paul's letter is where the mortal–venial distinction can be located. He also follows Melanchthon in the understanding that while the concupiscences arising from natural corruption are indeed sin, these sins are venial (i.e., forgiven) in the saints and not imputed as sin or guilt.[57] However, like Melanchthon's teaching,

---

55. See n52 above for direct comparison.

56. Emphasis mine. Vermigli, *In Epistolam S. Pauli Apostoli ad Romanos*, 209: "Ex hoc loco discrimen elicitor inter peccata mortalia, et veniala. Nam cum reclamamus, et resistimus cupiditatibus, motus illi turbulenti, et incitationes, ab insita pravitate erumpentes, quoniam legi Dei adversantur, peccata sunt: Sed tamen, quoniam illa nobis displicent, nosque illis reluctamur, et fidei, Deique spiritui locum in nobis aliquem relinquimus, ideo nobis condonantur, neque ad mortem imputantur. Contra vero, quum illis paremus, et divini spiritus impulsum repellimus, agimusque contra conscientiam, aut certe conscientia vitiate, ut quae mala sunt, dicamus bona, aut bona iudicemus mala, tum demum peccamus mortaliter. Peccatum enim in nobis regnare facimus."

57. For a deeper treatment of Vermigli's understanding of sin, and more specifically

these venial sins can become mortal when we obey them, stripping ourselves of the Spirit and allowing sin to reign within. For both Vermigli and Melanchthon, sins become mortal when a saint allows such corrupt desires to steer the ship of his soul, against the winds of the Spirit, conscience, and faith.

Vermigli is not alone among the sixteenth-century Protestant Reformed in following Melanchthon on this distinction. The commentary tradition on the Heidelberg Catechism—that is, the commentary that has been posthumously accredited to Zacharias Ursinus (1534–83), a friend of Vermigli and likely the chief producer of the Heidelberg Catechism— offers several different distinctions of sin.[58] (What follows is also found in Johannes Borg's notes on Ursinus's lectures on the Heidelberg Catechism, which seems to imply that this is a distinction Ursinus himself adopted.[59]) In this section of the commentary, it first maintains the fundamental distinction between original sin and actual sin. Next, it distinguishes between actual sins as sins of commission and omission. Then it makes a distinction between "reigning sin" (*peccatum regnans est*) and sin that does not reign (*non regnans peccatum est*). Following this closely are sins against the conscience and sins against the Holy Spirit.[60] These last two distinctions should by now be recognizable. The commentary directly quotes Rom 6:12 and 1 John 3:8 as support for the distinction between "reigning" sins, concerning which "the sinner makes no resistance through the grace of the Holy Spirit," and those "un-reigning" sins that "the sinner resists by the grace of the Holy Spirit."[61] The commentary re-

---

mortal and venial sins, see Donnelly, *Calvinism and Scholasticism in Vermigli's Doctrine of Man and Grace*, 101–23.

58. On the difficulty of attributing authorship of the commentary to Ursinus, see Wagner-Peterson, "Zacharias Ursinus"; De Wildt, "Commentaren Op de Heidelbergse Catechismus." Thanks to Damian Danke for bringing this problem of authorship to my attention. On the question of the authorship of the catechism itself, see Bierma et al., *Introduction to the Heidelberg Catechism*, 52, 67–74.

59. He connects reigning and unreigning sins to mortal and venial sins. See Borg, *Dictata seu explicate in catechis*, 15v. Thanks again to Damian Danke for making me aware of these lecture notes and pointing me to the section on hamartiological distinctions.

60. Here I am engaging *CHC* 43–54.

61. *CHC* 48–49: "*Secunda distinctio.* Peccatum aliud est regnas, aliud non regnans. *Peccatum regnans* est, cui peccans non repugnat per gratiam Spiritus sancti, ideoque fit obnoxius aeternae morti, nisi poenitentiam agat, et veniam per Christum consequatur. . . . De hoc dicitur: *Ne regnet igitur peccatum in mortali corpore vestro.* Item: *Qui facit peccatum*, id est, qui data opera peccat, et cum delectatione, *ex diablo est*. . . . *Non regnans* peccatum est, cui peccans repugnat per gratiam Spiritus sancti: ideoque non est obnoxius aeternae morti, quia poenitentiam agir, et veniam consequitur per Christum."

fers to this distinction as the "common distinction of sin into mortal and venial sin."⁶² It follows the typical Protestant pattern of noting that every sin by nature is mortal sin, yet following Melanchthon and Vermigli, it states that mortal sin becomes venial sin "when it becomes un-reigning sin in the reborn."⁶³ It is, according to the commentary, only in line with this new definition that the distinction between mortal and venial sin can be retained. The problem with the Roman Catholic view, it proceeds to say, is that it assumes that sins become mortal or venial based upon the "gravity" (*gravitate*) or "lightness" (*levitate*) of the sin itself.⁶⁴ It is for this reason that the commentary uses the categories of "reigning" and "un-reigning" sins in place of "mortal" and "venial" sins, as it places the distinction not in the sins themselves but in the person who either resists or concedes to them, while at the same time using Pauline language to draw the distinction.⁶⁵

These early Reformed and Lutheran traditions both seem to agree that this distinction can be maintained insofar as it does not minimize sin, yet at the same time, both traditions sought to affirm, following Paul, that the saints are those who actively resist sin. Both groups agreed that all sin is mortal but becomes venial among the saints on account of God's mercy alone, and while most Lutherans believed that venial sin can become mortal again, not all Reformed thinkers agreed. Some, such as Wolfgang Musculus (1497–1563), agreed that the difference between mortal and venial sin resides in the person committing the sin (and not in the sin itself), yet he explained this difference with the language of "the elect" and "the reprobate."⁶⁶ In other words, for the elect, the sins remain venial, whereas the sins of the reprobate are always mortal. This idea appears to establish itself with some regularity (though not without certain nuances) within post-Reformation Reformed theology, yet early

62. CHC 49: "Ad hanc distinctionem referri potest illa vulgaris, in *peccatum mortale et veniale*."

63. CHC 49: "Fit autem *veniale*, hoc est, non accersit mortem aeternam, cum fit non regnans in renatis."

64. CHC 50: "Et hoc quidem sensu distinctio *mortalis* et *venialis peccati* retineri potest: nequaquam autem eo sensu, quo a pontificiis usurpatur, quasi *mortale* sit quod sua gravitate mortem aeternam mereatur; *veniale*, quod propter levitate suam non aeterna morte, sed tantum temporali poena dignum sit coram Deo."

65. CHC 50: "Ego pro peccato mortali et veniali malim dicere peccatum regnans et non regnans."

66. Musculus, *Loci Communes*, 39: "Constituamus igitur primum de peccantium personis. Quod si illae in Christo sunt electe ac fideles, consequitur et illorum peccata mortalia non esse, sed veniala."

Reformed theologians' views on the matter were not entirely uniform.[67] We can say that both Lutherans and the Reformed tied the new Protestant mortal–venial distinction to the person committing the sin rather than the quality of the sin itself. Sin is still sin, whether it is simply felt or acted upon. However, the Lutheran and Reformed traditions generally appear to diverge on the point of whether a saint can fall back into mortal sin (i.e., can venial sin *truly* become mortal again?).[68] Lutherans tended to ground the distinction in the presence of the Spirit and faith in a person, whereas the Reformed tended to ground it in the state of a person, either elect or reprobate. Whatever the case, even despite their shifting hamartiologies, magisterial Protestants in the sixteenth century still sought to maintain certain distinctions within sin, such as original and actual, mortal and venial, and reigning and unreigning.

CONCLUSION: A PASTORAL DISTINCTION

Martin Luther's radical criticism of the medieval penitential system posed a new challenge for Protestants' understandings of the mortal–venial sin distinction. Whereas penance once played the role of remitting mortal sin, the traditional distinction between mortal and venial sin was essentially killed and reconverted according to a new theological and pastoral perspective. As evidenced above, this tradition of distinguishing sin (as far back as Ambrosiaster) in light of Rom 4:7–8 was largely discontinued in the Protestant traditions that emerged in the wake of Luther, who used this scriptural locus to redefine the old distinction. Following Luther,

---

67. On this point of mortal and venial sin in early modernity, see Hampton, "Sin, Grace, and Free Choice," 233–34. The early Reformed had very similar though slightly distinct views on mortal and venial sin. For example, Martin Bucer understood apostasy to be the only mortal sin in the righteous; see Lugioyo, *Martin Bucer's Doctrine of Justification*, 68. Heinrich Bullinger maintained the category of mortal sin but "used it in a variety of ways," applying it to more heinous sins among both the faithful and the unfaithful while also applying it to the sin against the Holy Spirit. He also saw a moral difference between concupiscence resisted and concupiscence indulged; see Stephens, *Theology of Heinrich Bullinger*, 237. John Calvin famously derides the mortal–venial sin distinction; however, he still retained a place for the distinction between "depraved lusts which gain consent" and "concupiscence which tickles and affects our hearts, but halts in the middle of being enticed" (*CO* 49:124). Cf. Raith, *After Merit*, 129–30. Zwingli's earlier view of original sin as "a defect which of itself is not sinful in the one who has it" also clearly marks a difference among Reformed and Lutheran writers on the matter of original sin being in itself mortal sin—as cited in Stephens, *Theology of Huldrych Zwingli*, 149.

68. For a Lutheran consideration of the topic, see Cooper, "Mortal and Venial Sin."

Melanchthon relocated this doctrine in Paul's discourse on the new and old man in Rom 6. A *locus classicus* was rejected in favor of a *locus Apostolicus*. Instead of mortal sin being of a different quality or quantity than venial sin and in need of remission via penance, it was re-understood in light of Paul's notion of "reigning sin." All sin in this new configuration was indeed considered mortal, but for those who are baptized, regenerated, and being vivified, concupiscence and evil desires are (although still guilty in themselves) no longer imputed as sin on account of one's faith in Christ. All the saints feel that pull of concupiscence and evil desire, yet it is the saint who resists with the wind of the Spirit at her back and Christ's righteousness in her stead. The mortal sin that becomes venial, for Melanchthon, is simply concupiscence resisted and not allowed to reign in a person. The later Lutheran tradition appears to have followed Melanchthon in this regard, and certain Reformed theologians, such as Peter Martyr Vermigli and Zacharias Ursinus, also directly followed Melanchthon on his reading of Rom 6 and his distinction between reigning and unreigning sins.

These Protestant reformers recognized that all sin violates the law of God and thus is mortal by its very nature. However, they did not maintain that all sin was necessarily of the same consequence, effect, or significance. There were strategic reasons for this—for example, they did not want to be identified with the Jovinianist heresy, which considered all sins to be equally evil—yet at the same time, there was a pastoral tension at the heart of it. To claim that all sin is mortal by nature was a soteriological move: to minimize the gravity of sin would be to minimize the gravity of Christ's atoning work. However, to claim that all sins, whether acted upon or not, are the same would be to refuse to acknowledge the work of the Spirit against sin in the lives of the saints. In other words, through their commentaries on Rom 6, these Reformation theologians, exegetes, and pastors sought to demonstrate a fundamental difference between "reigning" and "un-reigning" sin in the life of a person, one that would act as a bellwether of a person's spiritual condition and ward against fatalistic thinking about indwelling sin. Despite the evil desires that remain within the saints until the eschaton, this newly established distinction was just one way that these reformers sought to encourage others to follow the apostle Paul's lead in being sober-minded about sin yet ever persistent in the fight against it, trusting that the Spirit is at work within them and that Christ's righteousness is theirs by faith. As Theodore Beza once wrote to a group of pastors in Basel: "For in this life we have no more sure testimony of the life-giving Spirit in our hearts than the violent struggle of the flesh against the Spirit, whose full victory and full testimony is put off until the future age."[69] It is a gracious indication of the Spirit's work within believers that they are not spared a noble struggle with the sin that stirs within them.

BIBLIOGRAPHY

Ambrose. *De Poenitentia*. In *PL* 16.
Ambrosiaster. *In Romanos*. In *CSEL* 81/1.
Anderas, Phil. *Renovatio: Martin Luther's Augustinian Theology of Sin, Grace and Holiness*. Refo500 Academic Studies 57. Göttingen: Vandenhoeck & Ruprecht, 2019.
Aquinas, Thomas. *Super Epistolam B. Pauli ad Romanos Lectura. Commentary on the Letter of Saint Paul to the Romans*. Translated by F. R. Larcher. Edited by John Mortensen and Enrique Alarcón. Latin/English Edition of the Works of St. Thomas Aquinas 37. Lander: Aquinas Institute for the Study of Sacred Doctrine, 2012.
Augustine. *De Nuptiis et Concupiscentia*. In *PL* 44.
———. *Epistolae*. In *PL* 33.
Balduin, Friedrich. *Catechesis apostolica, hoc est, S. apostoli Pauli Epistola ad Romanos, commentario perspicuo illustrate* [. . .]. Wittenberg: Boreck, Selfisch, Helwig, 1620.
Batka, Ľubomír. "Luther's Teaching on Sin and Evil." In *The Oxford Handbook of Martin Luther's Theology*, edited by Robert Kolb, Irene Dingel, and Ľubomír Batka, 233–53. New York: Oxford University Press, 2014.
———. *Peccatum Radicale: Eine Studie zu Luthers Erbsündenverständnis in Psalm 51*. Frankfurt am Main: Lang, 2007.
Berkouwer, G. C. *Sin*. Translated by Philip C. Holtrop. Studies in Dogmatics. Grand Rapids: Eerdmans, 1971.
Beza, Theodore. *Correspondance de Théodore de Bèze*. Vol. 4, *1562–1563*. Edited by Alain Dufour, Claire Chimelli, and Béatrice Nicollier. Geneva: Droz, 1965.
Bierma, Lyle D., et al., eds. *An Introduction to the Heidelberg Catechism: Sources, History, and Theology*. Texts and Studies in Reformation and Post-Reformation Thought. Grand Rapids: Baker Academic, 2005.
Bizer, Ernst. *Theologie der Verheissung. Studien zur theologischen Entwicklung des jungen Melanchthon (1519–1524)*. Neukirchen-Vluyn: Neukirchen, 1964.
Borg, Johannes. *Dictata seu explicate in catechis: Heidelb: a Zacharia Ursino. In Aedibus Sapientiae incoepta Mense*. Manuscript (student lecture notes), Bibliotheca Palatina, Heidelberg, July 1572.
Briola, Lucas. "A Case Study of Scholasticism: Peter Abelard and Peter Lombard on Penance." *Journal of Moral Theology* 5 (2016) 65–85.
Calvin, John. *Commentary on Romans*. In *CO* 49.
———. *Institutes of the Christian Religion*. In *CO* 2.

---

69. Beza, *Correspondance*, 4:186: "Neque enim in hac vita certius vivificantis Spiritus testimonium in cordibus nostris habemus quam repugnantem carnis luctam adversus Spiritum, cuius plena victoria plenumque testimonium in futurum saeculum differtur."

Cicero. *On the Orator: Book 3. On Fate. Stoic Paradoxes. Divisions of Oratory.* Loeb Classical Library 349. Cambridge, MA: Harvard University Press, 1942.

Cooper, Adam G. "Mortal and Venial Sin: A Lutheran Distinction?" *Lutheran Theological Journal* 40 (2006) 117–25.

Cruciger, Caspar, Sr. *In epistolam Pauli ad Romanos scriptam commentarius* [. . .]. Wittenberg: Johannes Crato, 1567.

Cyprian. *De Opere et Eleemosynis*. In *PL* 4.

———. *De Oratione Dominica*. In *PL* 4.

De Bruyn, Theodore S., trans. *Ambrosiaster's Commentary on the Pauline Epistles: Romans*. Writings from the Greco-Roman World. Atlanta: SBL, 2017.

De Wildt, Kees. "Commentaren Op de Heidelbergse Catechismus." In *Handboek Heidelbergse Catechismus*, edited by Arnold Huijgen, John V. Fesko, and Aleida Siller, 85–95. Utrecht: Kok, 2013.

Donnelly, John Patrick. *Calvinism and Scholasticism in Vermigli's Doctrine of Man and Grace*. Studies in Medieval and Reformation Traditions 18. Leiden: Brill, 1976.

Durkin, Eugene F. *The Theological Distinction of Sins in the Writings of St. Augustine*. Mundelein, IL: Saint Mary of the Lake Seminary, 1952.

Froehlich, Karlfried, ed. *Biblia Latina Cum Glossa Ordinaria: Facsimile Reprint of the Editio Princeps (Strasbourg: Adolph Rusch, 1480/81)*. Turnhout: Brepols, 1992.

Hampton, Stephen. "Sin, Grace, and Free Choice in Post-Reformation Reformed Theology." In *The Oxford Handbook of Early Modern Theology, 1600–1800*, edited by Ulrich L. Lehner, Richard A. Muller, and A. G. Roeber, 228–41. Oxford: Oxford University Press, 2014.

Hause, Jeffrey. "Abelard on Degrees of Sinfulness." *American Catholic Philosophical Quarterly: The Journal of the American Catholic Philosophical Association* 81 (2007) 251–70.

Hughes, Kevin L. *Constructing Antichrist: Paul, Biblical Commentary, and the Development of Doctrine in the Early Middle Ages*. Washington, DC: Catholic University of America Press, 2005.

Hunter, David G. *Marriage, Celibacy, and Heresy in Ancient Christianity: The Jovinianist Controversy*. Oxford: Oxford University Press, 2007.

Jerome. *Adversus Jovinianum*. In *PL* 23.

Kolb, Robert, Torbjörn Johansson, and Daniel Johansson, eds. *Simul: Inquiries into Luther's Experience of the Christian Life*. Refo500 Academic Studies 80. Göttingen: Vandenhoeck & Ruprecht, 2021.

Lombard, Peter. *Magna Glossatura in Romanos*. In *PL* 191.

———. *Sententiae*. In *PL* 192.

Lugioyo, Brian. *Martin Bucer's Doctrine of Justification: Reformation Theology and Early Modern Irenicism*. Oxford: Oxford University Press, 2010.

Luther, Martin. *Lectures on Romans*. In *WA* 56; *LW* 25.

Major, Georg. *Primus Tomus Operum Reverendi Viri D. Georgii Maioris: Continens Enarrationes Epistolarum S. Pauli, electi organi Dei*. Wittenberg: Johann Krafft, 1569.

Melanchthon, Philip. *Commentary on Romans*. In *CR* 15.

———. *Commentary on Romans*. Translated by Fred Kramer. St. Louis: Concordia, 2010.

———. *Loci Communes (1521)*. In *CR* 21.

———. *Loci Communes (1521)*. Translated by Christian Preus. St. Louis: Concordia, 2014.

———. *The Loci Communes of Philip Melanchthon: With a Critical Introduction by the Translators*. Translated by Charles Leander Hill. Boston: Meador, 1944.

———. *Philipp Melancthon: Werke in Auswahl, Studienausgabe*. 7 vols. Edited by Robert Stupperich. Gütersloh: Bertelsmann, 1951–75.

Musculus, Wolfgang. *Loci Communes in usus sacrae Theologiae candidatorum parati*. Basel: Johann Herwagen, 1560.

Oberman, Heiko A. *The Harvest of Medieval Theology: Gabriel Biel and Late Medieval Nominalism*. 3rd ed. Durham, NC: Labyrinth, 1983.

O'Hagan, Peter. "Glossing the Gloss: Reading Peter Lombard's *Collectanea* on the Pauline Epistles as a Historical Act." *Traditio* 73 (2018) 83–116.

———. "Teaching the Tradition: Twelfth-Century Scholastic Commentaries on Paul's Letter to the Romans." PhD diss., University of Toronto, 2017.

Ott, Ludwig. *Fundamentals of Catholic Dogma*. Edited by James Canon Bastible. Translated by Patrick Lynch. 4th ed. Rockford, IL: Tan Books, 1960.

Pereira, Jairzinho Lopes. *Augustine of Hippo and Martin Luther on Original Sin and Justification of the Sinner*. Refo500 Academic Studies 15. Göttingen: Vandenhoeck & Ruprecht, 2013.

Pitkin, Barbara. "Nothing but Concupiscence: Calvin's Understanding of Sin and the *Via Augustini*." *Calvin Theological Journal* 34 (Nov. 1999) 347–69.

Raith, Charles, II. *After Merit: John Calvin's Theology of Works and Rewards*. Refo500 Academic Studies 34. Göttingen: Vandenhoeck & Ruprecht, 2016.

Reuchlin, Johann. *Ioannis Revchlin Phorcensis LL. doctoris in septem psalmos poenite[n]tiales hebraicos interpretatio de uerbo ad uerbum*. Tubingen, 1512.

Schaff, Philip. *Ante-Nicene Fathers*. Vol. 3, *Latin Christianity: Its Founder, Tertullian*, edited by Alexander Roberts and James Donaldson. Peabody, MA: Hendrickson, 1995.

Smalley, Beryl. "Gilbertus Universalis, Bishop of London (1128–34), and the Problem of the *Glossa Ordinaria*." *Recherches de Théologie Ancienne et Médiévale* 7 (July 1935) 235–62.

Stephens, William Peter. *The Theology of Heinrich Bullinger*. Edited by Jim West and Joe Mock. Reformed Historical Theology 59. Göttingen: Vandenhoeck & Ruprecht, 2019.

———. *The Theology of Huldrych Zwingli*. Oxford: Clarendon, 1986.

Tentler, Thomas N. *Sin and Confession on the Eve of the Reformation*. Princeton, NJ: Princeton University Press, 1977.

Tertullian. *Liber de Pudicitia*. In *PL* 2.

Vermigli, Peter Martyr. *In Epistolam S. Pauli Apostoli ad Romanos, D. Petri Martyris Vermilii Florentini, Professoris diuinarum literarum in schola Tigurina [. . .]*. Basil: Pietro Perna, 1558.

Wagner-Peterson, Boris. "Zacharias Ursinus und 'Seine' Auslegung des Heidelberger Katechismus." In *Geschichte und Wirkung des Heidelberger Katechismus. Vorträge der 9. Internationalen Emder Tagung zur Geschichte des Reformierten Protestantismus*, edited by Matthias Freudenberg and J. Marius J. Lange Van Ravenswaay, 87–109. Göttingen: Vandenhoeck & Ruprecht, 2013.

Wengert, Timothy J. "Philip Melanchthon and the 'Simul Iustus et Peccator.'" In *Simul: Inquiries into Luther's Experience of the Christian Life*, edited by Robert Kolb,

Torbjörn Johansson, and Daniel Johansson, 125–44. Refo500 Academic Studies 80. Göttingen: Vandenhoeck & Ruprecht, 2021.

Wigand, Johannes. *In epistolam S. Pauli ad Romano annotationes*. Frankfurt am Main: 1580.

Woodward, Michael Scott, trans. *The Glossa Ordinaria on Romans*. Kalamazoo: Medieval Institute Publications, 2011.

10

"Do Not Many of You Become Teachers"

Interpreting James's Directive About Teaching (3:1) in the Reformation

KIRK SUMMERS

JAMES'S DIRECTIVE TO HIS readers at 3:1 that "not many" of them "should become teachers" (διδάσκαλοι, or *didaskaloi*) has generated an assortment of disparate interpretations across the centuries. Modern interpreters typically understand the gist of the charge in two different ways. Some focus on the phrase that follows, that is, James's warning that "we who teach" will face stricter judgment than those who do not. For many commentators, the fact that James includes himself among the group designated by *teachers* implies that he is talking about a formal office of the church and thus means to discourage those aspiring to it, since few are really qualified in terms of intellect or disposition. The section that follows on the tongue and the difficulty of controlling it as the leading edge of the body's sin provides an additional explanation: teachers must maintain a high standard of morality. The preponderance of modern interpreters hold to some variation of this "formal office" or "leadership" view, including Davids, Adamson, Martin, Johnson, and Moo.[1] Moo believes

---

1. Davids, *Epistle of James*; Adamson, *Epistle of James*; Martin, *James*; Johnson, *Letter of James*; Moo, *Letter of James*.

that James uses this warning to those aspiring to be teachers simply as a way to launch into his next topic, the problem of the tongue and bitter, critical speech occurring in the churches.[2] Another related interpretation finds the key to the directive's meaning in the broader scope of the letter. In the buildup to this verse, James has been discussing the need for works of charity as evidence of one's faith, going so far as to assert that works justify us, since any faith that lacks them is a dead faith. In this view, James advises his readers not to neglect the essential works of charity in favor of teaching theology, or to sacrifice the labor of Christianity in favor of its intellectual aspects, a problem that we can surmise plagued the churches at the time of his writing. Lutheran theologian and pastor Johann Huther champions this interpretation.[3]

Theologians and commentators in the time of the Reformation, influenced by their own circumstances and the unique challenges facing the church, understood *teachers* in the passage differently. The urgent problems facing leaders of the Reformation—competing theologies and viewpoints that threatened to sow chaos and confusion; organizational needs, both on the micro and macro levels; the unique pastoral issues confronting second- and third-generation reformers—shaped perspectives on how James's directive should be applied. In this paper, we will review how Reformation commentators, especially Reformed and Lutheran, interpreted 3:1 and argue that, depending on time and place, they chose their interpretation, or were even steered into their interpretations, due to conflicts with the Anabaptists, concerns over policing morality, questions over how the church should be organized, and the pressing need for pastors and teachers for the nascent Reformation movement.

TRANSLATION

By far the majority of manuscripts, and the best ones at that, share the following reading of Jas 3:1:

---

2. Moo, *Letter of James*, 148.

3. Huther, *Critical and Exegetical Handbook*. Huther does not exactly associate the *teachers* of Jas 3:1 with the formal ecclesiastical office, but rather with "the free teaching in the congregation which was not yet joined to a particular office, but appertained to every one who felt himself called to it" (108). This work was originally published in German in 1882.

Μὴ πολλοὶ διδάσκαλοι γίνεσθε, ἀδελφοί μου, εἰδότες ὅτι μεῖζον κρίμα λημψόμεθα.[4]

Modern English translations universally render *didaskaloi* with *teachers*, while early English translations opt for the word *masters* (Tyndale, Wycliffe, Geneva Bible, KJV), though in the sense of the old word *schoolmasters*, that is, *teachers*. The earlier Latin translations show three variations: the Vulgate renders it *magistri*, as do the Latin Bibles and commentaries coming out of Zurich produced by Zwingli, Pellikan, Jud, Bibliander, and Bullinger, all published from the press of Christoph Froschauer.[5] Erasmus and Calvin, who were not inclined to stray far from the Vulgate, also choose *magistri*, as does Lucas Osiander on the Lutheran side.[6] Jacques Lefèvre d'Étaples translates it as *magistri* but glosses it in his commentary with *doctores* and connects it with the word *doctrina*.[7] Perhaps inspired by d'Étaples's note, both Beza and Piscator translate *didaskaloi* as *doctores*, though their interpretations differ from that of d'Étaples, as we will see.[8] Finally, Bern theologian Benedictus Aretius deviates from all these by choosing to render it *praeceptores*, perhaps thinking of the word the Vulgate uses at Luke 17:13 to translate how the ten lepers addressed Jesus.[9]

All these Latin words are interchangeable, in a broad sense, as much as *teacher* is with *schoolmaster*. Even so, they each represent a deliberate choice by the translators. D'Étaples's adoption of *magistri* says something about the predominate conservativism in translation at the time—few wanted to arouse prejudice among readers by challenging the familiar Vulgate rendering without sufficient cause—but his commentary suggests that other considerations were attracting him to a rendering that, in his view, would have greater nuance to it. Both Beza and Piscator, who

---

4. The *ECM* records one uncial and one minuscule that share the reading πολυδιδάσκαλοι, which is not a classical word but which would mean "teaching many things," as if James has in mind doctrinal uniformity.

5. See especially the following: Bullinger, *In omnes apostolicas epistolas*, 130 (pagination begins anew for the canonical epistles); Zwingli, *In evangelicam historiam de domino nostro Iesu Christo*, 552; Pellikan et al., *Biblia sacrosancta*, 100v (pagination begins anew for the New Testament).

6. Erasmus, *Novum Testamentum omne*, 497; Calvin, *Commentarii in Epistolas canonicas*, 122; Osiander, *Epistola ad Hebraeos Iacobi*, 125.

7. D'Étaples, *Commentarii in epistolas catholicas*, 9v.

8. Beza, *Testamentum Novum*, 417 (pagination begins anew after Acts); Piscator, *Analysis Logica*, 44.

9. Aretius, *Commentarii in epistolas canonicas*, 63.

were in frequent communication with each other concerning the translation of the New Testament and who were both interested foremost in precision, prefer *doctores* to *magistri*, but why is not altogether clear; perhaps they made the change from the conventional rendering to draw attention to their glosses or because *doctor* was the term applied to the office that certain unqualified people were usurping. Novelty may have motivated Aretius in his seemingly gratuitous choice of *praeceptores*, given that, in commenting on the passage, he quickly forgets the word *praeceptores* and instead discusses the word *doctores*. The variations themselves, however, do us a service in that they underscore the fact that the word *didaskaloi* presented not so much a translation problem, since in the final analysis each one of the existing translations works as well as the next, but an interpretation problem. James is urging the faithful universally not to aspire to be *didaskaloi*. Who exactly does James have in mind when he uses this term? And how much do the circumstances in which commentators find themselves influence their interpretations?

EARLY REFORMATION INTERPRETATIONS

At the outset of this essay, we quickly surveyed a sampling of modern interpretations of Jas 3:1 and noted the variety among them. Reformation commentators, who are the focus of this study, share a common way of talking about the passage (repeating frequently the words *ambition*, *calling*, and so on) but do not always draw the same conclusion as to its intent. Even though they have an obvious familiarity with the history of the passage's interpretation, they were not looking at the passage in an intellectual vacuum. To be sure, idiosyncratic hermeneutical principles or doctrinal allegiances led commentators to read James's intent differently, but at the same time it appears that the term *didaskaloi* could be somewhat malleable under the pressures of one's immediate social, theological, or personal circumstances, that it could shift in meaning—or, at least, in the understanding of its meaning—depending on factors external to the philological features of the text.

We begin with a reform-minded Roman Catholic who wrote during the early stages of the Reformation period and whose scriptural expositions many reformers consulted: Jacques Lefèvre d'Étaples, also known as Faber Stapulensis, who published a commentary on the catholic epistles at Basel in 1527.[10] D'Étaples begins his comments on Jas 3:1 by noting that out of the many throngs of people in the world, God in his goodness raises up only a small handful who are fit to obtain the office (*munus*) of teaching. He points out that God chose only four evangelists to tell the gospel story of Jesus and then added one more later (namely, Paul) to share the story with the nations. Therefore, by this example, d'Étaples argues, James urges that few "in communities" (*in communitatibus*) become teachers. He goes on to argue that James aims his directive at two problems: he wants to prevent the development of many doctrines (and here we see the connection with the Latin word *doctor*), and he is concerned that some take on the title of "teacher" solely out of a desire for status within the congregation. So, when James talks about "many teachers," says d'Étaples, he is looking more to the unity of doctrine than a simple number. In essence, we can think of the gospel writers, Paul, Peter, and James as one teacher, since they advocated one doctrine, taught in the school not of men, which inflates, but of the Holy Spirit, whose love builds up. "Therefore," he concludes, "the apostle does not prohibit teaching (*doctrinam*), rather, a multitude of teachings, which happens whenever people teach anything other than the pure and sincere Word of God expounded, when needed, purely and sincerely." D'Étaples points to Heb 13:9, where he says Paul exhorts his readers not to be carried off by such "diverse and strange" teaching that contradicts what he has taught them. The idea here, then, is that James does not deny the need for teachers in the church communities, so long as they all ground themselves in the one teaching that those to whom God gave the office put forward. In this way, given that they all speak with one unanimous voice about one doctrine, we can recognize that the church essentially has one teacher.

D'Étaples seems motivated by a concern to maintain the unity of the church and a respect for authoritative voices. He also mentions ambition as a particular concern of James in writing this directive about teachers. Many assume the role of teacher so that they can enjoy the prestige that accompanies it. He observes that the title "teacher" runs the risk of engendering in us the vice of ambition, so much so that Jesus forbade his disciples from applying it to themselves (Matt 23:8), as the scribes and Pharisees do: "Do not be called Rabbi, for you have one teacher, Christ, and all of you are brethren." The scribes and Pharisees love the honors they receive for their position, their special seats at feasts, their lofty place

---

10. D'Étaples, *Commentarii in epistolas catholicas*, 10r–v.

in the synagogues, the greetings they hear in the marketplace. People who love to teach, rather, to rule over others with their teaching, often fall into the same trap as those Jews in the time of Jesus, argues d'Étaples. They introduce novel doctrines to replace the word and place burdens on others that have no real purpose but to signal their own virtue. The real danger, however, and the reason they face a greater condemnation, according to James, lies in the responsibility and authority associated with teaching. The word of God as taught by the Holy Spirit leads people into the kingdom of God. But any teaching that deviates from God's word, which self-serving ambition taints, drags with it a multitude to perdition, even people who sincerely want to enter the kingdom.

D'Étaples's interpretation successfully preserves the office of teaching in the church with skillful dexterity. By restating *magistri* with *doctores*, he succeeds in drawing the association with the purity of *doctrina*, that is, doctrine or teaching. He then points out that regardless of how many people teach in the church, they all must ground themselves on one teaching, the teaching of those inspired truly by the Holy Spirit. Thus, in this way many teachers become one teacher, or, conversely, for "many not to become teachers" means "do not promote a teaching that deviates from the one teaching." Furthermore, by reading into James's words a warning about ambition and teaching, d'Étaples can point to Matt 23, where Jesus accuses the scribes and Pharisees of exemplifying the pitfalls that accompany positions of doctrinal authority. True teaching promotes charity and the kingdom of God, while false teaching—that is, teaching that promotes diverse and false views—imbues people with rivalry and bars them from the kingdom.

ZURICH

Besides stipulating that teachers expound the word "purely and sincerely," d'Étaples did not directly address the sticky issue of conflicting interpretations of the Scriptures or what role church tradition plays in the establishment of a single, unifying doctrine. He himself ran afoul of the Roman Catholic authorities at times for appearing to favor some of the new evangelical doctrines, especially regarding the question of justification, and for this reason may have been reluctant to wade into the finer questions hidden in these deep waters. The early reformers, however, felt obligated to resolve these problems, given that they themselves had fractured the visible church and feared further fracturing.

At Zurich, the commentaries of Heinrich Bullinger and Konrad Pellikan on the catholic Epistles reveal a shift in thinking about James's directive that more directly reflected their own circumstances. Heinrich Bullinger, who assumed the role of antistes in Zurich after the death of Zwingli, published his commentary on all the apostolic Epistles in 1537 at the press of Froschauer.[11] His comments on Jas 3:1 show both an awareness of d'Étaples's comments and a more immediate concern regarding theological and ecclesiastical conflicts with the Anabaptists in the area. Bullinger believes that Jas 3:1 marks a hard transition in the text. Here the apostle is no longer treating the relationship between faith and works, as he did in chapter 2, but rather a new problem prevalent in the ancient churches: the fact that many people without the proper training want to engage in public teaching. Bullinger immediately sees a parallel in his own time with the Anabaptists, a sect he deems every bit as "ambitious" (recalling d'Étaples's word) as they are ignorant. James's addition of the word *many*, in his view, recalls to his mind a distinctive feature of Anabaptism, in which everyone, without distinction and apart from being elected and called, can assume the office of teacher. He complains about this often, including in his 1560 book *Adversus Anabaptistas*, where he develops in detail the kinds of requirements the apostles demanded of those who want to teach.[12] For example, at 1 Cor 12, Paul makes clear that God distributes gifts as he wills and that not all have the same gift; therefore, not all can be teachers. At Heb 5, we are told that every person should have a calling if they want to teach, as Paul—and even Jesus himself—did. Paul's letters to Timothy and Titus are full of requirements for leaders in the church. He forbids neophytes to assume the office of teacher because they need time for preparation and study in true doctrines. Anabaptists, he complains, allow for uneducated people who can barely read, or who have not even taken time to open the Scriptures, to preach to others! Even Paul's exhortation to liberty at 1 Cor 14 has limits that do not support the Anabaptist positions. He then concludes with an exhortation directed at them that echoes these sentiments of James:

---

11. Bullinger, *In omnes apostolicas epistolas*.

12. Bullinger, *Adversus Anabaptistas*. Bullinger addresses the question of "many teachers" among the Anabaptists in the third book, 77r–117r. Bullinger published this work earlier in German; the Latin translation was done by Josias Simler.

> You, Anabaptists, and especially those who are leaders and teachers (*doctores*) of others, I exhort you to look at yourselves carefully in this mirror and take note of your enormous faults. Acknowledge, at least, your manifest lack of knowledge, that you are thus completely unsuited for this office. Do not hasten so to teach others when you yourselves have learned little or nothing at all. Or do you imagine that you will escape the judgment of God? We still have plenty of pious and learned ministers of the Church who will lead you truly and rightly in the way of righteousness and true salvation. So, stop your dissension and join with the true ministers of the Church and submit to them.[13]

The Anabaptists, unlearned and unprepared as they are, argues Bullinger, are putting themselves in serious moral jeopardy by trying to teach. They should listen and submit.

Returning to the commentary, we observe the same pattern in Bullinger's handling of Jas 3:1. He identifies a first point in James's exhortation—namely, that few are qualified to be teachers due to the lack of education and calling—but then sees in the rest of the verse two additional arguments to dissuade congregants from teaching publicly. James warns that teachers will face a greater judgment from God because, as Bullinger understands it, teaching is a hard business and one that makes the teacher responsible for the well-being of those being taught. And then, as a third point, James reminds his readers that "in many things we all fall," meaning, Bullinger says, "human weakness causes everyone to sin often enough on their own account without the need to appropriate sins from someone else and transfer them to themselves."[14] He deduces that this happens most easily when someone ambitiously takes on the office of teaching when they are unequal to the task. And he adds that James mentions the tongue in the very next verse as the instrument that leads to the most lapses in our character, because the teacher has the difficult task of using it for good (teaching the truth) while controlling it so as not to corrupt himself.

Bullinger's colleague at Zurich, fellow theologian Konrad Pellikan, published his own commentaries on the catholic Epistles in 1539, the final part of a larger commentary set that covered the entire Bible.[15] Like Bullinger, Pellikan was involved with the Carolinum at Zurich, where

---

13. Bullinger, *Adversus Anabaptistas*, 94r–v.
14. Bullinger, *In omnes apostolicas epistolas*, 2:130.
15. Pellikan, *In omnes apostolicas epistolas*. He discusses Jas 3:1 on 697–98.

he benefited from intense discussions about the proper understanding of the Scriptures. Unlike Bullinger, Pellikan was not inclined to engage directly with the Anabaptists in polemical disputes, preferring to concentrate his intellectual efforts on philological matters. This is apparent in his comments on the 3:1 passage, where Pellikan avoids mentioning the schismatics and their doctrine and instead ties James's directive about teachers to the broader scope of the entire Epistle (as opposed to Bullinger, who identifies 3:1 as the beginning of a new train of thought related to what he sees as the Anabaptist failing). In the previous chapter, James has been discussing the need for works as a proof of faith; now, according to Pellikan, he draws a further distinction that is also related to works: he censures those who aspire to the office of teaching out of a desire to pontificate about doctrine more than engage in the kind of works James has been commending, that is, visiting widows and orphans in their distress. James wants his readers to understand that the tongue has great utility, provided it promotes true piety, but that "it is a dangerous matter to undertake the office of teaching." A teacher requires a thorough grasp of evangelical doctrine coupled with an impeccable character, a knowledge of true doctrine coupled with pious works; "this person must do more than just teach right things but must direct all things to the glory of Christ." Successful teachers love what they teach; those corrupted with depraved desires (anger, hate, ambition, greed, lust, and so on) only wreak havoc on the people. Thus, Pellikan concludes, James warns against the ambition to be teachers and urges most to listen, since the church only needs a few educators. James is telling them to question whether they are really prepared to take on such an influential and potentially damaging office, laden with authority, for which they will have to give an account to the Supreme Judge. Pellikan contends that this warning anticipates James's subsequent harangue against the tongue: "The speech of a person is something that is very powerful and efficacious; it either plants or removes noxious opinions; it excites or calms hatred; it stirs people to war, it settles them down in peace; it drives the hearer this way or that way."[16]

Pellikan is touching on the same essential points as Bullinger did, but in his case without singling out the Anabaptists by name. Both, however, highlight deficiencies in the Anabaptists' understanding of how a congregation should function. Special qualities are required of those who seek leadership positions; not "many" are fit to stand before the

16. Pellikan, *In omnes apostolicas epistolas*, 697–98.

congregation to expound the word. Thus, Bullinger and Pellikan stress the kind of preparation and training involved in becoming a teacher; the need for moral self-reflection and purity of character that surpasses the ordinary (not to mention a complete lack of ambition); the grave responsibility that comes with the authority of instructing others; and the potential for incorrect dogma to send others, and eventually oneself, to perdition.[17] It is safer, in their opinion, to check the tongue, to be slow to express one's opinion, and to use one's ears to listen and learn. They certainly saw something else going on in the Anabaptist congregations.

GENEVA

For all the stress in Zurich on the qualifications needed for the *office* of teaching, others in the Reformed camp interpreted Jas 3:1 in a different light. Genevan commentators tended to shift their focus away from the office itself and who should hold it to the idea of lording over others as morally superior. Calvin's note on the passage in his commentary begins this way:

> The common and almost authoritative interpretation of this passage is that James is dissuading people from desiring the office (*munus*) of teaching. And this is because it is fraught with peril and liable to God's severe judgment if anyone is irresponsible in it. They think that he said *do not many be* because we must have some at least. But I take *teachers* (*magistri*) to mean, not those who hold the office (*munus*) in the Church, but who assume for themselves the right of criticizing others. Such are censors, who act as if they want to be considered teachers (*magistri*) of morals.[18]

Calvin explains the rationale for this change from interpreting these "teachers" as official teachers in the church to seeing them as self-appointed moral censors by appealing to the use of *didaskaloi* and *magistri* among the Greeks and Romans: The ancients called those who superciliously warn others *teachers*. James is induced to dissuade "many" from becoming this kind of "teacher" because, in fact, that is exactly what

---

17. Sebastian Castellio (*Biblia Sacra*, 343) appears to reach the same conclusion. He translates the verse with *magistri* and glosses the second half of it ("scienties nos graviores esse poenas daturos") with "magistros, si suo officio non fungantur," that is, "knowing that we teachers (if we do not fulfill our responsibility) will receive a more severe punishment." The first edition was published in 1551; I consulted the 1573.

18. Calvin, *Commentarii in Epistolas canonicas*, 122.

many do. Human nature has this disease: it wants to build itself up by tearing other people down, to promote itself by posturing as morally superior to others.

Calvin next begins to talk about a twofold vice involved in becoming this kind of teacher, one of bad preparation and one of bad intent. Here he is drawing directly from d'Étaples, as the correspondence in Latin shows, but he now makes a small alteration to avoid invoking the office of teaching, an interpretation he has already set aside. Instead of lamenting that too many become teachers even though they have not studied sufficiently, he instead observes that "although few possess an abundance of dexterity" (*quum pauci dexteritate polleceant*),[19] everyone indiscriminately rushes into being a teacher. Whereas d'Étaples and the Zurich theologians bemoan these would-be teachers' lack of biblical training, Calvin requires a natural disposition of adroitness and competence that aims at a person's well-being and salvation. He contrasts this with the deplorable, self-serving ambition and hypocrisy that typically motivate people. In other words, Calvin believes that James means too many become teachers who have a character problem. He is quick to say, however, that James does not intend to discourage the kind of gentle admonitions that Scripture often recommends within the Christian community, but only the eager desire to censure as a way of promoting oneself over others. Thus, regarding the next verse about the tongue, Calvin sees a continuation of the thought: Given our own inner struggles with sins, a good censor, one who has the "dexterity" mentioned above, will so be cognizant of their own failings and imperfect sanctity that they will treat others with meekness and kindness.

Calvin's comments on Acts 10:24 and the story of Cornelius, at first glance, seem to contradict this interpretation at Jas 3:1, but a closer reading shows that this is not the case. In the Acts passage, he raises many of the same points that he does in the James one. He praises the example of Cornelius for involving all his family and not wanting to set himself up as a teacher. "Many," he says, "are motivated by ambition to set themselves up as teachers." They are eager to babble incessantly yet are unwilling to listen. But even teachers, he notes, should be setting themselves under the word along with fellow believers. Their possession of the "faculty and grace" of teaching should be at the service of the kingdom, not their own preeminence; meanwhile, those who do not possess the skill should

---

19. Calvin, *Commentarii in Epistolas canonicas*, 122.

keep themselves within their limitations. At this point, Calvin mentions the Jas 3:1 passage, but with an important change in wording: "Neutri magisterium appetant," that is, "Let neither of them desire the role of schoolmaster."[20] The latter phrase could be rendered *mastery*, the point being that both teachers and learners in the church should abstain from assuming for themselves the right to criticize and berate others as if those others are beneath them morally and intellectually. We should all be building each other up in a way that is free from the ambition to have mastery, so that both learned and unlearned can rejoice to be brought into order.

While the presence of the Anabaptists around Zurich caused the pastors and theologians there to worry that too many were setting up themselves in an official capacity to teach, the situation in Geneva, with no Anabaptist presence to speak of, naturally differed. Given its close connection to the French churches and its sense of urgency about the need for well-trained pastors to fill pulpits there and elsewhere in Europe, Geneva undertook to train as many men as were willing to risk their lives to serve the kingdom. Undoubtedly, they could only imagine that James was addressing another problem, as Calvin's comments suggest, and not that too many wanted to assume the office of teacher. Meanwhile, the emphasis on church discipline and moral matters in the Genevan churches pointed to a somewhat novel and more relevant way to interpret Jas 3:1, one that focused on who and how to engage in the correction of a brother or sister.

Calvin was not alone in reading the passage this way; we see Theodore Beza attempting to steer the interpretation of *teacher* here away from teaching elders or pastors in the church, qualified people the church has plenty of need for, and to a secondary, less formal meaning of the word, which includes anyone in the church who assumes a superior position over another, especially regarding morals. Beza summarizes the verse in question as follows:

> Let no one usurp for themselves the right of stiff censure against others. This is something most do, driven by ambition. The reason is that those who so diligently and rigidly condemn others provoke God's severity against themselves since they themselves are found to be guilty as well.[21]

---

20. Calvin, *Commentariorum in acta apostolorum*, 132.
21. Beza, *Testamentum Novum*, part 2, 418.

Here again, *ambition* motivates the desire of many to teach, but not *to teach* in the way that d'Étaples and the Zurich theologians understood it, but as Calvin interpreted it—namely, *to censure*. Beza's annotation on *many teachers* reveals how and why he transitions from one interpretation to the other:

> The added word *many* indicates that he is not condemning the office that is divinely instituted for offering good and profitable instruction to people, since very few are autodidactic, and these are not always well-informed. No, he is dealing here with that disease which is widespread also in the case of physical ailments, where we end up with more doctors than sick people. Yes, most everyone considers himself more suited to teaching than learning. We should avoid this first and foremost when dealing with cases of conscience before God—not only when it is a question about doctrine itself, but when, and even especially so, we are talking about people's private affairs. In these scenarios, sinning happens all the time as some assume for themselves the role of censorious critic, as Christ himself experienced. See Matthew 7 and what the apostle hammers home in a thousand passages. Therefore, he is calling those who engage in correction and criticism *teachers*. You see, he censures that vice which is too widespread among people, whereby it happens that they severely condemn others but give license to themselves.[22]

At first glance, Beza appears to have simply borrowed from Calvin, but we can detect slight differences between the two. For Beza, the idea that many are becoming teachers indicates that James is talking about self-appointed teachers who have not gone through training but only want the prestige and feeling of superiority. Beza, as often in his annotations, stresses the need for the faithful to *listen* rather than teach. These types of people may ignorantly try to correct others' doctrines, to be sure, but the real danger comes when they try to be censorious teachers, that is, when they begin to criticize the behavior of others. Matthew 7:1 especially provides the parallel passage that explains this one. The Holy Spirit is not forbidding public, civil, ecclesiastical, or even private censuring when it is done in the right way by the right person, Beza says in his note there, but he does prohibit antagonistic and spiteful rebukes. The next note at Jas 3:1, on the phrase "we will receive a heavier judgment," continues this thought:

---

22. Beza, *Testamentum Novum*, part 2, 417–18.

Understand, "unless we cease from that censorious and completely arrogant criticism of others." We will be more harshly punished, the more severe and arrogant we will have been as wicked censors (Matt 7:2). The fact that he counts himself among those who struggle with this vice he does partly for instructional purposes and partly because there is no one who is completely immune from this vice.[23]

Beza has to explain the fact that James is including himself among the "teachers" to counter the argument that this proves James means the office of teacher. Still, Beza does not eliminate the usual meaning of "teacher"—that is, someone who expounds the word and instructs others in doctrine—but like Calvin he focuses on people's natural tendency to want to judge others harshly as a way to signal their own virtue.

HERBORN AND BERN

We have seen that in interpreting James's intent when he advises that not many be teachers, the Zurich theologians lay the stress on the formal office (*munus*) itself, arguing that very few will have the intellect and temperament to assume the role, while the Genevans understood James's word *didaskaloi* as a term that is broadly applicable to all the faithful. In the latter view, people in general should be hesitant to take on an air of authority whereby they set others straight, either doctrinally or morally, and, instead, should cultivate humility and be more inclined to listen and mutually support others in the body of Christ than to speak. Both interpretations agree that *ambition* commonly lurks behind the desire to take on the schoolmaster's role, especially when the proper qualifications are lacking.

At the Academy of Herborn, Reformed Bible scholar and Ramist theologian Johann Piscator published his own commentary on the catholic Epistles, to which he applied his *analysis logica*, or interpretation of the passage, within the progression of the apostle's argument.[24] He divides his analysis into three parts: (1) the analysis of the subject matter, (2) scholia, and (3) observations. The first part, the analysis of the subject matter, functions as a paraphrase of the passage so that the run of the argument becomes clear; the second part contains the more technical comments

---

23. Beza, *Testamentum Novum*, part 2, 417–18.
24. Piscator, *Analysis Logica*. He discusses Jas 3:1 on 44.

about language and parallels, while the third part interprets the overall meaning and thrust of the passage in an organized way with reference to similar passages in Scripture. His understanding of the passage shows the influence of the Genevan interpretation, even though many in the Reformed camp, especially Beza, had grave doctrinal differences with him.[25]

Piscator argues that James is rebuking those who have no calling to the office of teacher yet without sanction act as if they have the office and, "accordingly, motivated by ambition, appropriate and assume the authority to themselves to engage in unbending censure toward their neighbors."[26] He dissuades them from their arrogance and harshness in reproving and condemning faults, Piscator notes, by warning them that they are inviting a harsher treatment from God. Why? Because everyone sins; they have no fewer faults than the ones they condemn. But they bear a greater judgment because as teachers they sin, not out of ignorance, but against their conscience. In other words, they have set themselves up as knowledgeable about right and wrong, and yet they have been found to be doing wrong anyway. Piscator recalls that Paul says a similar thing at Rom 2:21, when he rebukes Jews who claim to instruct others in the law, who position themselves to be a guide of the blind and a light in the darkness, yet who do not teach themselves; they say not to steal, and yet they steal. In his scholia, Piscator follows Beza in drawing attention to Matt 7:1 as a parallel ("Judge not, lest you be judged"), but he also points to 1 Cor 11:31–32, where Paul tells the faithful to judge themselves and not others, because God castigates those who judge others. Piscator concludes in his observations that James is warning everyone against "arrogance and rigor" when chastising others for their faults; instead, they should examine themselves with this same degree of severity, only looking to

---

25. Piscator had an amicable relationship with Beza over the years, and the latter appreciated his meticulousness of scholarship, but the two clashed over the doctrine of justification and the "parts" of it as traditionally defined by the Reformed. Piscator argued that there is no reason why Christ's perfect obedience in this life, his active obedience, should be imputed to us as one of the causes of our justification; only his passive obedience to die on the cross and shed his blood accrues to justification. Beza objects that his death frees us from death but that his obedience to the law frees us from the condemnation of the law (as articulated in Calvin's doctrine of double justification). This has further ramifications for understanding the nature of sanctification and its relationship to justification. For Beza, regeneration is begun in the faithful but not yet perfected. On this see esp. *CB* 27 (1586), 49–63, and *CB* 30 (1589), appendices IIa–b. On Piscator's life, see Bos, *Johann Piscator*, 9–31. In 1603, the Synod of Gap condemned Piscator for his views on justification. For a full discussion of Piscator's views on justification, see De Campos, "Johannes Piscator (1546–1625)."

26. Piscator, *Analysis Logica*, 44.

correct others if the situation demands it, and then only in a gentle and loving way. Jesus, after all, advises us to find the log in our own eye before worrying about the splinter in someone else's.

Piscator's interpretation does not in any way discourage those who have the gift, calling, and training from becoming teachers; for him, James is talking about those who in a sense mock the office by grasping undeservedly at its authority. As he interpreted the passage, though, he may have been thinking of the personal intramural wrangling with several Reformed theologians over the doctrine of justification. His letters to Beza, for example, plead for civility and the continuance of friendship between them characterized by love and respect. Even so, his comments here concentrate more on the teacher's role as moral guide rather than defender of pure doctrine.

Benedictus Aretius (Bendicht Marti), theology professor at Bern, published his own commentaries on the canonical epistles in 1581.[27] Like Piscator, his comments on Jas 3:1 underscore the continuing tension in the passage between what would be the easiest and, to quote Calvin, long-accepted interpretation—namely, that James is cautioning that not many should aspire to the legitimate office of teacher—and the interpretation that sees here a warning for the smug and sanctimonious chastisers of others. Aretius's comments straddle both possible understandings. He writes:

> The sentiment here is that the pious should especially take care that they not assume for themselves the right to censure others harshly while forgetting their own sins. Therefore, I take *doctores*[28] to mean both those who take up for themselves the office of teaching and those who easily pass judgment on others. The two have similar characteristics, since typically those who aspire to the office of teaching are gabby, satirical in tone, and harsh in their censuring of others. First, then, young men should learn from this passage that a perverse eagerness for teaching is to be condemned. Jeremiah (23:21) prophesies for the Lord when he says, "They were running, but I did not send them." And the apostle at 1 Timothy 3:3 bids that they first be proven, and only then does he grant the power of being a minister. Second, he chastises the censorious power of those who take

---

27. Aretius, *Commentarii in epistolas canonicas*, 63–64.
28. But Aretius translates it *praeceptores*.

upon themselves the right to pronounce all sorts of things about others while having no sense of what is in their own backpack.[29]

Aretius then interprets the latter part of the verse, the statement about the "greater judgment," solely with an eye to those who become teachers without the proper qualifications and motivations. These types teach out of ambition and an eagerness to criticize. Such "censors and seraphic[30] doctors"[31] should beware the divine judgment, which will be greater and more severe for them, since they should have known that all people sin, including themselves. Everyone, says Aretius, can expect to face judgment, but those who act as rigid critics of others, who were never called to teach in the first place, and who did damage to those who heard them, can expect harsh treatment before the supreme Judge. Everyone, therefore, should pay heed to their own faults.

Aretius is able to navigate the problem of James's apparent misgivings about the office of *doctores* by turning the question into one of attitude and not the position itself. "Many" should not aspire to the office because many have not proven themselves to have the right motives and disposition. The church certainly has a place for those who will instruct others regarding the Christian life, but the pious ones who demonstrate their true calling with their success recognize how difficult it is to throw off the disobedience of the old self and put on the righteousness of Christ. They are self-aware of their own failings and sympathetic to the struggle of others. This is key. To walk around with airs and a supercilious posture while publicly denouncing the mistakes and failures of others misrepresents what a real *doctor* should be and redounds to one's own guilt.

LUTHERANS

So far, we have only considered Reformed commentators on Jas 3:1. However, the perspectives of Lutheran theologians Niels Hemmingsen and Lucas Osiander on the passage provide greater context and add nuance regarding the shift, in some quarters during the period, from understanding *didaskaloi* to mean *official teachers* to reading it as *carping censors*. For his part, Hemmingsen concedes the ambiguous character of James's

---

29. Aretius, *Commentarii in epistolas canonicas*, 63–64. A reference to the fable of Phaedrus 4:10.
30. We might say "holier-than-thou."
31. Aretius, *Commentarii in epistolas canonicas*, 64.

directive when considered per se but argues that the broader context in which it is stated strongly suggests that here James is thinking first and foremost about the vileness of the unbridled tongue speaking for a callous and insensitive human nature.[32] Hemmingsen explains that we can easily understand the sense of the directive, or *propositio*, by connecting it to the explanations that James gives to confirm it. These explanations, or *rationes*, all point to the petulant tongue, which helps us to understand that the word *teachers* here is used in the sense, not of a legitimate doctor in the church, but of those who assume censorious authority (*ius censorium*) over others and who "severely and strictly judge the actions of others without discerning their own faults." According to Hemmingsen, James is not condemning fraternal correction that is rooted in charity, something that Christ mandates and that is the foundation of all church discipline; rather, he denounces "shallowness, ambition, and haughtiness, which look, not so much to edification, but to an eagerness to rebuke and disparage." Hemmingsen, as others, draws the parallel with Christ's words at Matt 23, but he makes the point that Christ is not prohibiting people from being called teachers per se; our Lord simply wants them to recognize that they themselves are not the ultimate teacher but that he is their rabbi and the purpose behind their teaching. This recognition creates the right disposition within them, one that leads them to desire concord with their brothers and sisters in Christ free from ambition and contempt. Hemmingsen points out that Paul called himself the "teacher" of the Gentiles but in doing so did not violate Christ's mandates, since he himself remained obedient to him and taught that everyone should obey him. Thus, neither the mandates of Christ nor the words of James should be used to condemn academic preferments, he insists, since such condemnations "do violence to Scripture and undermine the useful administration of the Republic of Letters." Hemmingsen urges that everyone set aside ambition, subject themselves to Christ, and "respectfully preserve the economy of the schools."[33]

Hemmingsen clearly shows that a contextual reading of this verse—James flows immediately into a discussion of the unbridled tongue—as well as an analogy with other Scripture passages—Jesus warns his disciples at Matt 23 not to judge lest they be judged—precludes our interpreting James's directive as a disparagement of the office of teaching.

---

32. Hemmingsen, *Commentaria in omnes epistolas apostolorum*, 945.
33. Hemmingsen, *Commentaria in omnes epistolas apostolorum*, 945.

Teachers who are giving instruction to the faithful in an ambitious and supercilious manner are proving that they do not have a legitimate calling and should not be teaching. The church, however, needs pious and gentle teachers who will point sinners to Christ. The stress of James's directive, then, falls on the sinful desire to claim the office without delegitimizing the office itself.

Hemmingsen appears to be advocating for a general spirit of irenicism in the churches. Not long after Hemmingsen published his commentary at Frankfurt am Main, Osiander brought forth his own at Tübingen.[34] Like many of his predecessors, Osiander blames ambition for the issue being addressed in the passage, which even in the early church was causing problems. According to him, James is warning people against teaching "who are not suited to it and are not legitimately called." Such people, he says, should consider that if they mislead the church, they will have to give a serious accounting of their actions before Christ. Osiander is quick to add, however, that James does not intend to deter *suitable* candidates from ecclesiastical ministry, only those who "bewitched by the empty persuasion of erudition"[35] (that is, convinced how smart they are), seize upon the office of teaching (*officium docendi*), even though they lack the necessary gifts and calling. He describes such people as "drunk" with intellectual smugness yet completely unaware of how difficult it is to teach the church about true piety. Very few people should aspire to the office of teaching, he concludes, because of the likelihood that somewhere along the way they will commit a grievous sin. Osiander then moves on from his analysis of 3:1 and the problem of the ambition to teach what he considers a new thought on the part of James in the second half of verse 2, a section that he labels "other sermons." Now, he says, in contrast to the approach of Hemmingsen, James addresses a new problem, that of the tongue.

CONCLUSION

At the beginning of this paper, we quickly surveyed modern thinking about James's directive that not many be teachers but then turned our attention to the fortunes of the passage during the sixteenth-century, when the evangelical churches were in their nascent stages. We asked

---

34. Osiander, *Epistola ad Hebraeos*, 125–26.
35. Osiander, *Epistola ad Hebraeos*, 125.

how the unique circumstances of the sixteenth century and the birth of the evangelical movement shaped Reformational readings of Jas 3:1. Calvin informs us that the traditional and "received" interpretation of the passage holds that James is referring to the *munus*, or office, of teacher, to which few should rightfully aspire. D'Étaples reflects this tradition. In the evangelical movement, the office of *doctor* assumed an important place in the church. In his *Institutes*, Calvin, likely influenced by Martin Bucer, draws a clear distinction in the church between the office of pastor and that of *doctor*. *Doctores*, that is, teachers, protect the church through pure and sincere doctrine, but they do not bear the other responsibilities that the pastor also has, such as presiding over discipline, the administration of the sacraments, and admonitions. Pastors teach, but they also share the task of organizing the church and exercising discipline with ruling elders. In support of his views, he brings to bear Rom 12:7, Eph 4:11, and 1 Tim 5:17, along with their surrounding contexts. For our purposes, without wading into the complex evolution of these ideas to the present time, it is enough to note that the early evangelical churches generally recognized an office in the church wholly dedicated to orthodoxy and instruction, while modern evangelical churches put less stress on the distinct function and office of *doctor* (because of higher literacy rates and more accessible education?), though some undoubtedly hold that seminary professors fulfill this role for the church.

This brings us back to the interpretation of James's directive in the Reformation. We can detect in the interpretations of the period a strong desire to protect the uniqueness and importance of the teaching office in the church and to say that James was in no way undermining it. Depending on their circumstances, interpreters of the period tackled the issue in a variety of ways. The Zurichers faced the pressing problem of the Anabaptists, who were allowing untrained, uncalled people to teach in the churches, and so they focused on the preparation and responsibility of the teacher and followed d'Étaples in stressing doctrinal purity. Both Lutherans and the Reformed tie James's warning about *didaskaloi* closely to the homily on the tongue that follows. Anyone who claims the authority to tell others right and wrong—regarding doctrine, to be sure, but more often as a moral censor—should beware that the tongue has power to inflict all kinds of harm. Far from discouraging people from fulfilling an important office in the church, James, in this view, is urging circumspection and self-evaluation when speaking. Should I be listening or talking? When read in the light of Jesus's instructions at Matt 7 and

23, James's charge that few become teachers does not undercut evangelical ecclesiology as it was understood in the period of the Reformation; instead, it reinforces the notion that the church functions as a body that edifies itself to the benefit of all its members.

BIBLIOGRAPHY

Adamson, James B. *The Epistle of James*. The New International Commentary on the New Testament. Grand Rapids: Eerdmans, 1976.
Aretius, Benedictus. *Commentarii in epistolas canonicas facili et perspicua methodo conscripti*. Morges: J. le Preux, 1581.
Beza, Theodore. *Testamentum Novum, sive Novum Foedus Iesu Christi, D.N., cuius Graeco contextui respondent interpretationes duae: una, vetus: altera, Theodori Bezae, diligenter ab eo recognita*. Geneva: H. Étienne, 1589.
Bos, Frans Lukas. *Johann Piscator: Ein Beitrag zur Geschichte der reformierten Theologie*. Kampen: J. H. Kok, 1932.
Bullinger, Heinrich. *Adversus Anabaptistas Libri VI*. Translated by Josias Simler. Zurich: C. Froschauer, 1560.
———. *In omnes apostolicas epistolas divi videlicet Pauli XIIII et VII canonicas, commentarii*. Zurich: C. Froschauer, 1537.
Calvin, John. *Commentarii in Epistolas canonicas*. Geneva: J. Crespin, 1551.
———. *Commentariorum in acta apostolorum, liber I*. Geneva: J. Crespin, 1552.
Castellio, Sebastian. *Biblia Sacra*. Basle: P. Perna, 1573 [1551].
Davids, Peter H. *The Epistle of James: A Commentary on the Greek Text*. The New International Greek Testament Commentary. Grand Rapids: Eerdmans, 1982.
De Campos, Heber Carlos, Jr. "Johannes Piscator (1546–1625) and the Consequent Development of the Doctrine of the Imputation of Christ's Active Obedience." PhD diss., Calvin Theological Seminary, 2011.
D'Étaples, Jacques Lefèvre. *Commentarii in epistolas catholicas*. Basel: A. Cratander, 1527.
Erasmus, Desiderius. *Novum Testamentum omne*. Basel: J. Froben, 1522.
Hemmingsen, Niels. *Commentaria in omnes epistolas apostolorum, Pauli, Petri, Iudae, Iohannis, Iacobi, et in eam quae ad Hebraeos inscribitur*. Frankfurt am Main: C. Corvinus, 1579.
Huther, Johann Eduard. *Critical and Exegetical Handbook to the General Epistles of James, Peter, John, and Jude*. Translated by Paton James Gloag, David B. Croom, and Clarke Huston Irwin. Edited by Timothy Dwight. Peabody, MA: Hendrickson, 1983.
Johnson, Luke Timothy. *The Letter of James: A New Translation with Introduction and Commentary*. The Anchor Yale Bible Commentaries. New York: Doubleday, 1995.
Martin, Ralph P. *James*. Word Biblical Commentary 48. Nashville: Thomas Nelson, 1988.
Moo, Douglas J. *The Letter of James*. The Pillar New Testament Commentary. Grand Rapids: Eerdmans, 2000.
Osiander, Lucas. *Epistola ad Hebraeos Iacobi, Prima et Secunda Petri, Prima, Secunda, & tertia Ioannis, Iudae & Apocalypsis Ioannis*. Tübingen: G. Gruppenbachius, 1584.

Pellikan, Konrad. *In omnes apostolicas epistolas, Pauli, Petri, Iacobi, Ioannis, et Iudae* [. . .] *commentarii, ad collationem optimorum quorumque interpretum conscripti et aediti, in usum theologiae apostolicae studiosorum*. Zurich: C. Froschauer, 1539.

Pellikan, Konrad, Leo Jud, and Theodore Bibliander. *Biblia sacrosancta testamenti veteris et novi e sacra Hebraeorum lingua Graecorum fontibus*. Zurich: C. Froschauer, 1543.

Piscator, Johannes. *Analysis Logica Septem Epistolarum Apostolicarum, Quae Catholicae Appellari Solent*. 3rd ed. Siegen: C. Corvin, 1598.

Zwingli, Ulrich. *In evangelicam historiam de domino nostro Iesu Christo* [. . .] *annotationes D. Huldychi Zvinglii per Leonem Judae exceptae et editae*. Zurich: C. Froschauer, 1539.

Afterword

DOUGLAS A. SWEENEY

I FIRST MET SCOTT Manetsch in the winter of 2000. I was wooing him for a faculty position at Trinity, and he and his wife, Cathy, came to dinner at our house. Sometimes scholars are annoying. We can be self-absorbed, too eager to impress. So I was gratified to learn that Scott was not this way at all. He was humble and kind, most interested in getting to know Wilma and me and in finding ways to build us up in faith, hope, and love. He was learned, to be sure. His first monograph had just been released from the press. Entitled *Theodore Beza and the Quest for Peace in France, 1572–1598* (Brill, 2000), it treated an evergreen topic: Beza's ministry to migrants—in this case, Huguenot refugees from France who sought shelter in Geneva. It was very well researched. But when we met that day, Scott was much less interested in showing off his learning than in extending pastoral care, like Beza, to my family. Our conversation at dinner was largely spiritual and edifying. We discussed Scott's children, one of whom had recently been healed from her deafness through the prayers of a relative. We spoke about the church and our interest in serving it. My memory of such things is not usually good, but I remember this conversation vividly. Scott impressed me as a man who lived to care for other people—in his scholarship, of course, but in his daily life as well.

Scott joined us at Trinity, and he and I soon became lifelong friends, partners in scholarship, teaching, and ministry. We read each other's work before it saw the light of day, offering helpful feedback in advance of conference presentations, articles, and books. I recall quite clearly Scott's scholarly development. I learned so much from him about the Protestant Reformation and Calvin, especially. He gave blood, sweat, and tears to InterVarsity's Reformation Commentary on Scripture, serving with distinction as associate general editor and as volume editor for 1 and 2 Corinthians. He edited other volumes on the history of missions, the Reformation, Calvin, Beza, and more. He spent summers toiling in the archives in Geneva. And all of this culminated in two major projects: *Calvin's Company of Pastors: Pastoral Care and the Emerging Reformed Church, 1536–1609* (Oxford University Press, 2013) and a biography of Beza, not yet finished, which will be the standard work on Beza's life for years to come. If I were to summarize Scott's varied scholarly achievements, I would say that he has blessed the world with several scholarly books and several dozen learned articles on the history of gospel ministry, the ministry of the word in Reformed congregations, and the history of pastoral care in the age of Reformations.

But again, Scott has not left these interests in the past. They have shaped his own approach to Christian ministry today and, through his teaching, the approaches of several hundred students. Scott applies what he has learned as well as anyone I know. I have witnessed this firsthand for a quarter of a century. He and I were prayer partners for many years in Deerfield. I could bring you to tears with accounts of Scott's love and prayers for students and colleagues. He and I co-taught several classes together. I could make your heart sing by describing Scott's pedagogy in and out of the classroom. He is one of the best lecturers I have ever known. He won teacher of the year awards at Trinity more frequently than anyone on faculty. And Scott's pedagogy did not stop when he left the podium. He has spent thousands of hours with students one-on-one: in his office, in his home, and over coffee or lunch. Scott loves being with pastors and pastors-in-training. He speaks at pastors' conferences to universal acclaim. He also spends time with pastors in interpersonal settings: on the phone, in their churches, in restaurants, and hiking through the mountains of France, where he has shared the highs and lows of daily ministry with them. This book is not big enough to hold all the stories of Scott's pastoral care for the thousands of people for whom he has done his work and given his life through the years.

You will not understand the integration of Scott's academic work and his daily life unless I also say a word about his care for his family. He has never been one to put career above family. He loves his wife, Cathy, much as Christ loves the church. They raised two amazing girls to adulthood together. Both are now PhD students working in physics, one at Caltech and the other at MIT. More importantly, both love the Lord, love people, and serve God and neighbor with heart, soul, mind, and strength. Scott has also helped Cathy nurse an uncle through a long decline and a tragic, painful death and nurse parents through age-related illnesses as well. To quote the words of St. Paul, Scott does little from selfish ambition or vain conceit but humbly considers others better than himself (Phil 2). Or to quote Christ himself, Scott decided long ago to deny himself, take up his cross, and follow Jesus (Matt 16), to lose his life for Christ and thus find it for eternity (Matt 10).

Scott Manetsch has devoted every aspect of his life to the history and practice of pastoral care. I do not know anyone who has done so more consistently—with passion, energy, integrity, and joy. Thanks be to God for our friend, teacher, and pastor, Scott Manetsch.

www.ingramcontent.com/pod-product-compliance
Lightning Source LLC
Chambersburg PA
CBHW051642230426
43669CB00013B/2405